User-Centered Requirements Analysis

User-Centered Requirements Analysis

Charles Fontaine Martin, Ph.D.

Charles F. Martin Associates

Prentice Hall
Englewood Cliffs, New Jersey 07632

Library of Congress Cataloging-in-Publication Data

Martin, Charles Fontaine, (date)
  User-centered requirements analysis.

  Bibliography: p.
  Includes index.
  1. Computer software. 2. Data base management.
I. Title.
QA76.754.M37 1987   005.1   87-19138
ISBN 0-13-940578-X

67485

Editorial/production supervision
  and interior design: Sophie Papanikolaou and Jane Bonnell
Cover design: Wanda Lubelska Design
Manufacturing buyers: S. Gordon Osbourne and Margaret Rizzi

© 1988 by Charles Fontaine Martin

Printed in the United States of America

10   9   8   7   6   5   4

ISBN 0-13-940578-X   025

Prentice-Hall International (UK) Limited, *London*
Prentice-Hall of Australia Pty. Limited, *Sydney*
Prentice-Hall Canada Inc., *Toronto*
Prentice-Hall Hispanoamericana, S.A., *Mexico*
Prentice-Hall of India Private Limited, *New Delhi*
Prentice-Hall of Japan, Inc., *Tokyo*
Simon & Schuster Asia Pte. Ltd., *Singapore*
Editora Prentice-Hall do Brasil, Ltda., *Rio de Janeiro*

Contents

PART THREE
Functional Analysis

PART FOUR
Data Analysis

PART FIVE
Determining an Implementation Approach

PART SIX
Planning the Requirements Analysis

Preface

User-Centered Requirements Analysis describes an efficient process to define detailed requirements for new custom computer software applications. Emphasis is on applications that contain a high degree of user-computer interaction and centralize their information handling in an integrated data base. Such a process is increasingly important today, given the following trends:

- As hardware prices continue to decline, software is becoming an ever-increasing portion of organizational budgets for computer systems.
- Structured programming techniques and software development tools have become mature and effective, but structured analysis has lagged.
- System definition problems are now the most common sources of development overruns and failures.

In short, if you master the techniques in this book, you will be a more productive systems analyst or a more effective manager of software implementation projects.

The need for this book became clear as a result of my experiences training a business staff of systems analysts. Published methodologies, including the Yourdon functional analysis approach, as explained by Tom DeMarco, and modern data analysis, as described by James Martin, needed to be supplemented. What was missing was a clear guide showing how data and functional analysis should be combined in a well-structured sequence of steps. *User-Centered Requirements Analysis* began as an internal seminar to meet this need.

This book is designed to serve both graduate students in Computer Science or Management Information Systems programs and practicing requirements analysts. Teachers and seminar leaders should supplement the text with case studies to give their students a project-like hands-on experience. Discussion questions after each chapter point out subtle issues that lead to valuable classroom discussion. Practitioners can use the book on two levels. Lead systems analysts will benefit from the whole book to decide how to tailor user-centered requirements analysis to their current projects. Supporting analysts will want to concentrate on the instructions in Parts Three and Four which tell how to carry out functional and data analysis, while ignoring the discussion questions and comparisons of the standard approach with alternative techniques.

Prerequisites for readers of this book include a general knowledge of computer science principles and an introduction to modern data analysis principles. Common computer science terms like *software* and *mouse* are used without definition, based on this assumed computer science background. Chapter 10 gives a short summary of the data base concepts needed here; however, this summary may appear terse to students with no previous exposure to data base management systems.

A number of special terms appear in the book. For example, the term *user concept diagram* denotes a special kind of data flow diagram discussed in Chapter 6. For easier understanding, I spell out these special terms, rather than using acronyms like "UCD." Moreover, these terms are defined both in the text and in a glossary at the end of the book.

Throughout the book, the pronoun *he* is used for the third person singular. Use of *he or she* would be more accurate, but stylistically awkward. In particular, there is no intent here to discourage women from becoming systems analysts. I have not noticed any particular advantage of men over women or vice versa in this field.

I wish you success in applying these well-proven principles to your own exciting, challenging, analysis tasks.

Charles Fontaine Martin
Concord, Massachusetts

Acknowledgments

Many people have helped me to take the vague idea that requirements analysis can be made both well-disciplined and quick, and transform it into a useful, readable text. I am deeply indebted to the following people for their insightful technical and stylistic comments and continuing encouragement.

Past colleagues at Booz, Allen and Hamilton helped develop and test the approach and reviewed early drafts to compare user-centered requirements analysis with other methods used by the firm. Anupam Sachdev, Maryann Fabrizio, Keith Block, and Leonard Palmieri were particularly helpful in their questions and observations while using the emerging methodology on a dozen requirements analysis projects. John Robert Statz helped me with a preliminary description of user-centered requirements analysis for a major proposal. Will Mason, John Chasse, Brian Mallare, John Vosburgh, Paul Oliver, and Fred Cipriano read drafts of the book and suggested useful improvements.

Individuals outside of Booz, Allen and Hamilton read various drafts and supplied comments from the perspectives of commercial practitioners, government project managers, and university faculty. They were: William Frank of IISA, John Lehman of Advanced Decision Systems, Lt. Col. Robert Cutter of the Air Force's Electronic Systems Division, Eunice Cronin and Skip Ulman of the Air Force Geophysics Laboratory, Peter Coad of Project Concepts, Lavette Teague of

Cal. State, Tom Gildersleeve of Dean Witter Reynolds, and William Perry of Quality Assurance Institute.

My mother, Lillian Martin, made a heroic effort reading the entire first complete draft, despite a lack of computer science background. She pointed out sentences that were difficult to read and suggested improvements. Much of the clarity that has been achieved is due to her patient efforts.

Prentice Hall's professional support, led by acquisition editor Pat Henry, has been most helpful in focusing the book's target audience and bringing the book to publication.

Above all, I thank all of these people and my wife and children for encouraging me to complete the project at times when I felt like forgetting the whole thing and going off skiing or whitewater kayaking.

*User-Centered
Requirements Analysis*

PART ONE
Introduction

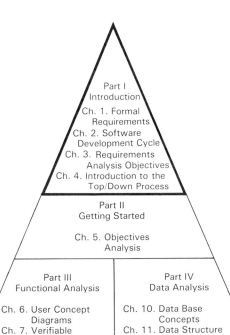

Part I
Introduction

Ch. 1. Formal
Requirements
Ch. 2. Software
Development Cycle
Ch. 3. Requirements
Analysis Objectives
Ch. 4. Introduction to the
Top/Down Process

Part II
Getting Started

Ch. 5. Objectives
Analysis

Part III
Functional Analysis

Ch. 6. User Concept
Diagrams
Ch. 7. Verifiable
Functional Requirements
Ch. 8. Tying Functional
Requirements to the
User Concept Diagrams
Ch. 9. Output Definitions

Part IV
Data Analysis

Ch. 10. Data Base
Concepts
Ch. 11. Data Structure
Diagrams
Ch. 12. Data Dictionary

Ch. 13. Detailed Data
Analysis

Part V Determining an Implementation Approach

Ch. 14. Performance Requirements
Ch. 15. Implementation Assessment

Part VI Planning the Requirements Analysis

Ch. 16. Automated Tools
Ch. 17. Requirements Documentation
Ch. 18. Project Planning

1

Why Bother with Formal Requirements?

REQUIREMENTS ANALYSIS HYPOTHESIS

This text's basic hypothesis is that important information system applications should be developed from clear, complete, agreed-upon descriptions. To be clear, the description must be in terms that both users and developers understand. Diagrams should be used where they help explain the concepts, and English-language and structured logic descriptions employed where more precision is required. To be complete, the application definition must fully describe what the new application must do, who it will support, and how well it must work in throughput and response performance. Users, sponsors, and developers must all agree that the application description is appropriate for the business need and is feasible to implement at the projected costs and schedule. This chapter discusses why computer applications should be developed from descriptions with these three quality criteria.

Systems Developed
without a Careful Description Usually Fail

The opening paragraph may sound self-evident. Yet, in actual practice most applications today are developed without having such a description. Typical projects work from informal requirements or have programmer-oriented requirements which are never thoroughly reviewed by users. Consider these two examples:[1]

Example 1:

One programming team was told: "Convert the shipments tracking system from our Wang computer to our new Data General computer as quickly as possible, leaving exactly the same functional capabilities." The original shipments tracker was undocumented, full of errors, and not validated to be providing user-desired functions. The manager asking for the conversion thought that the only reason the old version was not being used was poor accessibility of the Wang computer to the Shipping Department. The application was converted to the Data General at large expense, did indeed match the old system's functional capabilities, and was never used. It did not provide the support the shippers needed to do their jobs.

Example 2:

A second group was told: "We are going to need a system which tracks performance test results from our vehicle test program. We do not have a clear understanding of what the tests will be or details of the data, but we have some excellent data reduction algorithms. Build us a flexible data manager which takes care of anything we might want to do with these algorithms." Many thousands of lines of code later, software was available which required extensive engineering integration for each vehicle test. Software costs overran the original budget by a factor of three.

Since people seldom admit their development failures, it is not possible to get reliable statistics on the fraction of software applications that have worked successfully after being developed within their budgets and schedules. Exhibit 1-1 shows the results of a Government Accounting Office (GAO) study of nine software development projects for federal government agencies (1).

Less than 5 percent of the money put into the nine software developments resulted in software which could be used as delivered or with minor changes. Projects worth $5.1 million (75 percent of the total) failed to implement usable software. The report suggests that these systems were not properly described in the first place. To the developers, much of the software "worked," but to users the applications were worthless.

---

[1] All example situations in this book are fictitious, but similar in nature to many project situations the author has observed.

EXHIBIT 1-1. Results of Nine Software Developments Studied by GAO

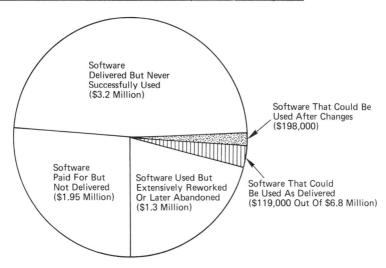

Usefulness of the System Description
Continues After System Implementation

Usefulness of a proper system description continues after initial development. Software maintenance, the continuing process of fixing problems and adding new functions, requires redevelopment of the software throughout its useful life. Most working applications have substantially higher total costs for maintenance than for initial development. Boehm estimates maintenance to be 60 to 80 percent of the total life-cycle cost of an application, with successful systems tending to the larger percentage because of a longer lifespan (2).

During the operational life of an application, people can lose control of it through the following common scenario. Users call up a programmer for a change. The programmer makes a quick change and becomes a hero in the users' eyes. This happens several times, and then the programmer moves to another assignment. Users now find another programmer responds to their call. He is much more cautious, since he is not certain what the software does after the previous programmer's undocumented changes. But, under pressure of continuing operations, he makes changes and hopes they work. After a while, nobody can understand the program. In fact, no one knows what the program does any more. Eventually, it becomes too expensive to patch the program, and it must be totally rebuilt. Rebuilding is an intellectual and financial challenge, because nobody understands what the operational application does.

A properly managed software application will generate a set of user requirements for the initial development and maintain that document through the various changes. Developers and managers may change, but the system keeps a life of its own, if properly documented. As a higher-level definition than the programmer maintenance manuals, the system requirements support user-oriented discussions concerning which software changes should be implemented, how much these changes will affect the rest of the system, and how the changes should be batched in version releases.

Reasons Why Many Systems Analyses Are Unsuccessful

So why is it so hard to get the comptroller or personnel manager to work with a systems analyst to describe an important application before software implementation? Perhaps because of previously unsuccessful attempts at requirements analysis.

Requirements analysis[2], the process of developing clear, complete, agreed-upon descriptions of feasible new software applications, is extremely difficult. Some key sources of difficulty include:

- *Insufficient time allowed.* Users are anxious; they want a working system immediately.
- *Insufficient or inefficient review with users.* Users may get an imposing three-inch thick document and not understand how to review it, or they may get trapped in long interviews or meetings which never get anywhere.
- *Differences of opinion.* Getting a number of people to agree on something is not easy; the analyst must be adept at achieving consensus among the people involved with the application.
- *Political twists and turns.* Decision makers can derail a project at any time. The analyst's best defense is to figure out who they are (this book uses the term *sponsor* to indicate individuals who can turn project support on and off) and keep them involved in the analysis process.
- *Lack of technical knowledge.* When the systems analyst and users do not understand state-of-the-art limitations with commercially available computer hardware and software, it is hard for them to define a good, feasible system.
- *Inability to write well.* Some methods try to avoid textual material, but this author's experience indicates that summary descriptions and textual requirements are necessary. The ability to write clearly is a necessary skill for the systems analyst.
- *Lack of structured analysis techniques.* It is not obvious without having had a great many requirements analysis experiences, or reading a text like this one, what should be included in the application definition and how this material can be generated.

---

2 *Systems analysis* is a slightly more general term covering both requirements and design. The combination is also referred to as systems architecture.

Thus, what a computer-knowledgeable writer needs to become a good requirements analyst is a well-defined system description approach which is quick and which involves not only the analyst, but the users and sponsors as well, in all important decisions.

Some Applications Succeed

Fortunately, there are many examples of successful applications built from solid system descriptions. Generally the moving force is an experienced systems analyst who has developed a personal style that worked well, at least on the set of applications encountered. These techniques get handed down within the organization by an apprenticeship approach.

Since the mid-1970s, theoretical bases for various styles of systems analysis have appeared in books and articles. These styles vary tremendously, and no one approach has emerged as the "right" way to describe an application. You might expect that there would at least be agreement on the content of the system description document, but this has not been the case. The lesson appears to be that each application should have some unique considerations in its description.

Nevertheless, experience shows that successful requirements analysis methodology can be described and learned. Work with actual applications is necessary for the requirements analyst to become proficient, but beginning with a clearly thought-out approach can save several years of floundering. The objective of this text is to describe methods which work and show how they can be used together in a total requirements analysis process. At Booz, Allen, and Hamilton, these techniques have enabled junior analysts to develop excellent application descriptions.

USER-CENTERED PHILOSOPHY

Two philosophical principles underlie the user-centered approach to requirements analysis. The first principle is that application descriptions should be oriented toward users rather than toward developers. In particular, the results of systems analysis should be written in terms easily understood by users and should clearly indicate how users will interact with the automated system. The second principle is that functional requirements (statements of the services the computer application must provide) and data requirements (description of the information handled by the computer application) are equally important in an application description and should be developed in parallel. This follows a modern trend to combine functional decomposition and data flow analysis (3) with analysis supporting integrated data base definition (4). This text contains unique insights into steps which can be followed to obtain successive levels of detail on both functional and data requirements. These methods support user involvement in decision making without requiring an inordinate amount of time from the users to prepare for these decisions.

ALTERNATIVE METHODS FOR SPECIAL SITUATIONS

Since every new application presents a unique challenge, the systems analyst must be prepared with a variety of techniques. The basic user-centered requirements analysis methodology works surprisingly well for a large variety of applications, but additional techniques are needed for special situations. For that reason, this book gives a model approach for each systems analysis step, and then compares that approach with other available techniques.

This introductory part of the book sets the stage for the detailed techniques described in Chapters 5 to 18. Chapter 1 indicates the importance of front-end requirements to success of computer application implementations. Chapter 2 discusses how the need for requirements stays constant with a great variety of different implementation styles. The ways the requirements are used will vary. Chapter 3 discusses the requirements quality factors (clarity, completeness, and agreement) in order to make the objectives of requirements analysis more specific. Chapter 4 then gives an overview of the user-centered requirements analysis process.

DISCUSSION QUESTIONS

[Author's note: Common sense is required for many of the difficult situations which arise in requirements analysis. Each chapter has a set of discussion questions which illustrate many of these situations. The questions can be used in group discussions or individual thought to consider analyst options. An instructor's manual is available to help teachers guide these discussions.]

1. Consider the following two software applications:

    Personnel Hiring System

    Expert Services Corporation finds that its growth is restricted by the difficulty of finding suitably qualified people to be consultants in the engineering areas the company serves. Expert's Vice President for Personnel has decided to build a management information system which tracks all employment candidates in the engineering areas that the company serves. Reports from this data base will insure timely processing of candidates in Expert's three divisions (with a total of 1,000 employees). Statistics from the system should answer questions like "What form of advertising was most successful in attracting candidates?" and "What types of people are most likely to accept Expert's employment offers?"

    Refinery Operation Optimization Program

    An operations analyst at the World Oil refinery in New Jersey has a mathematical model to optimize refinery control parameters to minimize the costs of production. His model is in the form of a linear program:

$$\text{Minimize cost} = c_1 x_1 + c_2 x_2 \ldots + c_n x_n$$

Subject to the constraints

$$a_{i1}x_1 + \ldots + a_{in}x_n = b_i, \text{ for each } i = 1, \ldots, m, \text{ and } x_j \text{ is non-negative,}$$
for each $j = 1, \ldots, n$.

The decision variables, x_j, represent controllable quantities such as pressure and temperature of the various refinery processes. In the operations analyst's model, there are 100 variables (n=100) and 200 constraints equations (m=200). There is a well known, easily programmed solution method called the Simplex Algorithm. The operations analyst wants you to develop a software application that assists his input and review of the linear programming parameters (a_{ij}, b_j, and c_j), solves his problem using the Simplex Algorithm, and presents the results using tabular and graphical displays the analyst has found useful. The software must run on his IBM PC AT™ personal computer with 512 KB main memory, and should be able to complete optimization and report generation within ten minutes to support the analyst's "what if" analyses.

a. What are the difficult and what are the straightforward aspects of development of the Personnel Hiring and Refinery Optimization applications?

b. Which system is more difficult to implement?

c. How much effort (in man-months) would you expect these two applications to require?

d. What skills are required for each application?

2. Globetrotters Athletic Equipment Corporation is a Fortune 500 company whose growth required a complete upgrade of its marketing and order entry systems. Two accounting-oriented analysts from the Globetrotters MIS department spent four months analyzing the existing Globetrotters marketing system and order entry system and new federal and state regulations. Then they spent another four months writing a detailed 200-page specification of a new integrated system. This document is now out for review to Globetrotters financial and product line managers to obtain approval for the specification and funding for development. The analysts are proud that they did not have to bother users with questions before generating a well thought-out draft specification.

a. What are the good and bad features of the analysts' approach?

b. Place yourself in the position of the comptroller. Your introduction to this project consists of the specification in your incoming mail with a note to return review comments in two weeks. What is your reaction?

c. What do you suspect will happen in development of the integrated application in the next year?

REFERENCES

1. General Accounting Office, "Contracting for Computer Software Development—Serious Problems Require Management Attention to Avoid Wasting Additional Millions," FGMSB-80-4, November 9, 1979.

2. Barry W. Boehm, *Software Engineering Economics*, Englewood Cliffs, N.J.: Prentice-Hall, 1981.

3. Tom DeMarco, *Structured Analysis and System Specification*, Englewood Cliffs, N.J.: Prentice-Hall, 1979.

4. James Martin, *Managing the Data Base Environment*, Englewood Cliffs, N.J.: Prentice-Hall, 1983.

2

The Software Development Cycle

Implementation of a computer application is such a complex process that managers need an intellectual model to plan and control the project. A software development cycle is an explicit breakdown of the work that is required to implement a new or modified software application. The steps in this breakdown should be primarily sequential. That is, the result of one step is required for the next step. Moreover, each step should have a reviewable output that allows managers to evaluate progress and to make schedule adjustments, based on comparing actual achievements with the goals of that step.

Three rather different kinds of software development cycles which have achieved widespread attention for information system applications are:

- Classical approach
- Prototyping
- Reusable code.

This chapter discusses each of these approaches and shows how requirements definition supports each implementation style.

CLASSICAL SOFTWARE DEVELOPMENT CYCLE

Exhibit 2-1 shows the kind of standard approach described in many software engineering books (1-4). Although often honored more in the breach than in the observance, it is widely felt that going through these steps results in a well managed, relatively predictable project. This approach relies on extensive paper documentation and approval of both requirements and design before coding the software.
Exhibit 2-1 shows what happens at each phase of the classical software development cycle. The first phase, concept identification, identifies an application need according to mechanisms such as:

- Feasibility study of the application (1)
- Organization strategic information planning study (5)
- Management fiat.

At the conclusion of this phase, an application charter is published and funding is made available to pursue the next step. The application charter is usually an informal statement of purpose of the system, such as: "Transfer the personnel files from our old brand X computer to our new brand Y model," or "Develop a system which reduces shipment time to customers by tracking orders and picking transportation options." Additional bounds which can be placed on the concept, such as identification of the main user types, help focus the systems analyst's time on the desired functions.

EXHIBIT 2-1. Classical Software Development Cycle

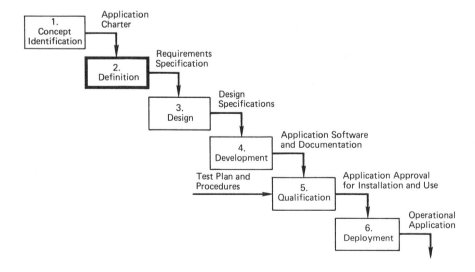

The second phase in the classical software development cycle is application definition. This phase is the subject of *User-Centered Requirements Analysis*. The output of this phase is a requirements specification, which is discussed in Chapters 3 and 17 of this book.

The third phase, design, describes the structure of the hardware and software solution. It is usually broken into two subphases: preliminary and detailed design. Preliminary design generates the overall structure of equipment configurations and software modules which will implement the application. It also determines the user interface menus, screen formats, and reports. Detailed design generates all the algorithms and logic detail that programmers need to know in coding the software. Usually the results of preliminary and detailed design are reviewed with users in formal preliminary design review and critical design review meetings. Documentation from this phase is collectively referred to as design specifications.

The fourth phase, development, generates all the programs, data bases, procedures, programmer manuals, and user manuals needed for the application. Internal testing in the development organization may occur on many levels, such as module, subsystem, and system-level tests. Generally the developer tests against his own design materials to see if the implementation correctly followed the design.

The fifth phase, qualification, tests the new application from the users' perspective. Alpha testing checks to see if the implementation meets all the requirements in the requirements specification. Beta testing involves a small group of users who try out the new software in performing their jobs. Invariably there will be problem reports from both alpha and beta testing which need to be resolved before widespread deployment.

In the final phase of deployment, the software is installed on operational machines, data bases are converted to the new formats, and users are trained and given access. Often a period of parallel operation of old and new systems precedes a cutover to complete reliance on the new application. As users gain experience with the new system, user requests for system changes and enhancements are collected and batched for new maintenance releases of the application.

In the classical software development cycle, the requirements specification has its largest impact on the design phase. It is also used as the basis for alpha testing in the qualification phase. Finally, it serves as functional-level documentation of changes, both during development of the application and for changes requested after the application becomes operational.

PROTOTYPING SOFTWARE DEVELOPMENT CYCLE

Many software implementation managers prefer a development approach which stresses development of preliminary versions of the application rather than creation of paper designs. A realistic version of the system allows users to be more involved and to make comments which refine the system concept.

Modern application development environments supplied with major data base management systems make it possible for the developer to construct prototypes of applications in the same time that it used to take to document a design. As a result, it is possible to show users how the entire user interface (menus and screen displays) will appear, and obtain user reactions. Advantages to this approach include:

- The developer obtains more user involvement and feedback, because the screen displays are more interesting than design documentation.
- Once the screen displays in the prototype are approved by users, their definitions may be used for the mature application.

As indicated in Exhibit 2-2, the prototyping phase in this approach combines aspects of design, development, and qualification of the classical cycle. Actual achieved efficiencies will not be quite as dramatic as suggested by Exhibit 2-2, because algorithmic processes must still be designed using standard structured logic documentation approaches.

EXHIBIT 2-2. Prototyping Software Development Cycle

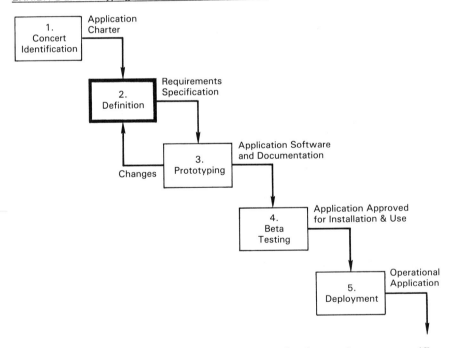

In the prototyping software development cycle, the requirements specification drives the prototyping phase. In return, the prototyping yields more user changes to the requirements than in a classical design approach because of the prototype's realism. The requirements specification should still be kept up to date to maintain configuration control. Testing tends to be less formal and more iterative, with far more versions to test than is possible with the classical approach.

REUSABLE CODE SOFTWARE DEVELOPMENT CYCLE

In a third approach to software development, employing reusable code, the objective is to implement the new application with as much existing software as possible. Such an approach can cut both the manpower and calendar time required for development, but is complicated by the need to make modules sufficiently general to apply to new applications. The larger the software development organization, the greater the chance that any particular function has already been implemented. Hence, the reusable code concept has been an important part of some recent "software factory" concepts.

The application software is designed in a different way under this philosophy. A clever design may allow use of more existing modules. Moreover, when new modules are developed, additional time is spent adding generality and careful module documentation.

Exhibit 2-3 shows how the classical software development cycle is modified with reusable modules. As in the other two cases, a requirements specification drives the rest of the implementation. In this case design (phase 3) starts with an assessment of which functions can be implemented with existing modules. New modules may be designed and developed (phase 4) in either a classical or prototyping style. System integration melds the old and new modules into a working system.

An important variant of the reusable code approach to software development is use of commercially available software packages. Vendor software is often the most efficient way to implement standard applications like accounting, manufacturing resource planning, and marketing systems. When commercial software is available, phase 3 (code reuse assessment) becomes an analysis of the vendor offerings which could best satisfy the requirements specification. The specification supports objective selection of the most effective software product, rather than being overly influenced by a fast-talking salesperson or by features which demonstrate well, but have little practical use.

SUMMARY OF THE ROLE
OF REQUIREMENTS SPECIFICATIONS

In all three of the sample software development cycles discussed in this chapter, requirements must be generated in an early definition phase (highlighted in Exhibits 2-1, 2-2, and 2-3) in order to manage the implementation properly. Even if the development is carried out in an MIS or data processing department in the same overall organization as the user departments, the requirements specification is a valuable tool as an internal contract between the sponsor and the developer. It

EXHIBIT 2-3. Reusable Code Software Development Cycle

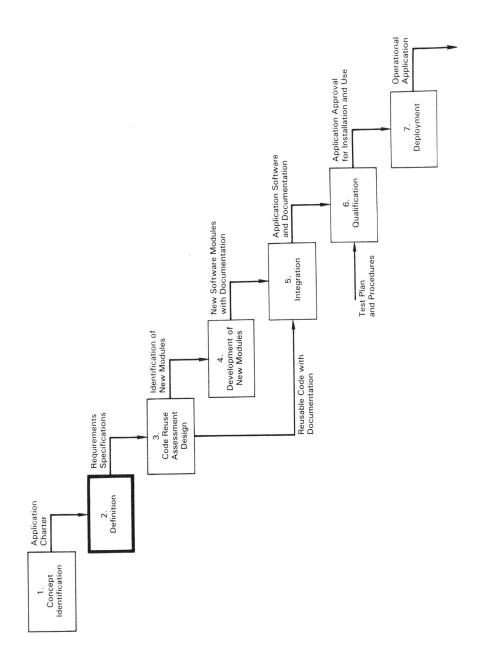

protects both parties, since it helps the users and sponsor to indicate clearly what they expect, and it protects the developers who can request more time and resources if major changes are introduced.

Requirements differ in nature from design specifications. The requirements need to be *user-centered* (that is, clearly expressed in terminology the user groups understand), so that they can be fully coordinated among the users. Design specifications should be *programmer-centered* (that is, expressed in a form which most helps the efficient development of error-free software). Because of this difference in orientation, it is difficult to find a single engineering methodology and set of tools which can successfully carry an application through the requirements, design, and development phases. For example, Higher-Order Software's USE.IT™ methodology (6) tries to decompose the problem gradually, using provably correct formal rules that eventually reach atomic definitions which are computer-executable. But the process is programmer-centered, and does not support effective requirements interaction with users. Hence, such an approach should be reserved for system software, rather than for applications with extensive user interaction. Chapter 16 discusses modern trends in computer-aided software engineering tools which combine user-centered and programmer-centered techniques to support multiple phases of implementation.

DISCUSSION QUESTIONS

1. Software engineering and software project management texts commonly show views of the development steps that look like Exhibit 2-1. Yet it is more common in practice to see managers taking a laissez-faire approach like the one shown below in Exhibit 2-4, which gives little opportunity for management review of project progress. A programming team is given a general statement of the problem to be solved and then left to implement a solution.

    a. Why don't more managers use the standard development approach?

    b. What problems arise from the approach shown in Exhibit 2-4?

EXHIBIT 2-4. Laissez-Faire Software Development Cycle

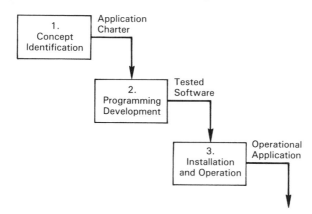

2. An interesting phenomenon on very large MIS programs is the emergence of two or more different views of the program's software development cycle within different participating organizations.
   a. What is the impact of having multiple, inconsistent views of the development process?
   b. How can managers assure a single view of the software development cycle among all participants?

3. On small projects, the requirements specification and design specification are often melded into a single document.
   a. Why should larger projects split out requirements specification as a separate effort?
   b. What guidelines should be used to determine whether a given application can get by with a single specification document covering both requirements and design?

REFERENCES

1. David King, *Current Practices in Software Development*, Englewood Cliffs, N.J.: Yourdon Press, 1984.

2. Dennis Connor, *Information System Specification and Design Road Map*, Englewood Cliffs, N.J.: Prentice-Hall, 1985.

3. Peter Freeman and Anthony I. Wasserman, Editors, *Tutorial on Software Design Techniques*, Silver Spring, MD: IEEE Computer Society Press, 1983.

4. "Department of Defense Standard 7935: Automated Data Processing System Documentation," Department of Defense, 1983.

5. Mark L. Gillenson and Robert Goldberg, *Strategic Planning, Systems Analysis & Database Design*, New York: John Wiley & Sons, 1984.

6. James Martin, *Software Design from Provably Correct Constructs*, Englewood Cliffs, N.J.: Prentice-Hall, 1985.

3
Requirements Analysis Objectives

As hypothesized in Chapter 1, the objective of requirements analysis is to obtain a clear, complete, agreed-upon requirements specification for a feasible software application. This chapter describes the three components of this objective, so that criteria will be available for discussing good and bad features of various systems analysis techniques.

CLARITY

Before discussing what makes specifications clear, it is helpful to examine two types of requirements specifications which are unclear. The first type is *vague generalities*; the second is the *mammoth list*.

In the vague generalities specification, typically an excited proponent of the application describes it briefly in glowing terms such as "... provides an integrated data base of personnel information" or "... has a state-of-the-art user-friendly interface." Although such a document may be a useful executive summary and could help sell the system concept, it is not a requirements specification. How does one verify whether a user interface is friendly? Verifiable requirements are stated in such a manner that different people examining the final product will agree whether or not the requirement is satisfied. For example, a user-friendliness requirement could be stated in a verifiable way as follows: "All data input shall be accomplished using menu-driven data input screen displays, formatted according to Section 3 of Xenon Corporation's User Interface Standards Document, dated June 1983." The other major flaw of the vague generalities document is that it fails to answer questions about which capabilities will be in the application and which are excluded. Both users and developers are left guessing. They will invariably guess differently, leading to serious misunderstandings when the system is designed and programmed.

The mammoth list heads toward the opposite extreme: tremendous detail. It might be 300 pages of detailed tidbits of functional, design, and operations characteristics of the system. Verifiability is solid. Each characteristic is expressed in precise terms. The problem is that the reader gets totally lost after 10 to 20 pages of this gruesome specification prose. There is no overall organization that helps the reader understand how all the requirements fit together. He is forced to develop his own model on the side, testing hypotheses of what the system might be against the mammoth list. The mammoth list specification also gives the uninitiated reader little help in telling whether a specific capability is included in the system. Answering the question requires scanning through the whole specification and perhaps finding the appropriate requirement if it is there.

For clarity, a requirements specification must do the following:

- Define all special terms used.
- Follow the principle of successive elaboration, describing the application first in very general terms, and then giving increasing levels of detail.
- Display simple pictorial models of the system.
- Key all requirements to the pictorial models.
- Define requirements to the first testable level, but no lower.
- Insure that all parts of the specification are consistent with each other.

Following these principles, readers can quickly orient themselves to general applications concepts, and then check out details. Once the reader understands the pictorial models, he can quickly find out whether a specific capability will be included in the application.

Incidentally, the principle of successive elaboration is a key to success in the application definition process itself. The analyst works first with the users on the broadest issues of functional and data base characteristics. Then they look at one small subset of these agreed-upon diagrams to get the next level of detail. These in turn are subdivided, as required. In any given technical discussion, the next higher level view of the system has already been decided. This is what people mean when they say they have a top-down approach.

COMPLETENESS

A question which stumps most systems analysts in their first few assignments is, "What material should be included in the requirements specification?" The author used several different formulas over a period of several years trying to pick a good approach. Experience with increasingly successful documentation led to the conclusion that the following principles apply to the contents of requirements specifications. The requirements specification should:

- Tell what users need and how well this must be accomplished, not how the software should be constructed.
- Include:
  - Functional requirements (what the new application will accomplish for users)
  - Data base requirements (data items and groups of items to be stored in the application's data base)
  - Performance requirements (user population, data base size, throughput, and responsiveness characteristics of the application)
- Tell what computer hardware and system software must be used to implement the application, if a particular environment is required.
- Indicate whether the application will be developed in a monolithic or a multipart (phased) implementation.

Exhibit 3-1 shows the general contents of a requirements specification which uses the methodology presented in this book.

In general requirements specifications should avoid material discussing how the application should be designed. For example, if the requirements analyst specifies screen formats, then the developer may be stuck with formats which are difficult to implement with his favorite screen painting tool. Even if the same systems analysts are carrying through both the requirements and design, it is best to leave design details till requirements have been agreed upon. Then design analyses will not have to be thrown away just because requirements have evolved.

However, it is never clear cut exactly where requirements should end and design should start. Subjects which can go either way include:

- User interface definition
  - Menus
  - Screen displays
  - Reports
- Algorithms and detailed logic
- Detailed tracing of data structures and elements used in functional processes.

EXHIBIT 3-1. User-Centered Requirements Specification Components

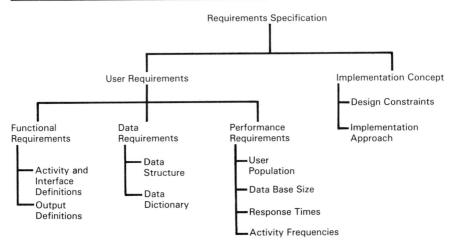

In order to avoid a lot of argument, the lead analyst should set dividing lines and make sure everyone involved understands what they are.

Two general rules which help set the boundary between requirements and design are:

- If the subject is an important issue for some user, it should be added to the user requirements.
- If the subject cannot be resolved independently, but must get user input to decide what is needed, then it should at least be considered for inclusion in the user requirements.

The first rule sometimes pushes toward varying levels of detail for different requirements. For example, most report requirements can be specified in a general manner, indicating options, sort orders, and data fields. But critical reports, central to the users' business area, may be defined with a complete page layout format and logic for computing each field from items in the data base. The second rule helps speed up the design and development phases, by concentrating analyst-user discussions in the requirements definition phase.

Although the requirements specification should not be a design document, it must provide design ground rules which help the developer to make a cost estimate. Is the application intended for a particular computer facility or type, or will the developer be able to choose hardware for the application? Must a standard operating system and data base management system be used, or can the developer use the system software environment he is most familiar with? What procedures will be employed to initialize the data base while maintaining parallel operation of the old system? These issues must be resolved to the level of detail needed by the developer in order to make estimates of cost and schedule that he is willing to stand behind. If there are areas of high risk to the developer, decisions should be made whether to make a more complete risk assessment before accepting the requirements specification, or to start development despite the risks in these areas.

AGREEMENT

A clear, complete requirements specification documenting a brilliant system concept is still worthless without one additional ingredient: agreement that these requirements are what the sponsor and users want, and that they are feasible for the developer. Formally, agreement is certified by a sign-off page which contains the approval signatures of managers representing the sponsor, user, and developer organizations. Informally, it means that everyone agrees that these requirements represent the automation need, and that they will drive the implementation.

Proceeding with the analysis in a top-down fashion lets all implementation participants contribute to major decisions along the way. There should not be a major hurdle in getting managers to look at a voluminous document and comment on it. They should already be familiar with the requirements concepts. The document itself should be accompanied by an explanation of major recent changes and decisions.

However, sign-off can be hard to obtain, even after working closely with these managers and having successful analysis sessions. The gnawing feeling "What if we don't have these requirements quite right?" makes people reluctant to sign off. For example, there may have been a requirements review which decided the Two-Year Forecast Report could be omitted from the new marketing system. But the Director of Marketing keeps wondering "Do I lock myself out of that report if I sign the requirements specification?"

The analyst must remind these managers that the requirements specification document is a living document and will evolve, but changes will cost money. The developer needs a concrete set of requirements in order to make a cost estimate, determine his manpower needs, and create a schedule. The Two-Year Forecast Report decision should be clear when planning the development program. Then, if the decision changes later, the requirements specification document can be changed accordingly, *after agreeing on the corresponding schedule and price changes*. Remember the rule with any engineering job: Changes during development are increasingly expensive the longer one waits to make the changes.

A mechanical need that comes up with changes to the requirements is the need to be able to modify the document in a simple, controlled, correct manner that reflects decision changes. One hopes to minimize the number of sections which have to be rewritten because of a new requirement. Redundancy is the enemy of maintainability. When a requirement specified in two places must later be changed, there is a tendency to make the change in one place and to neglect the other. This leaves an inconsistent requirements specification, clearly an undesirable outcome.

In summary, agreement may be obtained by a requirements analysis process which does the following:

- Develop and review the requirements specification in a process of successive refinement.
- Include a formal sign-off page for the requirements specification.
- Have managers formally sign off any changes to the specification.
- Keep the specification current with agreed-upon engineering changes.
- Eliminate redundancy as much as possible to facilitate specification maintenance.

SUMMARY OF REQUIREMENTS ANALYSIS GOALS

In the application definition step of MIS implementation, requirements analysts work with sponsor, users, and developer to obtain a conceptual view of the application. Results are documented in a requirements specification which must be clear, complete, and agreed-upon (Exhibit 3-2).

All three of these qualities take time. Clear writing, completeness of detail, and patiently explaining concepts to all the individuals involved require more effort than sloppy writing, high-level descriptions, and back-room writing without

EXHIBIT 3-2. Quality Principles for MIS Requirements Specifications

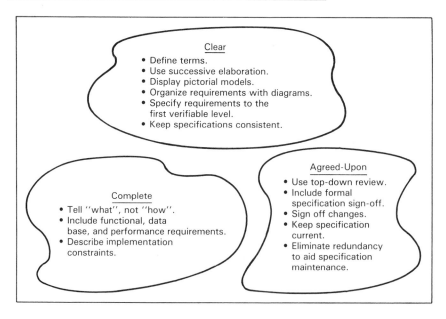

Clear
- Define terms.
- Use successive elaboration.
- Display pictorial models.
- Organize requirements with diagrams.
- Specify requirements to the first verifiable level.
- Keep specifications consistent.

Complete
- Tell "what", not "how".
- Include functional, data base, and performance requirements.
- Describe implementation constraints.

Agreed-Upon
- Use top-down review.
- Include formal specification sign-off.
- Sign off changes.
- Keep specification current.
- Eliminate redundancy to aid specification maintenance.

coordination. What brings ulcers to the systems analyst is that the sponsor invariably presses for quick results. Each analysis must therefore be a compromise between the ideal and the need to produce a requirements specification quickly.

DISCUSSION QUESTIONS

1. As manager of a large MIS shop, you are shown a recently assembled requirements specification.
   a. How will you judge the quality of that specification?
   b. How good is "good enough"?
   c. Your schedule shows that this requirements specification is due this week. Does that change your answer to (b)?
   d. What problems will crop up later if the requirements specification is not clear, complete, and agreed-upon?
   e. Should you defer these questions to the comptroller who is sponsoring the application?

2. Invariably one of the top managers asks what computer the application should run on, long before user requirements are obtained.
   a. Why is it dangerous to decide hardware environment at the start of analysis?
   b. Suppose corporate regulations make computer acquisition a one-year ordeal, and you must order the computer now to have it available for the application. How should you handle this situation?

4

*Introduction
to the Top-Down Process*

How do you prepare the clear, complete, agreed-upon requirements specification? The precise sequence of steps turns out to be very important. By looking at specification components in a particular order, the concepts flow in a natural process of successive elaboration which is easy for users and analysts to deal with. Other orders result in many awkward iterations of steps, either taking longer than necessary or not achieving the desired level of specification detail.

The definition phase of the chosen software development cycle (Exhibit 2-1, 2-2, or 2-3) can be broken into four subphases, as shown in Exhibit 4-1. The rest of this chapter provides an overview of these four requirements analysis steps.

OBJECTIVES ANALYSIS (PHASE 2.1)

As shown in Exhibit 4-2, objectives analysis has two steps, which result in the application concept and a rough estimate of costs.

The first step is to refine the application charter to a working definition of

EXHIBIT 4-1. Definition Subphases

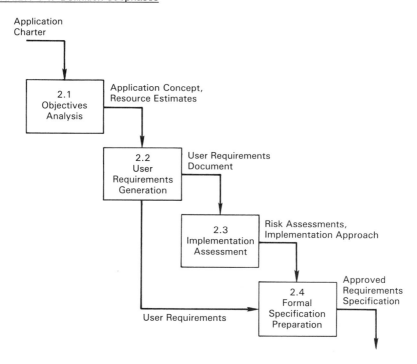

the new application. This application concept consists of three major parts:

- Objectives
- User identification
- Terminology.

Each part is necessary for planning and scheduling the rest of the analysis.

The objectives statements give an overall description of the functions and data content of the system. This is accomplished in a few written pages which successively elaborate from purpose to objectives to features of the new application.

User identification obtains agreement on who the direct and indirect users of the system will be. Direct users will interact from terminals or workstations to enter and maintain data and obtain system outputs. Indirect users supply data and use system reports but do not work with the automated system. Once user types are identified, representatives are selected to assist the implementation. Emphasis during user requirements generation is on the direct users.

Every application requires special terminology to talk about the concepts. You need to identify key terms and then work with the user representatives to obtain definitions all involved can agree upon. Agreeing on definitions early spares you a great deal of argument throughout the analysis.

EXHIBIT 4-2. Objectives Analysis Components

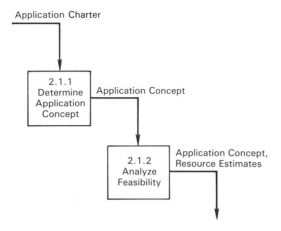

The second step of objectives analysis is the feasibility study. This analysis of benefits and projected costs helps to determine whether the project should proceed. In addition, it should indicate details concerning support from business area experts and other resources required to complete the definition phase.

USER REQUIREMENTS GENERATION (PHASE 2.2)

The heart of requirements analysis is generation of the users' requirements for the application. These can be classified in three general groups:

- Functional description
- Data base description
- Performance requirements.

The order in which these three types of requirements are compiled makes a difference in how efficiently the analysis proceeds. An important principle of the user-centered requirements analysis approach is that the functional and data base requirements should be developed *together*, followed by compilation of the performance requirements. Parallel top-down development of the functional and data base requirements differs from the classical systems analysis approach of defining functional capabilities first and then determining the supporting data requirements. It also differs from the approach taken by some data base practitioners: "Define and implement the data base and the necessary reports will take care of themselves with the 4th generation language capabilities."

The approach in this book recognizes that functional and data base requirements are *equally* fundamental for applications constructed around an integrated data base. Moreover, they are highly interrelated, so that elaboration of one requires the previous preliminary results about the other. They must both be described in user-oriented terms which are independent of the physical implementation tools (for example, operating system and data base managements system) to be chosen later with the implementation assessment or in the design phase.

Exhibit 4-3 shows the five major steps in user requirements generation. The first three steps (2.2.1-2.2.3) develop both the functional description and data base description in a top-down manner. The fourth step (2.2.4) compiles performance requirements. The last step (2.2.5) formally documents the results of the other steps.

The functional description tells what this application will do for users. Generation of functional requirements starts in step 2.2.1 with a special type of data flow diagram, called user concept diagrams. These identify automated processes from the users' perspective and trace the flow of data through the processes. The diagrams themselves have a hierarchical nature so that they start with a system overview and then decompose first the major functional areas and

EXHIBIT 4-3. User Requirements Generation Components

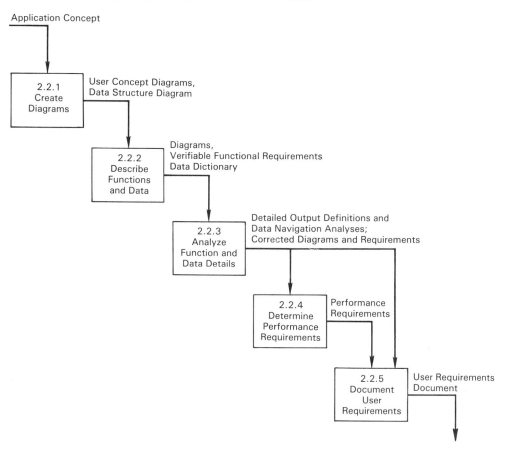

then more detailed functional activities as necessary to obtain a comprehensive view of the system. User concept diagrams give special attention to identification of the type of user anticipated for each process and how that user will interact with the system. Exhibit 4-4 shows a simple example of a user concept diagram.

The diagrams give pictorial views of the system—the artist's conception. In step 2.2.2, analysts must add the precise written statements which formalize detailed agreements concerning what the software must accomplish. In keeping with our user orientation, these verifiable functional requirements primarily use English-language statements, rather than programmer-like languages. However, detailed logic sometimes requires tools like decision tables and structured English. The verifiable functional requirements are tightly connected to the user concept diagrams for easy reference. They can be applied to all levels of the functional decomposition, and include nonperformance quality characteristics, such as graphics output pixel density and reference to local installation standards.

Definition of interfaces with external systems occurs with the functional description. The user concept diagrams have a special six-sided polygon symbol which designates an external system. Arrows between the external system symbols and function blocks identify transfer of interface data between the application being defined and other systems. The verifiable functional requirements describe the kinds of data which will be transferred, and how these transfers will appear physically to users. Detailed definition of interface data files occurs in the design phase.

Reports and other output definitions can be thought of as functional requirements. However, experience shows that outputs require additional detail and close correlation with the data base description. Hence, definition of critical application outputs can be considered a more detailed step (2.2.3) beyond verifiable functional requirements.

Elaboration of the data base description proceeds in parallel to the functional description using analogous techniques. An artist's conception is portrayed in step 2.2.1 with a single diagram called the data structure diagram. The data entities (conceptual record types) are indicated in boxes. Arrows show one-to-many relationships between the entities. Exhibit 4-5 gives a simple example which corresponds to the user concept diagram in Exhibit 4-4. Following generation of the data structure diagram, the analyst compiles lists of all data items in data dictionary tables in step 2.2.2. A final step (2.2.3) is an analysis of input and report processes or user views to determine if the data base description does in fact carry all the information required to support the application's functional requirements.

The data base description is independent of choice of data base management system (DBMS), or even the use of a DBMS. The approach in this book, however, is based on a philosophical bias toward integrated data bases managed by a modern data management software package. Instead of having functional processes that interface with each other, functions communicate through the master data base. Such an approach yields outstanding software maintenance

EXHIBIT 4-4. Library System Sample User Concept Diagram

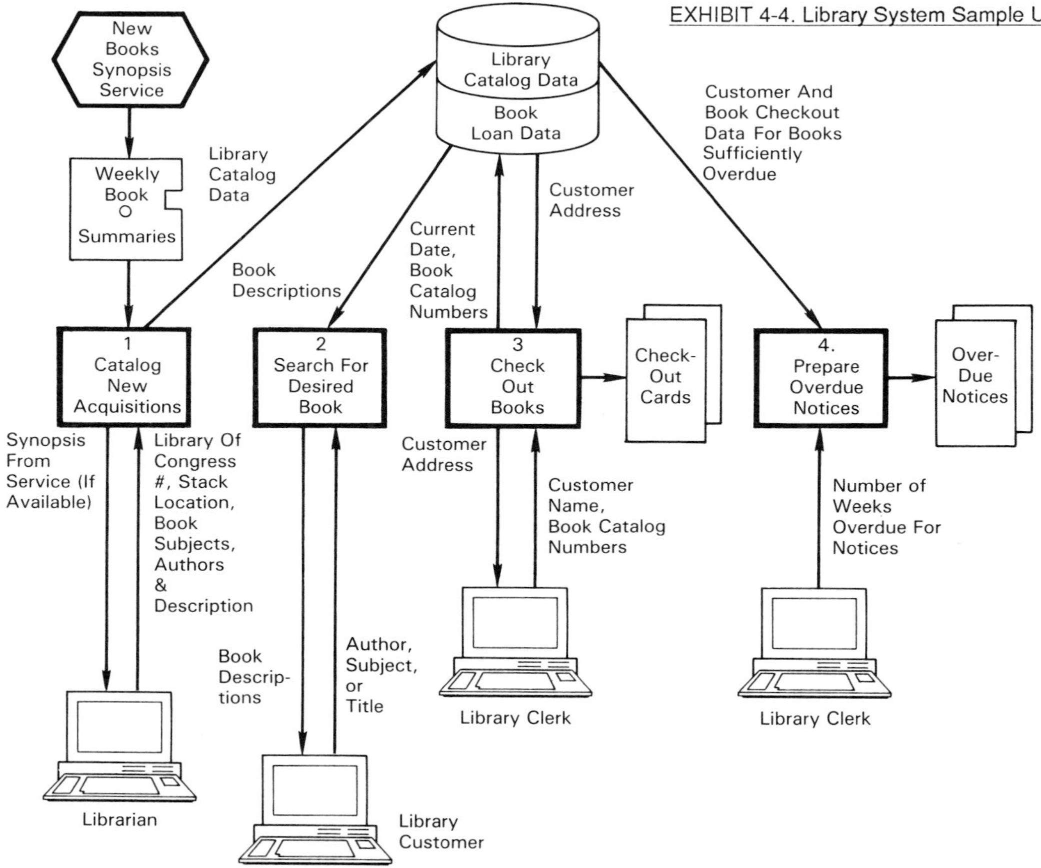

EXHIBIT 4-5. Library System Sample Data Structure Diagram

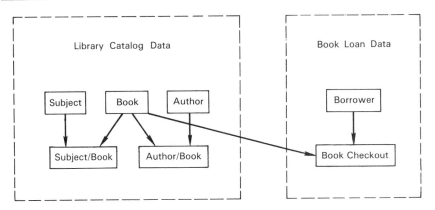

improvements and ad hoc reporting productivity gains over older process interface approaches, most typified by standard COBOL programs. In addition, requirements analysis based on an integrated data base is much faster than analysis based on detailed decomposition of data flows.

Detailed process data flow analysis is usually performed in the design and development phases. It may, however, need to be performed in the definition phase. In either case, a top-down method using data structure diagrams quickly focuses attention on the key data issues with each process.

Performance requirements indicate how well the application dispatches its workload. These requirements consist of:

- User population (number of users of each type)
- Data base size (number of occurrences of each entity type)
- Throughput (frequency that each functional activity is performed)
- Interactive response (reaction times).

As previously mentioned, other quality-oriented parameters, such as display size and number of colors on a graphics display terminal, are handled as part of the verifiable functional requirements.

Draft performance requirements (step 2.2.4) are best determined in group sessions. Performance estimates must then be checked for feasibility. This is a difficult technical matter which is often analyzed later as part of risk assessments.

The user requirements document (step 2.2.5) assembles the functional, data base, and performance requirements into a single document which allows all the user requirements to be reviewed as a whole. In the requirements generation process, analysts review preliminary requirements with users in a fairly informal manner. Paper handouts, briefing charts, and computer-aided software engineering workstation displays are typical media used for discussions aids. Now that the application concept, functional description, data base description, and performance requirements have been obtained, the analysts must package all of this material in a working document.

The user requirements document is the proper vehicle for publishing these results. It uses all of the materials generated so far, and adds the stylistic glue necessary to make the document readable. In this more formal form, the user requirements can be reviewed by a larger audience of interested people than the small core group involved in every analysis step. The user requirements document acts as an initial draft of the requirements specification. As indicated in Exhibit 3-1, the user requirements document contains most of the material published in the final specification.

IMPLEMENTATION ASSESSMENT (PHASE 2.3)

Following publication of the user requirements document, the analysts and developer bring technology realities into the picture (Exhibit 4-6). Can everything in the user requirements be implemented under a reasonable schedule and budget using available development personnel? Risks of any state-of-the-art functions, difficult performance requirements, algorithms, and so on must be assessed to bring these risks under control. Some nonoperational prototyping, including benchmarking, is usually necessary. Examination of alternative implementation approaches is also part of this step. Following risk assessments, an implementation plan must be assembled. This plan describes development phases, schedule, and estimated cost of the recommended implementation approach. Iteration with the application sponsor brings the scope of user requirements to the available resources.

EXHIBIT 4-6. Implementation Assessment Components

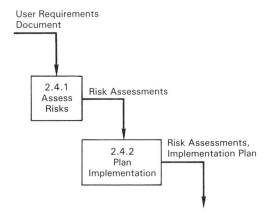

FORMAL SPECIFICATION PREPARATION (PHASE 2.4)

The user requirements document and implementation assessment lead to the final result of the definition phase: the requirements specification. As illustrated in Exhibit 3-1, the user requirements document appears to comprise most of the requirements specification. Only design constraints and implementation approach need to be added from the Implementation Assessment. However, the requirements specification often contains substantial differences from the user requirements document. These changes to functional, data, and performance requirements come from additional review by users, developer comments, and rescoping decisions which resulted from the implementation assessment. In a sense, the user requirements document acts as a model of the system which can be examined and changed much less expensively than an operational prototype.

The definition phase ends when the requirements specification is formally approved by the managers involved with the application. The specification is then used to guide the rest of the selected software development cycle.

THE PYRAMID MODEL

A condensed model helps to visualize the total user-centered requirements analysis approach. It should show the steps in Exhibits 4-1, 4-2, 4-3, and 4-6 on a

EXHIBIT 4-7. The Top-Down Process of User-Centered Requirements Analysis

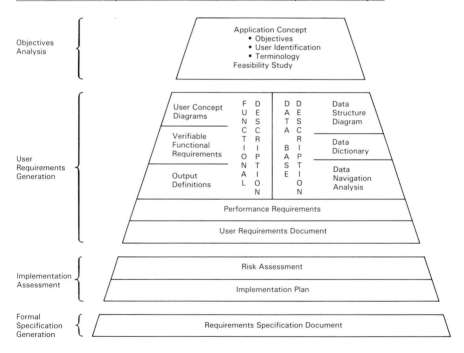

single diagram which can be used as an overall roadmap to the methodology. The pyramid diagram in Exhibit 4-7 serves this purpose. Read the steps downward from the top of the pyramid as a reminder that the methodology follows a top-down successive elaboration approach. The diagram reminds us that functional and data base requirements are generated in parallel, once an overview concept of the application has been established. For both functional and data base requirements, successive elaboration starts with diagrams, continues with detailed requirements, and may proceed to more comprehensive analyses that also could be

EXHIBIT 4-8. Organization of Chapters

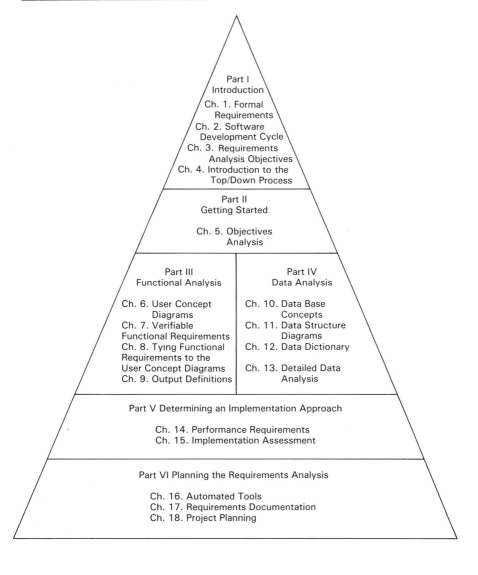

Part I
Introduction
Ch. 1. Formal
Requirements
Ch. 2. Software
Development Cycle
Ch. 3. Requirements
Analysis Objectives
Ch. 4. Introduction to the
Top/Down Process

Part II
Getting Started

Ch. 5. Objectives
Analysis

Part III
Functional Analysis

Ch. 6. User Concept
Diagrams
Ch. 7. Verifiable
Functional Requirements
Ch. 8. Tying Functional
Requirements to the
User Concept Diagrams
Ch. 9. Output Definitions

Part IV
Data Analysis

Ch. 10. Data Base
Concepts
Ch. 11. Data Structure
Diagrams
Ch. 12. Data Dictionary

Ch. 13. Detailed Data
Analysis

Part V Determining an Implementation Approach

Ch. 14. Performance Requirements
Ch. 15. Implementation Assessment

Part VI Planning the Requirements Analysis

Ch. 16. Automated Tools
Ch. 17. Requirements Documentation
Ch. 18. Project Planning

left until the design phase. Since the two subjects are worked at the same time, a single set of user interviews can discuss both the user concept diagrams and data structure diagrams. And both types of diagrams will be available for the next step of generating verifiable functional requirements and the data dictionary.

The user requirements document is really a draft of the requirements specification. Feasibility of the user requirements should be shown in an implementation assessment step. This is followed by preparation and sign-off of the requirements specification, which then drives design and development.

The remaining chapters of this book closely follow the pyramid model (see Exhibit 4-8). Some liberties were taken to add performance requirements to Part V (Determining an Implementation Approach), although performance requirements are really part of user requirements generation. Also, because the user requirements document and requirements specification are so closely related, they are described in a single chapter, Requirements Documentation (Chapter 17).

The Introduction has described the underlying philosophy of user-centered requirements analysis. Requirements are important to implementation success, whether a classical, prototyping, or reusable code software development cycle is employed. They should be clear, complete, and agreed upon. A top-down approach summarized in Exhibit 4-7 compiles the requirements through a combination of analysts generating strawman concepts (and providing technical expertise) and user representatives and the sponsor deciding what they want. The rest of the book takes this philosophical background as given, and describes each of the analysis steps and techniques in detail.

DISCUSSION QUESTIONS

1. A common alternative to analyzing risks in the definition phase is to go ahead and build the application, see where operational problems occur, and fix them. This is particularly true of performance goals, which are difficult to analyze before the fact.

    a. How should a manager decide which risks to analyze at the system definition step, which should be analyzed at system design, and which should be examined after building the application?

    b. What is the effect of application size on these decisions?

2. One style of systems analysis concentrates entirely on the definition of the data base. This approach has been popularized by James Martin in his prolific writings on this subject (1). The concept is that if you can generate an integrated data base which effectively models the business, then this data base will serve new applications as well as the applications which are known today. Hence, functional capabilities are looked at primarily for their data base implications. Implementation starts with construction of the data base and then gradually adds analysis and output capabilities, mostly using user-controlled 4th generation languages.

    a. What problems are caused by taking this approach of concentrating on the data base definition?

b. Which situations would be most amenable to the James Martin approach, and which require the kind of balance between functional and data base definition which is discussed in this text?

3. Ken Orr (2) takes a stance quite different from James Martin. Orr's view is that systems analysis should concentrate on the outputs of the system. The outputs (reports, decision-support queries, etc.) are the visible products of the system. Users (and hence the sponsor) will be happy if these products come out the way they want them. They do not care about data base and functional niceties, or how the application was thrown together.

a. What problems are caused by concentrating the systems analysis on definition of the main application outputs?

b. What kinds of applications would be served best by Orr's approach? Which would be served worst?

4. The definition phase is sometimes broken into two efforts with separate formal documentation. As described by David King, these two steps produce requirements definition and system specification documents (3). The requirements definition gives a high level view of the system, slightly more detailed than the application concept and feasibility study from objectives analysis. A software development organization takes the requirements definition and adds considerable detail about user functional and data requirements. The resulting system specification corresponds to this book's requirements specification. The main differences between the approach described here in Exhibit 4-2 and the two-step approach described by King are described in Exhibit 4-9. Most of the techniques of user-centered requirements analysis can be used in the two-step model described by King.

EXHIBIT 4-9. Primary Differences Between the 1-Step and 2-Step Models

Characteristic	Process to Generate Requirements Specification (Exhibit 4-7)	Requirements Definition and System Specification Process (Ref. 4-3)
Organizations analyzing user requirements	Single group of analysts	Two different groups; developer produces system specification
Number of formal requirements documents	One — the requirements specification	Two — the requirement definition and system specification
Need for developer involvement in user requirements	Small — developer can start with design phase	Large — detailed knowledge needed for system specification

a. In which situations would each approach be most useful?

b. Is it a good or bad idea for the developer to have a large role in determining user requirements?

REFERENCES

1. James Martin, *Managing the Data-Base Environment*, Englewood Cliffs, N.J.: Prentice-Hall, 1983.

2. Ken Orr, *Structured Requirements Definition*, Topeka, Kansas: Ken Orr and Associates, 1981.

3. David King, *Current Practices in Software Development*, Englewood Cliffs, N.J.: Yourdon Press, 1984.

PART TWO
Getting Started

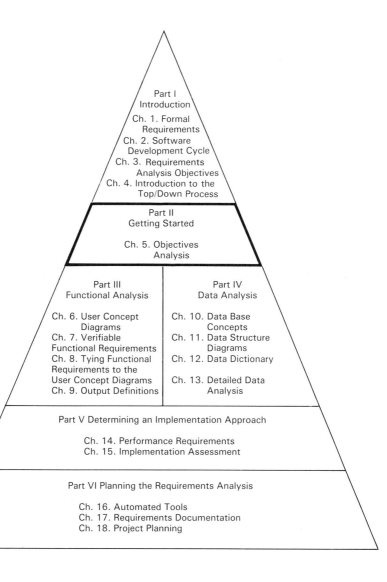

Part I
Introduction

Ch. 1. Formal
Requirements
Ch. 2. Software
Development Cycle
Ch. 3. Requirements
Analysis Objectives
Ch. 4. Introduction to the
Top/Down Process

Part II
Getting Started

Ch. 5. Objectives
Analysis

Part III
Functional Analysis

Ch. 6. User Concept
Diagrams
Ch. 7. Verifiable
Functional Requirements
Ch. 8. Tying Functional
Requirements to the
User Concept Diagrams
Ch. 9. Output Definitions

Part IV
Data Analysis

Ch. 10. Data Base
Concepts
Ch. 11. Data Structure
Diagrams
Ch. 12. Data Dictionary

Ch. 13. Detailed Data
Analysis

Part V Determining an Implementation Approach

Ch. 14. Performance Requirements
Ch. 15. Implementation Assessment

Part VI Planning the Requirements Analysis

Ch. 16. Automated Tools
Ch. 17. Requirements Documentation
Ch. 18. Project Planning

5

Objectives Analysis

Starting can be the most difficult part of systems analysis. All you have is a vague application charter. Called in to be the systems analyst for this application, you probably know very little about the user organization or the subject of the application. People you talk to know very little about systems analysis. How do you break the ice and get moving?

You have three ways to get information to start putting bounds on the new application:

- Interview business area experts.
- Read relevant reports and manuals.
- Exercise existing automated systems.

The problem is that it is easy to drown in details from any or all of these sources.

A life raft that keeps you from drowning is the concept of successive elaboration. From the tremendous amount of data available to you, you want to start the requirements analysis by obtaining a few high-level descriptions which bound the new application. That is the idea behind objectives analysis.

Exhibit 5-1 emphasizes the varied data sources possible for the two steps of objectives analysis: determine the application concept and study feasibility. The

EXHIBIT 5-1. Overview of Objectives Analysis

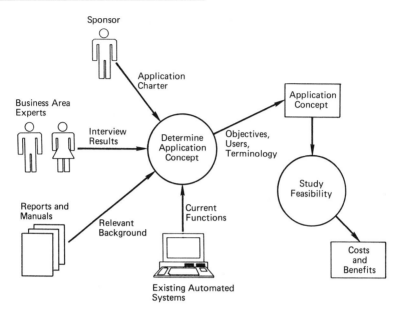

main problem is how to compile the available facts into an application concept in the first step. The second step takes a quick look to see if this application concept would be worthwhile to the business.

Common sense says that you will use different strategies depending upon the relative availability and relevance of each of the three types of information sources. Hence, this text does not try to suggest a "cookbook" approach for determining the application concept. However, when you customize your approach, you should consider:

- Organizational data flow analysis
- Critical success factor interviews
- Application concept components.

The first two are specific techniques to help gain an understanding of the environment and application charter. The third is a set of guidelines concerning the material which you need to compile. This chapter discusses each of these three points, and then explains how to perform the feasibility study.

ORGANIZATIONAL DATA FLOW ANALYSIS

In organizational data flow analysis, a systems analyst interviews people working in the business areas to be affected by the new application. The objective is to obtain clear diagrams showing how information *currently* flows within the existing organization. Exhibit 5-2 shows an example organizational data flow diagram

EXHIBIT 5-2. Time Sheets Example, Organizational Data Flow Diagram

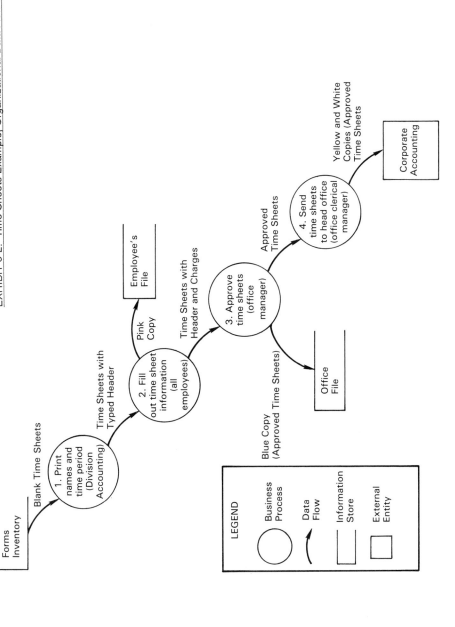

LEGEND

◯ Business Process

↗ Data Flow

▯ Information Store

▢ External Entity

for processing of time sheet forms through a professional office. Circles describe activities performed by particular individuals or organizations and arrows indicate flow of information between activities. In this case, the time sheets get progressively more information about individual charges and approvals until all copies are distributed to the right places.

Organizational data flow diagrams are a useful starting device when the current processing is confusing and when the scope of the new application is so large that nobody understands all the organizational interactions.

As an example of a confusing situation, consider production planning for a factory in which several different groups are involved with planning and scheduling factory processes and inventory movement. Organizational data flow diagrams may prove that the different planners perform parts of a unified hierarchical planning process with varying levels of scheduling detail. But the flows may also show that redundant (and conflicting) schedules are being kept by several different groups due to lack of communication or political empire building. In that case, the organizational data flow diagrams point out defects in operational policy which need to be worked out before determining requirements for supporting automation.

As an example of a large problem, consider a successful startup company which is making the transition from small entrepreneurial firm to a $100 million business and now needs a complete upgrade of its accounting systems. Organizational data flow diagrams may be necessary to establish a firm baseline of the current accounting practices. The accounting needs have expanded so rapidly that no single person understands what is supposed to happen across the various accounting groups. Organizational data flow diagrams, perhaps packaged in a procedures manual, can bring a measure of management control to such a situation.

A substantial theory exists to describe effective ways to generate organizational data flow diagrams of the current situation. DeMarco's (1) and Gane & Sarson's (2) books are widely used, helpful guides to this process. It is only briefly described here with Exhibit 5-1, because the organizational issues this technique addresses should really be addressed as part of concept identification before starting to generate requirements for a specific automated application.

Some writers insist that all new MIS applications should start with organizational data flow diagrams showing the current procedures. However, this extra work is unnecessary if the current situation is already well documented in procedures documents. It may also be unnecessary if new procedures will be followed with the new automated application, so that the current processes have limited relevance.

CRITICAL SUCCESS FACTORS

The technique of critical success factors was introduced by John Rockart in a *Harvard Business Review* article in 1979 (3). Critical success factors (CSFs) are the few key areas of activity in which favorable results are absolutely necessary for a particular manager to reach his goals. CSF analysis uses interviews with key managers to successively determine the following (4):

- Organization objectives (general statement of intended business directions)
- Goals (specific targets intended to be reached at a given time)
- Critical success factors
- Measures (specific standards which allow calibration of performance for each CSF, goal, or objective)
- Reports (information required about measures)
- Data bases (automated or manual systems required to generate the reports).

The analyst explains what these terms mean, and then asks for the information in direct questions (What are your organization's objectives? What are your goals?). By focusing on the important business issues (CSFs), this process isolates the kinds of information which are essential for MIS applications to make available to top management.

An example helps illustrate Rockart's special terms. Exhibit 5-3 shows the kinds of information about objectives, goals, CSFs, and measures which come from the interviews.

Critical success factor analysis aids statement of the application charter. It is particularly helpful to determine objectives of an executive information system designed to provide top managers with indications of their organization's status and trends. When used as part of a complete systems analysis approach, CSF in-

EXHIBIT 5-3. Sample Critical Success Factor Interview Results

Organization Objective: PlumTech Corporation aims to be the dominant commercial supplier of mass spectrometers worldwide.

Goals: 25% world market share by 1987
50% world market share by 1989

Critical Success Factors:
- Incorporate the latest microprocessor automation in each spectrometer product.
- Achieve and hold the lowest manufacturing costs.
- Increase world-wide awareness of PlumTech and our products.

Measures:
- Fraction of spectrometer units sold which employ modern (less than five years old) microprocessors.
- Ratio of PlumTech manufacturing cost per unit to the leading competitor's cost, by product.
- Fraction of target population of laboratory researchers who are aware of PlumTech.

terviews yield the perspective of top management in short interviews which focus on global issues. The details of requirements for the information system are then worked out with lower level people in the organization.

Critical success factors will not solve all your problems in getting started with an analysis. You must also obtain other information, such as definitions of key terms. Moreover, CSF interviews with a number of managers will be confusing, because what is critical depends on the organization view held by each manager based on his responsibilities. When you use the CSF technique, you should restrict the CSF interviews to a few top managers who need to get information from the new system.

SAMPLE PROBLEM: ACE AEROSPACE CONTRACT TRACKING SYSTEM

Before describing the components of the application concept, this section introduces the sample problem which will be used for a consistent set of examples throughout this book. The subject is a contract financial management system for a fictional aerospace defense firm. It is small enough to talk about in a textbook and has features representative of custom applications for both government and commercial organizations.

Ace Aerospace Corporation is a defense-oriented engineering firm with yearly revenues of $200 million. The company grew from a Los Angeles-based start to six locations nationwide. The Virginia office has grown rapidly from business in Washington, D.C. Dr. Steven Brass, manager of the Capital Region Division based in Arlington, Virginia, has the following problems:

- Several projects recently ran into large, unexpected cost overruns at the end of the projects.

- The larger, more complex projects have been modified so often that it is increasingly difficult to price and track new changes. A government auditor was not satisfied with a recent explanation of costs and is now looking for evidence of fraud.

- Personnel actions have been reactive rather than planned. Mass hiring occurs when new projects come in. When projects wind down, it seems as if there are always more people to place than other projects can absorb. The resulting layoffs are costly to morale.

Dr. Brass decides that Ace Aerospace's corporate accounting system is not meeting all his needs. It must be supplemented by a local system which serves his program managers and "rolls up" data on a plantwide basis for more up-to-date projections of financial and personnel numbers for each division. He commissions a systems analyst to be the architect for the new application. The project starts with an objectives analysis, based upon interviews with Dr. Brass and program managers.

APPLICATION CONCEPT

The purpose of the application concept is to add sufficient detail to the application charter so that all individuals working on the requirements specification will have a good working definition of the purpose and bounds of the application. The feasibility study then indicates whether this concept appears to be implementable in a manner which makes the benefits worth the costs. The application concept contains three parts:

- Objectives of the application
- Identification of system users
- Definition of special terms.

This material should be available for reference in all later steps. When questions arise which suggest a change in scope of the application, there must be agreement among the analyst, the sponsor, and user representatives concerning any changes to the application concept.

Objectives analysis can often be attacked directly from the application charter, using interviews of key managers. When this is possible, it saves considerable time and effort over the organizational data flow approach (Exhibit 5-2) in beginning the requirements analysis.

Objectives of the Application

A good approach for listing objectives is to have a three-level set of successively more detailed concepts:

- Purpose (one sentence describing the overall reason the application should exist)
- Objectives (three-to-seven sentences describing basic services to be provided by the application)
- Features (ten-to-twenty noun clauses describing particular application capabilities which help characterize the special aspects of this application).

For Ace Aerospace, the analyst started with discussions of system purpose with Dr. Brass, the contract tracking system sponsor. In his usual outspoken style, Dr. Brass described exactly what he wanted from a new automated system. The analyst asked a number of questions which were answered by the Capital Region manager, but many of Dr. Brass's concepts were still not clear. The analyst then obtained details of current project accounting and contract management practices from the local accounting staff, a Capital Region contracts administrator, and some relevant corporate practices manuals. As clear and consistent objectives began to emerge, the analyst interviewed two project managers to try out the initial objectives. Finally, the objectives statement shown in Exhibit 5-4 was typed and reviewed with Dr. Brass and these project managers.

EXHIBIT 5-4. Ace Aerospace Contract Tracking System Objectives Statement

Purpose: The Contract Tracking System will provide current
        status of contract financial, personnel, and technical
        status for the Capital Region program managers and
        senior staff.

Objective:
• Maintain contract information to be up to date within
  one week at all times.
• Insure consistency of the Contract Tracking System data
  with the Ace Aerospace Corporate Accounting System.
• Provide current status, by program, to program managers.
• Generate contract status briefing charts for monthly
  project status reviews the division manager holds with
  his project managers, director of contracts, and division
  comptroller.

Features:
• interactive entry of data through data entry screen
  displays
• data entry of employee time charges from standard Ace
  Aerospace time sheets
• automated checks of input data for consistency and
  reasonableness
• ability for program managers to define their own queries
  and reports using ad hoc query and ad hoc report
  languages
• automatic generation of the contract status and contract
  line item status reports
• ability for project managers to provide comments to be
  incorporated on project status review briefing charts
• color printout of project status review briefing charts
  on either plain paper or transparencies used for overhead
  projection
• softcopy access to briefing charts at graphics terminals

The objectives statement helps readers to understand the general idea of the
application. It is not sufficiently detailed to give to a software developer or tester.
It does, however, provide bounds on the application to guide the rest of the systems
analysis. When critical success factors interviews or organizational data
flow diagrams are used, their results should still be interpreted in an objectives
statement (Exhibit 5-4).

Identification of System Users

The second part of the application concept is identification of the types of
people who will be using the system. In some cases this will be specific individuals,
but usually the user identification is by work function. It is helpful to add
some indication of characteristics of the user types. These characteristics will be
taken into consideration when analyzing the requirements and design of man-
machine interactions for each user type.

Based on the same discussions which generated the Ace Aerospace objectives
statement, the systems analyst compiled an initial list of user types shown in
Exhibit 5-5. This list identifies four types of direct users who will interact with
the system. Division executives (Dr. Brass and his staff) and contract administra-

EXHIBIT 5-5. Contract Tracking System User Types

User Type	Characteristics
Direct Users	
Project Managers	These managers need to be able to obtain financial status of a particular project quickly without knowing much about the contract tracking system. They also need to be able to display project briefing charts with very little knowledge of the system.
Division Financial Analysts	These individuals have a great deal of computer experience, based on extensive use of personal computer tools like electronic spreadsheets.
Data Entry Clerks	These people will not have the "big picture" of the contract tracking system. They need to be able to enter quantities of contract characteristics and financial data quickly and accurately. When mistakes appear in input records, they need to be notified as quickly as possible to make the necessary changes.
Contract Tracking System Administrator	This individual is responsible for overall contract tracking system integrity. He needs tools to understand the current status of the system and to make necessary changes. Emphasis is on control of user permissions, but tools to control format and content of the data base are also required.
Indirect Users	
Division Executives	Dr. Brass and his staff want to see reports and briefing charts which are clear, uncluttered, and polished. He also wants to be able to change the output formats when he thinks of better ideas. He might become a direct user in running the briefing chart displays. That capability must be made absolutely crash-proof, in order to maintain his confidence in the system.
Contract Administrators	Contract administrators will feed information to the system by paper work sheets. They need contract status summary reports which are consistent with their contracts paper work.

tors will be indirect users who supply paper inputs and use reports and charts generated by the system.

Definition of Special Terms

The third part of the application concept is definition of special terms. Every application has a few words or phrases used in a special way. Understanding the special meaning of these terms is central to understanding the application. The terms are easy to identify, since they are the terms the systems analyst has the most difficulty fully understanding in the early interviews. Defining them is the hard part.

You should face the issue directly by asking questions about these terms and then coming up with strawman definitions as in Exhibit 5-6. When the managers being interviewed see these suggested definitions, they get a better understanding of how the term is unclear to you, and they can then help to iterate the definitions to agreed-upon statements. For a complex term like work breakdown structure, a special diagram like Exhibit 5-7 will often be needed.

EXHIBIT 5-6. Example Definitions of Special Terms

Term	Definition
Deliverable Item	Document, briefing, or product which must be formally delivered to a client official in a manner specified in the contract. The format, delivery schedule, number of copies, and recipients will be specified.
Work Breakdown Structure (WBS)	Hierarchical breakdown of an entire contract into successively more detailed work elements. Government contracts usually have the highest 2 or 3 levels specified by the government. Ace Aerospace fills in lower levels. After work starts, work breakdown structure changes are the responsibility of the Ace Aerospace program manager. By company policy, the same type of WBS is also used for contracts with commercial organizations.

FEASIBILITY STUDY

The purpose of an early feasibility study is to take a quick look at the application concept to determine whether the automation application appears to be implementable in a practical manner. An automation idea may be a great productivity tool if it can be implemented with a couple of personal computers and commercial software at a cost of three man-weeks of training and $15,000 of hardware and software purchases. But the same idea may make no sense at all if it will take a million dollars to implement and 18 months to develop.

By nature, the feasibility study is loosely structured and dependent on the experience and personality of the systems analyst. However, the study should address the following subjects, based on the application charter and application concept:

- Implementation costs and schedule
- Quantifiable and intangible benefits
- Detailed estimates of resources and time required to generate the requirements specification.

EXHIBIT 5-7. Contract Work Breakdown Structure Example

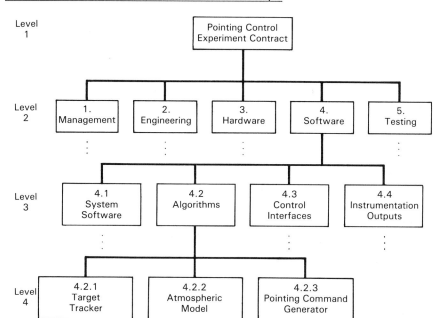

David King offers a good description of the feasibility study (5). He includes the application concept as part of the study. In the author's experience, the feasibility study often takes the form of a proposal to perform the definition phase analysis.

The sponsor uses the feasibility study results to determine whether the analysis should proceed through the definition phase. If the decision is affirmative, then the sponsor must make sure that the time and financial resources required by the analyst(s) will be made available. In addition, user representatives must be identified and have time set aside to assist.

To summarize, projects often get overwhelmed by details at the start, and fail to develop momentum. Objectives analysis develops a top-level description of the application, including a statement of objectives, identification of users, special terminology, and projected costs and benefits. By concentrating on these high-level concerns, the analyst avoids entrapment by details, and produces a description which guides the rest of the requirements analysis. Two specific techniques can help the analyst get started in objectives analysis. Organizational data flow diagrams are useful when there is no other way to understand the business area to be served than by mapping out current process flows. Critical success factor interviews help to clarify the top managers' needs, particularly for an executive information system. These techniques should be used only when clearly needed.

Objectives analysis should be performed quickly in days or weeks, not months. The primary requirements analysis effort is construction of the functional and data base descriptions. Those efforts are guided by the results obtained in objectives analysis.

DISCUSSION QUESTIONS

1. Giving a short, accurate, comprehensible description of a software application is always difficult. Give it a try with an application you are familiar with.
    a. Give a one-sentence statement of purpose.
    b. List the major objectives.
    c. Indicate features characterizing the application.
    d. Characterize the intended direct users.
    e. Define special terms used by this application.

    Check what you've written.   Are there general "motherhood" statements which could apply to any application, or have you succeeded in characterizing the unique aspects of this one?

2. Your company has a year-end accounting application which is undocumented. The programmer who patched it up last year left the company, and management wants you to figure out what the code does, how it should be used, and what changes are required to accommodate recent tax law changes.   How should you start this task?

REFERENCES

1. Tom DeMarco, *Structured Analysis and System Specification*, Englewood Cliffs, N.J.: Prentice-Hall, 1979.
2. Christopher P. Gane and Trish Sarson, *Structured Systems Analysis Tools and Techniques*, Englewood Cliffs, N.J.: Prentice-Hall, 1979.
3. John F. Rockart, "Chief Executives Define Their Own Data Needs," *Harvard Business Review*, March-April 1979.
4. Christine V. Bullen and John F. Rockart, "A Primer on Critical Success Factors," CISR No. 69, Center for Information Systems Research, Sloan School of Management, Massachusetts Institute of Technology, June 1981.
5. David King, *Current Practices in Software Development*, Englewood Cliffs, N.J.: Yourdon Press, 1984.

PART THREE
Functional Analysis

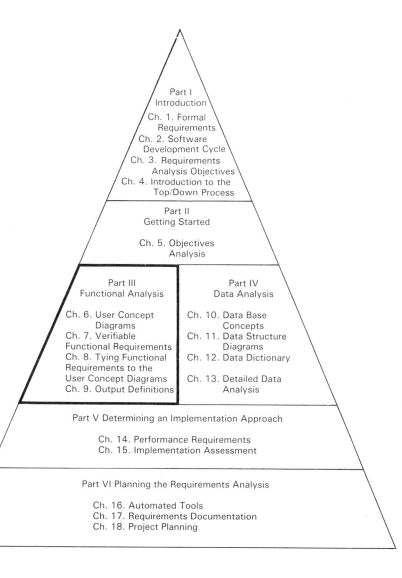

Part I
Introduction

Ch. 1. Formal
Requirements
Ch. 2. Software
Development Cycle
Ch. 3. Requirements
Analysis Objectives
Ch. 4. Introduction to the
Top/Down Process

Part II
Getting Started

Ch. 5. Objectives
Analysis

Part III
Functional Analysis

Ch. 6. User Concept
Diagrams
Ch. 7. Verifiable
Functional Requirements
Ch. 8. Tying Functional
Requirements to the
User Concept Diagrams
Ch. 9. Output Definitions

Part IV
Data Analysis

Ch. 10. Data Base
Concepts
Ch. 11. Data Structure
Diagrams
Ch. 12. Data Dictionary

Ch. 13. Detailed Data
Analysis

Part V Determining an Implementation Approach

Ch. 14. Performance Requirements
Ch. 15. Implementation Assessment

Part VI Planning the Requirements Analysis

Ch. 16. Automated Tools
Ch. 17. Requirements Documentation
Ch. 18. Project Planning

6

User Concept Diagrams

In any kind of analysis, it is easier to proceed when there is a simple picture giving insights about the structure of the problem at hand. In systems analysis, user concept diagrams are remarkably successful in portraying the major characteristics of the software application. These diagrams do not themselves express requirements. However, as suggested by Exhibit 6-1, they give a framework for viewing the various components of the system which must be specified. Because the diagrams can be kept rather simple, they are a good way to start the functional analysis and serve as an introduction to functional requirements in the requirements documents.

The systems analyst can be compared to an architect. Both start by finding out about the client's objectives. Then they show the client sketches of what the result could look like.

In the architect's case, the most attention is given to floor plans, using conventions for room layouts, windows, doors, stairs, electrical outlets, and special materials. Detailed construction specifications (materials, workmanship, finishing details) must be written up and keyed to the floor plans. Other diagrams showing elevations and special details will be required. But most of the architect-client interaction is focused on floor plans with the living-space details which will make all the difference in how the client uses the structure.

EXHIBIT 6-1. Content of User Concept Diagrams

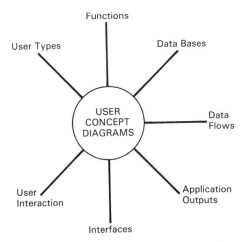

In the systems analyst's case, the most attention is given to user concept diagrams, which show the characteristics outlined in Exhibit 6-1. Detailed requirements must be specified and keyed to these diagrams. Other diagrams showing the data base structure and special details will also be needed, but most of the discussion concerning what the system must accomplish will be centered around the user concept diagrams.

In both cases, agreement on the diagrams lets the professional and the client talk about the details in a systematic way. Should the bathroom have a bathtub, or will a smaller shower stall suffice? Should salary figures be available to all system users, or just to higher management personnel?

OUTLINE OF THE USER CONCEPT DIAGRAM DISCUSSION

As Exhibit 6-1 suggests, a number of features of user concept diagrams need to be learned in order to employ the technique successfully. It is important to know both the rules for constructing the diagrams and the analysis steps which compile the information necessary to construct them.

This chapter makes heavy use of comparisons with other techniques and the architect analogy in order to present the major ideas behind user concept diagrams. A discussion of the older HIPO and DeMarco techniques helps clarify the concepts of hierarchical functional decomposition, data flow diagrams, hierarchical diagrams, and future physical models. Following this background, several sections present the symbols and construction rules for user concept diagrams, using examples from the Ace Aerospace problem. Finally, a comparison with DeMarco and structured analysis and design technique (SADT™)* diagrams

---

*SADT is a trademark of SofTech, Inc.

shows that other data flow diagramming styles can be stretched to satisfy most of the objectives portrayed in Exhibit 6-1.

THE EVOLUTION FROM HIPO TO DATA FLOW DIAGRAMS

The first widespread systems analysis technique was the HIPO (hierarchical input-process-output) chart, introduced by IBM around 1970 (1). The technique is based on two main ideas:

- The application functions should be decomposed hierarchically.
- Each functional breakout should be defined by inputs, processing, and outputs of that function.

Exhibits 6-2 and 6-3 show how the simplest form of HIPO could be applied to the Ace Aerospace example. The hierarchical decomposition of functions is shown in a tree diagram. Each function then has an input-process-output description.

It is important that a hierarchical decomposition should in fact be a decomposition. That is, each row of the chart should be a breakout of the entire system into nonoverlapping parts. It can be extremely difficult to follow a concept when the function blocks overlap. For example, suppose the "Corporate Accounting Comparison Report" function fell under both "Manage Contract Data" and under "Generate Standard Reports" (see Exhibit 6-2). The problem of

EXHIBIT 6-2.   Hierarchy Chart for Ace Aerospace Contract Tracking System

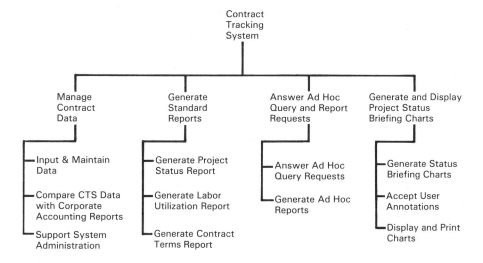

EXHIBIT 6-3. Example Input-Process-Output Chart for Ace Aerospace

Project Status Report		
Input	Process	Output
Contract modifications Work breakdown structure Milestones Cost items Manpower utilization	• Format data for each subreport • Check for inconsistent data • Print results or send to a remote terminal	Contract Change subreport Milestone Status subreport Financial Status subreport Labor Application subreport Other Direct Costs subreport
Labor Utilization Report		
Input	Process	Output
Contracts Salary levels Application of salary level manpower to contracts	• Find salary level application by month, • Check for abnormal, changes • Sum up charges over all contracts • Print results or send to a remote terminal	Overall salary level application trends subreport Individual contract salary level trends subreport Major changes management-by-exception report

overlapping functional areas is one of the most common sources of confusion in real projects. To avoid overlap, the systems analyst must constantly refine and monitor function boundaries. With HIPO charts, these boundaries are determined by the process statements.

A second comment on the HIPO technique is that hierarchies can be displayed in other notations. Exhibit 6-4 shows two common alternative notations. The Warnier-Orr notation (A) is sometimes useful when working at a blackboard. The indented list notation (B) is the simplest to produce with a typewriter or word processor.

HIPO charts were popular in the 1970s, because they provided a simple way to decompose large problems into smaller ones which could be understood in detail and programmed. The technique is still commonly employed as a system design tool.

Systems analysts found that HIPO was somewhat awkward to use, because consistency of inputs and outputs needed to be checked on a system-wide basis. Are the inputs for function 2.3 all set and maintained by other functions? What happens to a particular kind of data as functions act on it throughout the application?

One direct way to answer these questions is a set-use matrix, such as shown in Exhibit 6-5. The matrix has rows and columns identified by functions and data aggregates. Each cell tells whether that function sets or uses information in the

EXHIBIT 6-4. Alternative Hierarchy Notations

(A) Warnier-Orr Bracket Notation

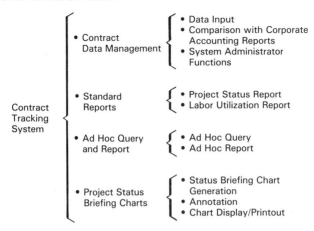

(B) Indented List Notation

Contract Tracking System

    1. Contract Data Management
       1.1 Data Input
       1.2 Comparison with Corporate Accounting Reports
       1.3 System Administrator Functions

    2. Standard Reports
       2.1 Project Status Report
       2.2 Labor Utilization Report

EXHIBIT 6-5. Example Set-Use Matrix

FUNCTION	DATA AGGREGATE			
	Contract Structure	Contract Modifications	Corporate Rates	Cost Elements
1.1 Contract Data Input	S	S	S	S
1.2 Comparison with Corporate Accounting Reports	U	U		S/U
1.3 System Administration Functions	U	U	U	U
2.1 Project Status Report	U		U	U

Key: S — Function sets (inputs or modifies) data
          in this data aggregate
        U — Function uses data in this data aggregate
      S/U — Function both sets and uses the data
            aggregate

EXHIBIT 6-6. Input-Process-Output Diagram Schematic

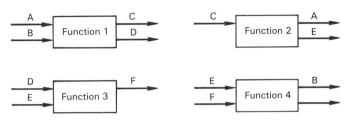

indicated data aggregate. Programmers have been using such matrices to help debug applications for the last 30 years. Why not use this technique and HIPO for systems analysis?

The reason set-use matrices do not quite suffice is that they do not show the flow of data. Which function sets the data initially? Which one acts on the data next? Before function 2.3 acts on the data, what must be present in the data set? A diagramming style needs to be used which shows a logical sequence of transformations of the data.

Data flow diagrams are now the generally accepted way to combine functional decomposition with a view of the sequence of transformations on data. They are now usually generated without starting with a HIPO representation. However, it is useful to see the close connection between the two techniques. Exhibits 6-6, 6-7, and 6-8 illustrate a mechanical procedure for transforming input-process-output diagrams to data flow diagrams.

Start the procedure by reformatting the input-process-output chart as shown in Exhibit 6-6. Place functions in boxes. Represent inputs as labeled arrows coming into the left side of each function box and outputs as labeled arrows emerging from the right side of each function.

EXHIBIT 6-7. Conversion to Data Flow Diagram

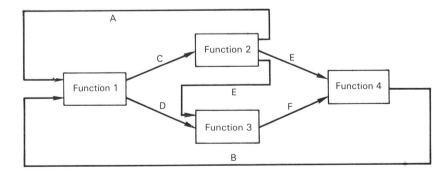

EXHIBIT 6-8. Simplifying Data Paths and Adding Data Stores

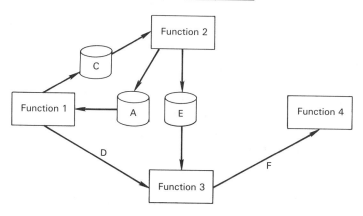

Next, link up all output and input arrows which have the same labels, as shown in Exhibit 6-7. In practice, the difficult part of this step will be maintaining the appropriate data nomenclature consistency to achieve the proper matchups. Naming consistency is important to have, and an initial benefit of data flow diagrams.

Exhibit 6-7 suffers from data flow lines being too "busy" on the page. A rigid adherence to inputs coming in on the left side and outputs leaving the right side make flows like A, B, and E have long, roundabout paths.   In real applications, such depictions of data flows make for a cluttered diagram which is hard to read. This is the prime objection to SADT diagrams, as will be discussed later in this chapter. The solution to this problem is to relax the left-side/right-side restrictions and rely only on the arrow direction to tell whether the data flow is an input or output from that function.

The diagramming style in Exhibit 6-7 also suffers from its lack of discrimination between transient and stored data. If function 1 sends data flow C to function 2 solely to support function 2's next processing step, and no function will ever need to look at this data later, then it is transient data. An example might be the set of parameters required for execution of a special report. If the data should be available later for these functions and others (including user queries) to access, then it must be stored by the system. Given the importance of integrated data bases, identification of data flows which must be stored is of critical importance to the systems analysis.

Exhibit 6-8 shows how the sample looks when relaxing the input-left/output-right restriction and adding a can symbol for data stores. The exhibit shows that data flows D and F are transient, and all other flows must be stored for repeated access.

Analysts have found that data flow representations, like Exhibit 6-8, are much easier to work with than HIPO charts of an application. Working through the data flows often results in a more systematic decomposition of functions than is obtained using HIPO.

HIERARCHICAL DIAGRAMMING

In principle, any hierarchical layer of a functional decomposition of an application (for example, Exhibit 6-2) can be portrayed in a single data flow diagram. Gane and Sarson describe an entire application with a single diagram containing 22 functions and about three times that number of data flows (2). In practice, such concentration of information on one page is awkward for these reasons:

- Making changes to this master chart is difficult, expensive, and takes a lot of time.
- The chart observer tends to be overwhelmed by so much information.

Various psychological studies have shown that the human mind has difficulty comprehending more than seven concepts at once (3). Therefore, good analysis practice tends to limit data flow diagrams to no more than seven functions.

Hierarchical data flow diagrams restrict the density of detail on any one diagram, while retaining an overall sense of the hierarchical decomposition of the application. The literature also uses the term *leveled data flow diagrams*, which DeMarco used to describe hierarchical diagramming (4).

Exhibit 6-9 illustrates the fundamental idea behind hierarchical diagramming: Each function in a data flow diagram may itself be expanded into a more detailed data flow diagram. Thus, the hierarchy shown in Exhibit 6-2 could lead to 15 separate data flow diagrams, one for each function shown in that exhibit.

There is no one correct diagram for an application. Each systems analyst will diagram an application differently, just as a group of programmers attacking a problem with the same programming language will each come up with different instructions for doing the job.

THE DEMARCO PROGRESSION

One of the subtle questions which the systems analyst must answer is "What is the subject of the data flow diagrams?" Should the diagrams describe the overall business system, consisting of people, procedures, and automated support? Should concentration be on how business is currently being performed or on how it should be accomplished with improved methods?

Tom DeMarco suggested a valuable intellectual model of the types of data

EXHIBIT 6-9.   Hierarchical Data Flow Diagramming Concept

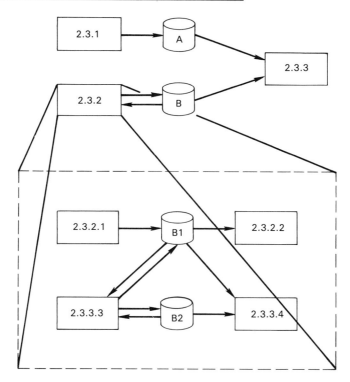

flow diagrams (4). In this model, the diagrams may be classified in two ways:

- Degree of abstraction
  - Logical
  - Physical
- Relevant time period
  - Current practice
  - Future, using new system(s).

These two choices give four basic types of data flow diagrams, as shown in Exhibit 6-10.

According to DeMarco, systems analyses naturally flow through all four of these possibilities, in the following order: current physical, current logical, future logical, and future physical. His current physical diagrams are the organizational data flow diagrams described in Chapter 5 (Exhibit 5-1 is an example). They describe flows of actual documents and computer data among particular individuals, organizations, and machines. In current logical diagrams, a more abstract view focuses on today's basic business functions which must be performed, types of people involved, and logical flow of data through the current

<u>EXHIBIT 6-10.</u>   Types of Data Flow Diagrams

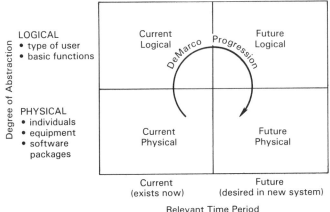

Relevant Time Period

functions. It is a simplified abstraction of the current physical diagram, and helps to point out the fundamentals of the activities being performed. The future logical view shows how the basic business functions could be streamlined or changed to improve efficiency or to satisfy some new business need. Finally, the future physical view gets to the details of which people will work with particular workstations and computers when the new system is built. The future physical model is the basis for DeMarco's structured specification.

DeMarco's theory was extremely attractive. Most of requirements analysis was reduced to data flow diagramming. Analyst training consisted of an introduction to the concept of data flow diagrams and instructions on achieving the transition through the four steps of the DeMarco progression. It was an elegantly simple concept which was easily automated in computer aided software engineering environments (Chapter 16). As a result, the DeMarco approach became a de facto standard for structured requirements analysis by 1986.

Unfortunately, elegance of concept does not always guarantee success in practice. Two major problems come from the straight DeMarco approach:

- It takes too long.
- It concentrates too much on data flows, and not enough on data base definition.

The first problem is that the four-stage DeMarco progression takes too much time and manpower. Analysts found that they could obtain just as good a definition of the new system without following the four stages, and take much less time. Moreover, there has been a tendency for projects using the DeMarco progression to become stuck on the current physical diagrams. McMenamin and Palmer refer to this problem as the "current physical tarpit" (5).

The goal is the future physical data flow diagrams which serve to tie together the functional, data, and interface requirements of the system. The user-centered requirements analysis steps develop the future physical model based on a streamlined objectives analysis. Why spend tremendous effort analyzing today's methods if people know already what they want to do in the future? This approach is consistent with McMenamin and Palmer's advice to "blitz an essential model" of the new system. It also is consistent with Ed Yourdon's admission that his firm (which developed the techniques described by DeMarco and Gane & Sarson) has "virtually eliminated" analysis of the current system (6).

The second problem is that DeMarco's approach puts too much emphasis on decomposition of data flows and insufficient emphasis on modeling the integrated data base. Chapter 13 gives an in-depth discussion of this issue. Here, it suffices to say that use of modern data analysis techniques early in the requirements analysis process makes it much easier to describe and understand data relationships than the hierarchical decomposition of data flows usually adopted by DeMarco-style analysts.

SYMBOLS FOR USER CONCEPT DIAGRAMS

User concept diagrams are a special kind of future physical data flow diagram which show what an automated information system will do for users. This section discusses the special symbols used in these diagrams.

Simple diagrams like Exhibit 6-8 with function boxes, data store cans, and data flow arrows are insufficient, because they fail to show any interfaces with the outside world. What data come from people performing interactive input or from other systems? What reports, displays, and data transfers come out of the system? Symbols are needed for external entities, so the data flows which come into and out of the automated system can be clearly indicated.

Many analysts use a single symbol for all external entities interfacing with the system. This type of abstraction leads to ambiguity in the diagrams and increases the difficulty of explaining the diagrams to user representatives. Returning to the architect analogy, the architect uses special symbols for doors, stairs, windows, and so on. These are pictorially more suggestive of the objects they represent than a single "nonwall" symbol would be. Likewise, symbols suggesting terminals, sheets of paper, and so on help the systems analyst.

In addition, the type of user interaction with the system is so important that a special notation should be used for this kind of data flow. The user type needs to be identified also, so that the style of the interaction can be designed to be compatible with the intended users.

A final requirement of the symbolism is that it be simple to draw using either standard flow chart templates or a computerized interactive graphics package. User concept diagrams will change rapidly in the early stages of analysis, and hence they must be simple to modify or redraw.

Exhibit 6-11 shows the symbols used in this book for user concept diagrams. There is nothing magical about this particular set. Additional symbols would have to be chosen for voice input, bar-code readers, mouse cursor control, and so on. The symbols should be visually suggestive and consistent throughout an individual application. Rationale for the symbol choices in Exhibit 6-11 is as follows:

- Boxes are used for functions, because they are easy to draw, can hold a long textual title, and stand out well on a page as a prime component of the system.
- Labeled arrows for data flows are standard for all data flow diagrams.
- Cans for on-line data stores are suggestive of disk drives, the usual kind of direct access storage today.
- Notched squares with a hole inside portray floppy disk storage of data.
- The circular reel with dangling line is suggestive of magnetic tapes.
- The hexagons are used for external systems, because they stand out clearly as being different from the function boxes for the system being defined.
- Two symbols are used for the user workstation interface. The rounded rectangle (suggestive of a keyboard) is quick for hand drawings. The terminal drawing is more graphic and just as quick with interactive graphics support when that symbol is prestored in a library. The user or user type is indicated with a label inside or below the terminal symbol.
- Hardcopy reports are indicated by vertical rectangles suggestive of 8.5" x 11" paper. Shadow copies of these rectangles are used to indicate multiple report formats in the same labeled family of reports.
- Softcopy displays are indicated by a rounded horizontal rectangle, suggestive of the video display on users' terminals. Again, shadow copies of the softcopy display symbol indicate multiple formats.
- Wide-screen projected displays have a wraparound screen symbol. This is a special type of output used in the Ace Aerospace example.

When the rounded rectangle is used to represent a terminal, the standard IBM flowchart template can be used to create these symbols.

Often system outputs can either be viewed interactively in a screen display or printed out in a report. Exhibit 6-12 shows how the hardcopy and softcopy output symbols can be used together, one in front of the other. The symbol shown in front represents the more usual form of this particular output. For example, an output usually viewed as a screen display, but available in printed form, can be represented with a report rectangle mostly covered up by a softcopy display symbol.

EXHIBIT 6-11.   Example User Concept Diagram Symbols

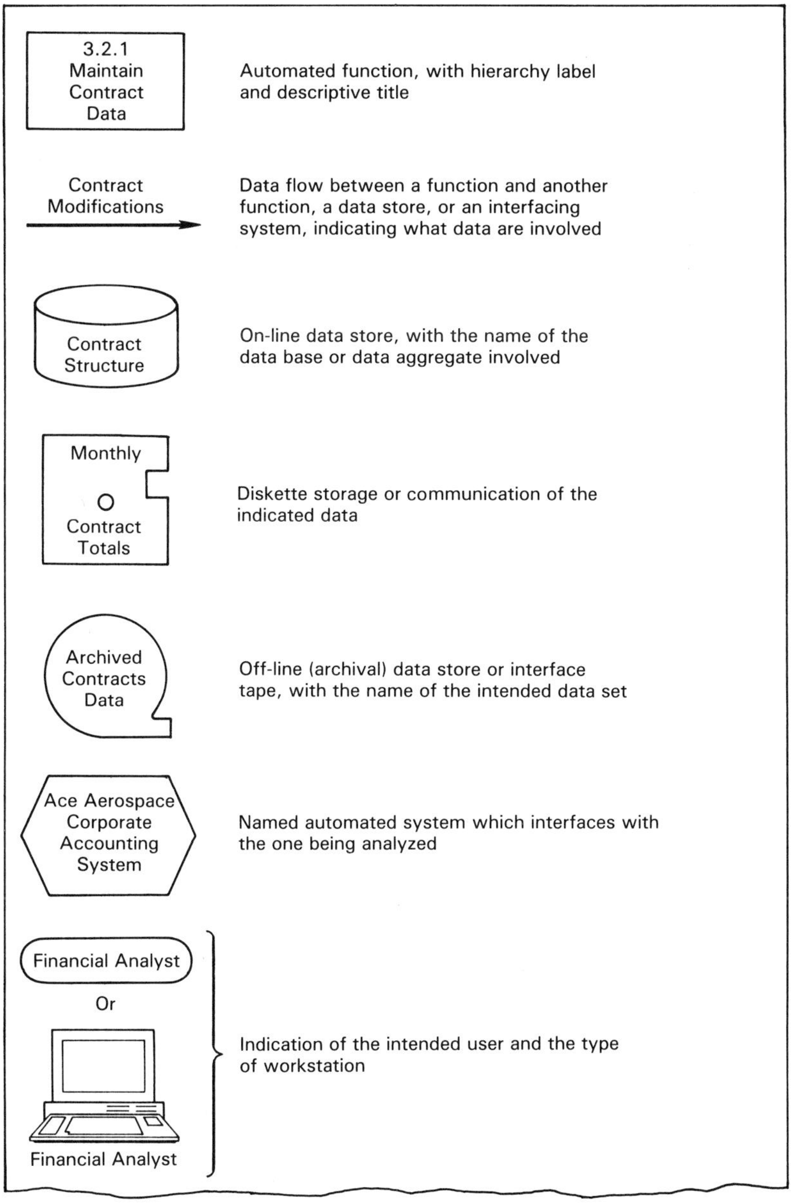

```
┌─────────────┐
│    3.2.1    │        Automated function, with hierarchy label
│  Maintain   │        and descriptive title
│  Contract   │
│    Data     │
└─────────────┘

    Contract            Data flow between a function and another
  Modifications         function, a data store, or an interfacing
  ──────────►           system, indicating what data are involved


   Contract             On-line data store, with the name of the
   Structure            data base or data aggregate involved


    Monthly
                        Diskette storage or communication of the
      O                 indicated data
   Contract
    Totals


    Archived
   Contracts            Off-line (archival) data store or interface
     Data               tape, with the name of the intended data set


  Ace Aerospace
   Corporate            Named automated system which interfaces with
   Accounting           the one being analyzed
    System


  Financial Analyst

       Or
                        Indication of the intended user and the type
                        of workstation



  Financial Analyst
```

EXHIBIT 6-11.   Example User Concept Diagram Symbols (Continued)

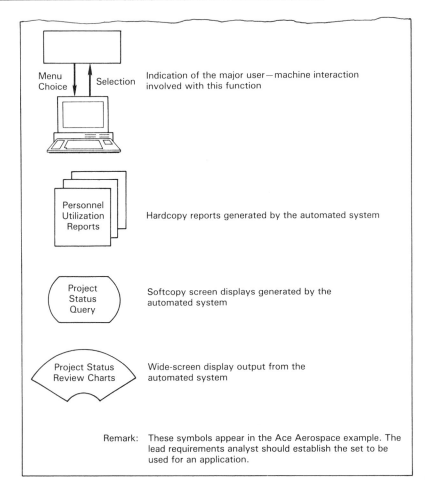

Menu Choice ↓ ↑ Selection — Indication of the major user—machine interaction involved with this function

Personnel Utilization Reports — Hardcopy reports generated by the automated system

Project Status Query — Softcopy screen displays generated by the automated system

Project Status Review Charts — Wide-screen display output from the automated system

Remark: These symbols appear in the Ace Aerospace example. The lead requirements analyst should establish the set to be used for an application.

EXHIBIT 6-12.   Softcopy/Hardcopy Preference Indication

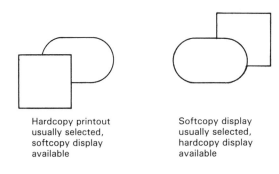

Hardcopy printout
usually selected,
softcopy display
available

Softcopy display
usually selected,
hardcopy display
available

GENERATING USER CONCEPT DIAGRAMS

Development of user concept diagrams for an application is a creative effort which deserves the systems analyst's best efforts. It is similar to the architect's conception of the right structure for his clients to place on a particular lot.

Top-Level User Concept Diagrams

The first decision is how to divide the entire system into functional divisions. This is an important decision, similar to the style of structure the architect and clients choose. The way the user concept diagrams break out the system will determine how people think and talk about it. There is no single correct way to divide up an application, but some ways are distinctly superior to others.

Four possible ways to start dividing an application into functions are by:

- User type
- Steps in a total planning and production cycle
- Input, processing, and output breakouts
- Functional areas meaningful to the client.

These will give quite different views, as Exhibit 6-13 shows.

EXHIBIT 6-13.   Comparison of Alternative Top-Level Decompositions of the Ace Aerospace System

Type of Decomposition	Top-Level Functions

By User Type	Support Division Executives' Decisions
	Support Financial Analysts and Contract
	    Administrators
	Support Project Managers
	Support Data Entry Clerks
	Support Contract Tracking System
	    Administrator

By Planning and Production Steps	Maintain Corporate Rates Establish Contracts and Contract Modifications Schedule Contract Milestones Enter Costs Support System Administration
By Input-Processing-Output	Manage Contract Data Generate Standard Reports Answer Ad Hoc Query and Report Requests Generate and Display Project Status Briefing Charts Support System Administration
By Functional Areas	Maintain Contract Parameters Track Contract Actual Costs Track Personnel Utilization Plan and Track Projects Administer Contract Tracking System

Note that you will need to consider the special functional area of system administration for most applications. This includes all operational checks needed to maintain system responsiveness, integrity of the data base, and user access. It is sometimes divided into subfunctions with names like data base administration, security officer, and so forth.

Which decomposition approach is best for the application depends on both the analyst's sense of balance and the user's feeling of comfort with the chosen approach. There should be approximately equal magnitudes of subfunctions and functional requirements under each major function. The breakout should match existing user business functions and terminology wherever possible.

Names of functions should be a composite of an active verb and an object, such as "Generate Standard Reports." Such a combination is clearer than naming with the object ("Standard Reports"), since it indicates more clearly what processing the system will perform. The functions "Generate Standard Reports" and "Retrieve Prestored Standard Reports" act on the same object, but apparently have nonoverlapping responsibilities. It pays to spend time replacing vague verbs like "process" with more descriptive ones like "optimize," "validate," or "combine," particularly with detailed functional breakouts. Proper choices of both the verb and noun parts of function names help to provide immediate conceptual bounds for the function.

For Ace Aerospace, the systems analyst leans toward the input-process-output style of decomposition. Before leaping too far with this approach, he confers with Dr. Brass's Administration Director, Bill Block. The discussion includes consideration of the three other decomposition approaches, and why the analyst recommends the input-process-output style for the Contract Tracking System. Bill agrees to try this approach.

Now it is time to diagram. What should the highest-level diagram look like? This can also be a tough decision. User concept diagrams are much easier to continue decomposing once you've generated the top level or two in a way which is natural for the application.

Some natural choices for the first diagram are:

- Context diagram containing a single function (the whole application)
- Skeleton diagram showing the first level of functional breakout of the system, and how those functions generally interact with the data base
- Full user concept diagram of the first level of funtional breakout, including interactions with external entities.

Exhibits 6-14, 6-15, and 6-16 show how each of these three choices appear for the Ace Aerospace example. The first two are drawn manually from an IBM flowchart template. This illustrates the manual approach which can be compared with the interactive graphics approach illustrated in Exhibit 6-16.

The context diagram (Exhibit 6-14) shows all the external inputs and outputs of the entire system. For small applications with a small number of external

EXHIBIT 6-14. Ace Aerospace Context Diagram

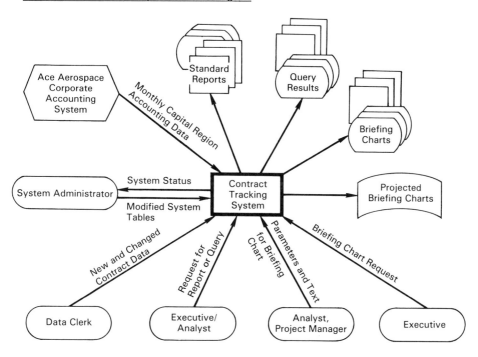

entities, this is an excellent place to start. But as systems get more complex, the number of distinct external entities (even when aggregated into a general type like "standard reports") can get unmanageably large. Besides making the context diagram hard to draw, a large number of external entities makes the resulting diagram difficult to read, as previously discussed (3).

For larger systems, it makes sense to start with a skeleton diagram like Exhibit 6-15. It shows only the top-level functions and gives a broad sense of how these functions interact with the main data base(s). The arrow from the first function, Manage Contract Data, to the Contract Tracking System Data Base indicates that this function's main purpose is to change the contents of the data base. The other three functions have data flow arrows from the main data base to the function, indicating that these functions primarily use but do not change the main data base. When the skeleton diagram is used for a large application, the next hierarchical level of diagrams will show decompositions of each of the top-level functions. These will start to show the context of external entities, as well as major breakouts of the data base into data aggregates.

The top-level functional breakout user concept diagram (Exhibit 6-16) can be used either in concert with a context diagram or as the diagramming starting

EXHIBIT 6-15.   Ace Aerospace Top-Level Functional Breakout Skeleton Diagram

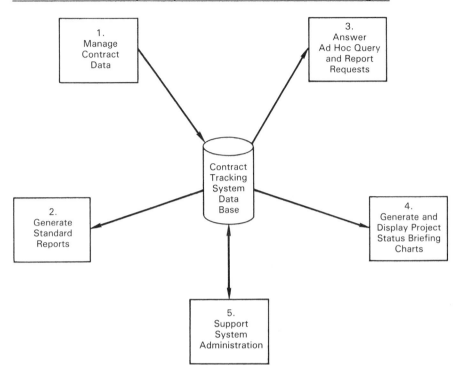

point. When used with a context diagram, it decomposes a function (the whole system) using the technique of hierarchical diagramming previously discussed. If the application is small enough, the context diagram may be too trivial to worry about, and then the top-level functional breakout diagram becomes a good starting overview level.

Note that the top-level functional breakout user concept diagram (Exhibit 6-16) is the same as the skeleton diagram (Exhibit 6-15), with the addition of external entities, data aggregate decomposition of the application data base, and data flow labels. User type indicators are often left out of this level if they would cause the diagram to be too cluttered.

Detailed User Concept Diagrams

Decomposing one of the top-level functions shows what happens with the detailed user concept diagrams.   Exhibit 6-17 shows a user concept diagram decomposing the first top-level function, Manage Contract Data. Evidently there is a significant increase in detail shown here over the definition of "Manage Contract Data" shown in Exhibit 6-16.   Some of the principles illustrated by Exhibit 6-17 include these:

EXHIBIT 6-16. Ace Aerospace Top-Level Functional Breakout User Concept Diagram

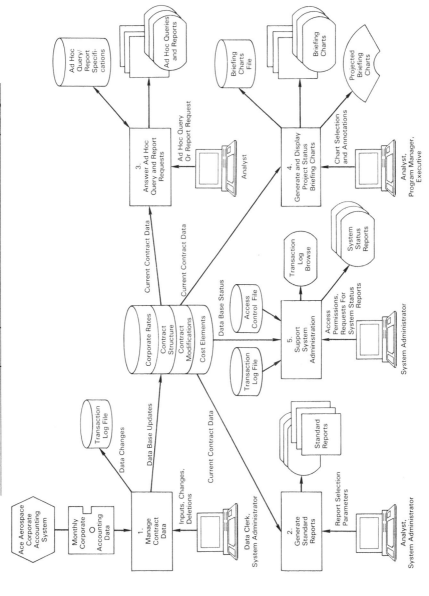

EXHIBIT 6-17. User Concept Diagram for Function 1, Manage Contract Data

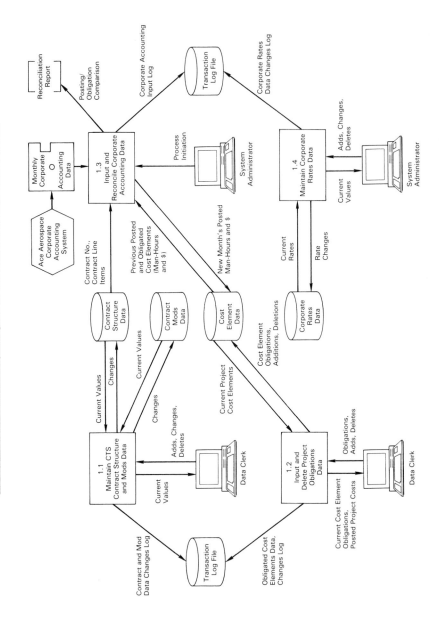

- The integrated data base is now broken down to individual data aggregates whose interactions are shown separately.
- A data store may be shown twice on the same page to simplify data flow lines (e.g., the Transaction Log File).
- Labels on data stores should correspond to data aggregate or record names in the data model.
- Data flow labels should be kept as concise as possible, while indicating the nature of the flows. Data flow labels are the hardest parts of the diagrams to draw and maintain.
- Numbering of the functions uses the standard decimal hierarchy numbering notation shown in Exhibit 6-4B. This helps the reader to travel up and down as well as laterally across levels of the functional decomposition hierarchy. (Note: The numbering system will be modified as to be discussed in Chapter 7.)
- The user interaction labels suggest the nature of the user interface. For example, in function 1.3, the user need only initiate the process, so that function appears to be an automated batch process which examines the entire monthly corporate accounting floppy disk without requiring user interaction.

Completing the User Concept Diagrams

When should the hierarchical user concept diagrams stop and decompose no more? The number of levels should be kept to the minimum needed to establish function-data relationships. In general, the tendency is for junior analysts to carry the diagrams too deep in hierarchical detail. Keep in mind that the user concept diagrams provide a conceptual framework to structure the verifiable functional requirements (Chapter 7). They do not themselves specify requirements. Some helpful guidelines follow:

- Too many diagrams or a large number of hierarchy levels becomes hard for readers to follow.
- Each user concept diagram should have between three and seven functions.
- A function which has a number of different kinds of things happening is a good candidate for decomposition.
- In particular, if users cannot get a reasonable general understanding of a function from its function block, flows, and some verbal comments, then it probably needs to be decomposed in its own diagram.
- Bottom-level functions should be describable in one or two pages of verifiable functional requirements (see Chapter 7).
- Unbalanced decompositions where some functions have many more subfunctions and/or hierarchy levels than others should be reorganized to obtain better balance. This usually reduces the number of diagrams.

A bottom line figure to shoot for is two, three, or at most four levels of decompositions only. Thus, function 1.3.2 in the third level of decomposition could be decomposed once more to functions 1.3.2.1 to 1.3.2.4, but further decomposition is likely to be counterproductive. If you are inclined to go further, check first for an unbalanced decomposition.

Another possibility is that the application is huge. When five-level decompositions appear to be inevitable, it is generally a sign that the application is unwieldy and should be divided into subsystems before using the techniques in this book. Methods to divide very large applications into manageable subsystems are often called business systems planning or strategic information planning techniques. They do *not* generally give the same results as the first level of functional decomposition here, because they strive to guarantee a coordinated decomposition of functional areas and subject data bases. These methods are outside the scope of this book. The interested reader may find out more by consulting IBM literature (7) and Gillenson and Goldberg's survey (8).

Data Store and Data Flow Labels

User concept diagrams help to link the functional requirements with the data base requirements. This linkage is provided by the data store and data flow labels.

Chapters 10 to 13 show how to use data analysis principles to structure the data base description. In this approach, there are four hierarchical levels of data base decomposition:

- Entire integrated data base
- Data aggregates
- Record types
- Data items.

Names used for the data base, data aggregates, record types, and data items should be used for user concept diagram data store labels and, where applicable, in data flow labels. This naming consistency achieves the desired connection between the functional description and data base description.

The level of detail of data stores increases with the level of detail of the user concept diagram. For example, Exhibit 6-15, a top-level functional breakout skeleton diagram, uses a single data store for the entire data base. Exhibit 6-16, a top-level functional breakout user concept diagram, also has a single data store symbol, but its label shows the data aggregates involved in the integrated data base. Exhibit 6-17, which details one function from Exhibit 6-16, has separate data store symbols for each data aggregate. When another level of detail is used, it may have a combination of data aggregate and record type data stores. In addition, the particular record types used from a data aggregate may be indicated with the technique of bands in the data store symbol, as shown in Exhibit 6-16.

There are five kinds of data flows needing labels:

- Flow between a function and a data store
- Interface with an external system
- Data output
- User interaction with the system
- Flow between two functions.

Each type of data flow has unique labeling considerations.

Flows between a function box and a data store "drum" are the most common and the most important ones to coordinate with the data base description. These flows may either be general or specific. A general flow may contain any of the data indicated by the data store which sends or receives the flow. For example, in Exhibit 6-17, the data flow from Function 1.1 to the contract structure data aggregate may contain any data in the aggregate. Hence, the label does not have to list the record types involved or repeat the aggregate name. Instead, it indicates the nature of this general flow: "Changes." A specific data flow contains only specific record types or items from the associated data store. In this case, the data flow label indicates what these are. For example, the data flow in Exhibit 6-17 from the contract structure data aggregate to function 1.3 consists of a specific data item (Contract Number) and a record type (Contract Line Item) in that data aggregate.

A data input from an external system or an output to an external system is handled as a labeled interface data set. The label is placed on the symbol indicating the interface medium (magnetic tape, electronic communication, etc.). In Exhibit 6-17, there is one external input, the monthly corporate accounting data from the Ace Aerospace corporate accounting system. Such interface data sets can be explicitly defined either in the verifiable functional requirements (Chapter 7) associated with the function handling the interface or in the data base description (Chapter 12).

A data output flow connects a function to the output it generates. The output itself is represented by a symbol showing the output medium and a label giving its title. For example, in Exhibit 6-17, function 1.3 generates the "Reconciliation Report," shown with the rectangular hardcopy printout symbol. Such outputs are defined in a special section of the user requirements document, using techniques explained in Chapter 9. The output data flow arrow often needs no label, since the flow generates the entire report. However, a label may be added with the arrow to indicate report version or comments. In the example just cited in Exhibit 6-17, there is a comment with the data flow arrow indicating that the reconciliation report contains a comparison of posted and obligated costs.

User interaction flows are labeled to show the general nature of the user interface. They may show important record types or data items transferred between the computer system and the user, but these labels make no attempt to characterize the entire man-machine dialogue. For example, in Exhibit 6-17 the user interaction with Function 1.3 labeled "Process Initiation" indicates that the system administrator will cause function 1.3 to execute but will not need to interact with this fully automated input function. The actual mechanization of this will require a menu screen or some other way for the system administrator to initiate the process, a way to abort execution, and so on. These design details ordinarily are left out of the user concept diagrams, unless of great interest to users. They can be placed in the verifiable functional requirements associated with this function.

The last kind of data flow is a flow directly from one function to another, such as flow "D" on Exhibit 6-8. These are relatively rare when following an integrated data base philosophy, but they do still occur. Such flows should be given labels similar to the "general" and "specific" labels with flows between functions and data stores. If more detail on the flow is required, the detail usually belongs with the verifiable functional requirements for either the sending or receiving function. However, if the flow has a complex structure of its own, it can also be explained in the data base description by treating this complex data flow as another data aggregate.

INTERACTION BETWEEN THE REQUIREMENTS ANALYST AND USERS

How should the systems analyst work with users when generating the user concept diagrams? This is a key issue in obtaining agreement, one of the three key characteristics of requirements specifications. The following sequence works well to generate user concept diagrams to the second and third level:

1. Analyst generates initial diagrams to the second level, based on the application concept discussed in Chapter 5 and all available documentation concerning the business area.
2. A working session with users marks up these diagrams.
3. The analyst works from the diagram markups and working session notes to create a second set of diagrams (to the second and third levels) which is logically consistent.
4. Another working session marks up the new diagrams.
5. The analyst reworks the second set based on markups and discussion notes to obtain a third, relatively stable set.

After Step 5, the analyst is ready to discuss verifiable functional requirements with users. These discussions will lead to some further user concept diagram evolution, but most major decisions will have been made in steps 1 to 5 as listed.

A common misconception is that the requirements analyst has done a poor job if the working session in step 2 generates a lot of changes. Actually, the reverse is true. If there are very few changes at that stage, it generally indicates that the users do not understand the systems analyst's material. Was the material poorly presented? Were the people at the working session not representative of the intended users? Or did the analyst not use the terminology common in the subject business area? In any case, *lack of extensive markups of the first draft of user concept diagrams is a danger signal.* When it happens, the analyst needs to understand why and should change procedures accordingly. User commitment will only come from user involvement.

When iterating the user concept diagrams and data structure diagram (Chapter 11) with users, an important task for the requirements analyst is to maintain consistency between the two. Data aggregates, record types, and data items become better understood over time. The analyst must occasionally review the user concept diagrams to ensure that data store and data flow labels use the new names. User representatives should concentrate their limited time on the fundamental requirements issues, leaving these technical consistency checks to the analyst.

AUTOMATION SUPPORT FOR USER CONCEPT DIAGRAMS

Use of templates for hand-drawn diagrams yields quick sketches but suffers from these shortcomings:

- Hand-drawn diagrams look unprofessional in a published requirements specification or user concept document. A reader observing crude-looking diagrams will probably question the adequacy of the analysis.
- When changes need to be made, the analyst needs to start from scratch and draw another diagram.

Sending the diagrams to graphics artists will produce excellent-looking results, but tends to require extensive lead times. Given the strawman nature of user concept diagrams, it hardly makes sense to delay a working session with users for three weeks so you can get crisp diagrams drawn, only to mark them up at the meeting.

What is needed is a way for systems analysts to generate and to modify good quality diagrams quickly. This capability exists in expensive computer-aided design (CAD) packages and now can be acquired as moderately priced personal computer software. Apple Computer started with the LISA DRAW™ software for LISA™ computers, which was converted to MAC DRAW™ on Macintosh™ computers. Other drawing packages, such as GEM DRAW™ perform a similar function for IBM and compatible personal computers.*

These software drawing packages allow users to draw line figures, copy them, shrink and expand them, move them on the page, and so on. They can be

---

*LISA, Macintosh, LISA DRAW, and MAC DRAW are trademarks of Apple Computer. GEM DRAW is a trademark of Microsoft.

labeled with text which itself can be enlarged or reduced and moved on the page. By making a library of the symbols in Exhibit 6-11, it is possible for the systems analyst to generate computerized diagrams almost as rapidly as the manual template drawings. Changes can be made by editing the computer version of the drawing, similar to word processing edits of text.

Software now exists from a number of vendors which combines systems analysis diagrams with a data base of information about the application requirements. These will be discussed in Chapter 16, along with other automated tools for managing requirements.

Experience in the author's systems analysis group has shown that the interactive graphics approach is a both a benefit and a bother. Analysts can and do use the computer support to make nice-looking diagrams, but they tend to produce them less rapidly than they produce the hand-drawn variety. Invariably there are steps which should be easy to work with the computer, but are not. For example, it turns out to be very difficult to generate a nice-looking "drum" symbol in GEM DRAW. Innocent looking changes to a diagram can cause so much disturbance to the original drawing that one needs essentially to redraw it. Diagram printouts tend to require two to fifteen minutes each on inexpensive dot matrix or laser printers.

Requirements analysts like to have a personal computer drawing package available to use when they are on their own (say over a weekend) and need to generate reasonable-looking drawings. But as a general practice it has been better to use a specialist who is very familiar with the drawing package to generate the diagrams. New software tools which use special characteristics of the analysis diagrams to lay out the diagrams automatically may provide both the quality and production efficiency which analysts need.

COMPARISON WITH OTHER DATA FLOW DIAGRAMMING STYLES

A comparison of the user concept diagram style with other popular styles of data flow diagrams helps to point out some of the subtle options available to the analyst.

Exhibit 6-18 is a simple user concept diagram which models a library system. It shows how three main automated functions interact with two data aggregates and an external system. All conventions used here have already been described in this chapter.

The Yourdon style of data flow diagramming, popularized by Gane & Sarson and DeMarco, has only four distinct symbols. They represent functions, external entities, data flows, and data stores. Exhibit 6-19 shows the same library system example in the Yourdon style, using "bubbles" for functions, as recommended by DeMarco. Gane and Sarson left Yourdon to set up their own firm, Improved System Technologies, and changed the bubble shape to a rounded

EXHIBIT 6-18.   Library System Sample User Concept Diagram

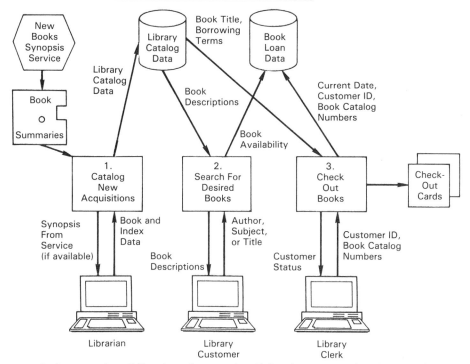

vertical rectangle.   Likewise, they made slight changes to the data store and external entities symbols, while retaining the basic Yourdon data flow diagramming approach.

Exhibit 6-19 shows that the Yourdon style leaves out many of the physical details shown in user concept diagrams.   External entities are shown with the same symbol whether they are system users, interfacing external systems, or people who act as data suppliers or consumers.   The example shows how the external entity symbol can be used in Yourdon diagrams to represent user interaction with the system.

DeMarco shows data flows with curved arrows.   These are harder to draw than straight arrows, but are felt to be more aesthetically pleasing when connecting the round function bubbles.

The structured analysis and design technique, SADT, was developed by Douglas Ross of SofTech (9).   It has had a large impact beyond systems analysis of software applications, including use as a design tool for such diverse areas as manufacturing lines and components of integrated circuit chips.   Under contract to the Air Force in the integrated computer-aided manufacturing program (ICAM), SofTech repackaged SADT as the "IDEF$_0$" language.

Exhibit 6-20 shows how the library system example looks using SADT. Although Ross's paper lists 40 language features, the basic symbols for information systems analysis are function boxes, data flow arrows, and data store parallel

EXHIBIT 6-19.   Library System Sample Yourdon (DeMarco) Diagram

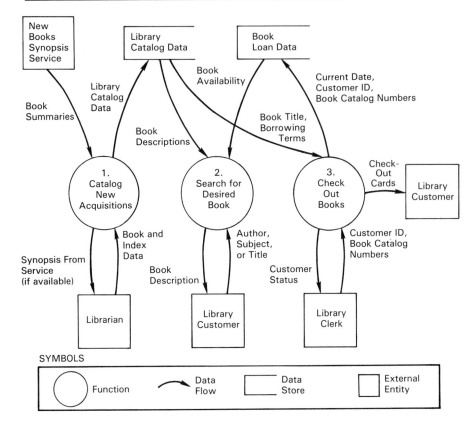

lines. SADT differs from the previously discussed data flow diagram techniques in these ways:

- Function boxes must be arranged in the upper-left to lower-right "waterfall" pattern, similar to the software development cycle diagrams in Chapter 2.
- SADT demands rigid adherence to the convention that data flows must have inputs pointing to the left side of a function box and outputs pointing from the right side of the function box.
- New symbols are added for "controls" and "mechanisms," represented as arrows pointing to the top and bottom of function boxes (see the symbol explanations at the bottom left of Exhibit 6-20).

SADT tends to be more difficult to use successfully than the other methods. Most people find that the rigid adherence to the input-left/output-right convention is awkward, since it leads to long, looping data flows. The exact conventions for controls and mechanisms used on a particular application must be spelled out

EXHIBIT 6-20. Library System Sample SADT Diagram

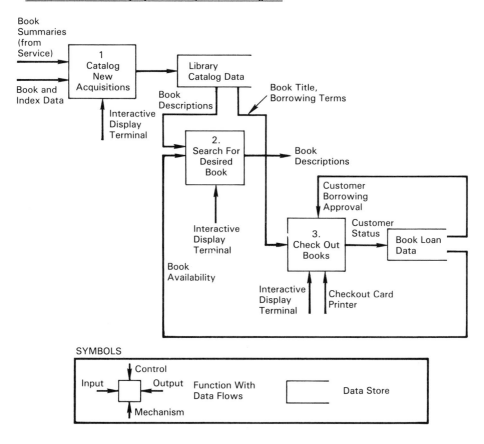

carefully so that multiple analysts will use these terms in a consistent manner. Finally, the lack of symbols for external entities makes it difficult to indicate type of user and the nature of interfaces with users and with external systems.

However, the similarities of user concept diagrams, Yourdon diagrams, and SADT diagrams are much more significant than their differences. All can use hierarchical diagramming, and all can be used to show how a hierarchical functional decomposition and a structured view of the data base (Chapter 11) interrelate.

SUMMARY OF HOW USER CONCEPT DIAGRAMS FIT THE ANALYSIS OBJECTIVES

In summary, user concept diagrams provide a visual tool which assists understanding of the structure of an application's user requirements. Their useful characteristics include:

- The goals shown in Exhibit 6-1 are satisfied. These diagrams portray functions, user types, user interactions, data bases, data flows, interfaces, and outputs.
- Simple structure and suggestive symbols make the diagrams easy for users to read and understand, thus aiding the process of obtaining user agreement.
- User concept diagrams may be drawn with either an IBM flowchart template or an interactive drawing package, so they are reasonably quick to draw and change.
- If drawn using personal computer drawing software, the diagrams look professional, thus giving the analysis results a degree of credibility not present with pencil- and-template sketches.

These diagrams help support the initial levels of functional decomposition. After the third level of decomposition, data flow diagrams rapidly decrease in value for user-centered requirements. Other techniques should be used to specify detailed functional requirements.

DISCUSSION QUESTIONS

1. Hierarchical (leveled) data flow diagrams have supporters and detractors. Some people would like to have everything in one picture, so that all flows can be immediately traced. Moreover, if a local standard requires at most two levels of diagrams, then the degree of detail will be kept at a summary level.
   a. Take a simple three-level set of data flow diagrams, starting with a context diagram, and flatten it onto one sheet by replacing high-level functions with their entire diagram. What problems do you encounter? In what ways is the result easier to examine?
   b. Does a functional hierarchy diagram like Exhibit 6-2 help you to compre-hend the structure of hierarchical data flow diagrams?

2. An objection to the symbols on user concept diagrams which represent physical objects (terminals, disks, tapes, etc.) is that they overly constrain the design solution. If an output report is required, for example, the designer of that function should decide the best physical mechanism for communicating the results to users. The converse argument is that user concept diagram symbols show how users want to interact with the system, and such physical characteristics are valid user requirements. Discuss the pros and cons of the physical media symbols (Exhibit 6-11) versus the general symbols used by DeMarco (Exhibit 6-19).

3. Data flow diagrams for complex applications sometimes end up with all the diagrams looking like context diagrams, as shown in the following illustration:

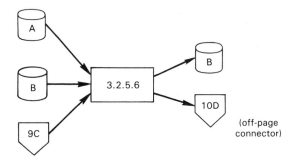

Such diagrams have no more information than input-output-process charts (Exhibit 6-3) and are harder to produce. Likewise, a similar problem is commonly encountered with a single data base unit accepting all data flows, as illustrated in the following diagram:

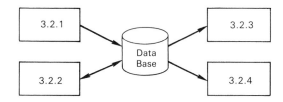

This diagram also has no more information content than input-processing-output charts. User concept diagrams are useful when they show how various functions interact with various data base components, so that flows among the functions may be traced through the data base components. How can the two "degenerate" styles of diagrams be modified to obtain more useful data flow diagrams?

REFERENCES

1. J. F. Stay, "HIPO and Integrated Program Design," *IBM Systems Journal*, vol. 15, no. 2, 1976.

2. Chris Gane and Trish Sarson, *Structured Systems Analysis*, Englewood Cliffs, N.J.: Prentice-Hall, 1979. See especially pages 44-45.

3. G. A. Miller, "The Magical Number Seven, Plus or Minus Two: Some Limits on Our Capacity for Processing Information," *Psychological Review*, vol. 63, March 1956.

4. Tom DeMarco, *Structured Analysis and System Specification*, Englewood Cliffs, N.J.: Prentice-Hall, 1979.

5. Stephen M. McMenamin and John F. Palmer, *Essential Systems Analysis,* Englewood Cliffs, N.J.: Yourdon Press, 1984.

6. Edward Yourdon, "What Ever Happened to Structured Analysis?" *Datamation,* vol. 32, No 11, June 1, 1986.

7. International Business Machines Corp., *Business Systems Planning — Information Systems Planning Guide,* GE20-0527-3, 1981.

8. Mark L. Gillenson and Robert Goldberg, *Strategic Planning, Systems Analysis, & Database Design,* New York: John Wiley & Sons, 1984.

9. Douglas T. Ross, "Structured Analysis (SA): A Language for Communicating Ideas," *IEEE Transactions of Software Engineering,* vol. SE-3, no. 1, January 1977.

7

Verifiable Functional Requirements

As shown in Exhibit 4-7, analysts first work with users to develop user concept diagrams (Chapter 6) and the data structure diagram (Chapter 11). Armed with these road maps to the application functions and data base, they can then proceed to develop the functional requirements (this chapter) and data dictionary (Chapter 12).

Functional requirements are written specifications of the actions that the automated system must perform. These requirements must indicate *what* must be done and associated quality factors. Questions concerning *how* the automation of these functions will be mechanized should be left to the later design stage.

With verbal precision similar to a lawyer's, the systems analyst strives to create statements of requirements which are verifiable, consistent, nonredundant, and which go only to the level of user needs.

Effective requirements statements are remarkably difficult to write. This chapter will give qualitative principles and examples. Chapter 8 will cover the more mechanical concerns of labeling requirements and explicitly matching requirements to the functions on user concept diagrams.

VERIFIABLE REQUIREMENTS

It must be possible to verify whether the implemented system meets the functional and performance requirements. Verification may be performed in four different ways: *inspection, analysis, demonstration,* and *testing.* In inspection, requirements are compared to obvious external characteristics of the delivered system. For example, does a graphics display screen have the required pixel density? Does the delivered source code comply with required commenting standards? In analysis, the systems analyst performs computations which are based on design parameters or on observable execution characteristics. These computations lead to numerical conclusions about characteristics which cannot easily be observed. For example, a performance requirement to complete an automated computational function within five minutes 95 percent of the time may be most appropriately verified by making a few benchmarking tests and then estimating the expected response frequency distribution in a paper-and-pencil analysis. In demonstration, a required capability is demonstrated in one case or a small number of cases representative of normal operational conditions. In testing, the requirement is checked against operational performance in a set of test cases carefully constructed to create a wide range of operating conditions possible for that function.

Verifiable requirements allow the implementer to have confidence that he has a valid design which, if implemented successfully, will pass the acceptance tests. Consider the pseudo requirement: "The scheduler will optimize allocation of resources." Such a requirement is so vague, it is difficult to tell if an implemented solution meets it or not. What resources should be allocated and what optimization criterion should be used? A better statement would be: "The scheduler shall assign people and equipment to work tasks in a manner which minimizes total production costs while meeting required due dates on all deliverable items." Even this statement may not protect users' interests if they have a specific algorithm which they know works well for their situation. In that case, the requirement might be: "The scheduler shall assign people and equipment to work tasks using the dynamic programming algorithm described by Mary Johnson in internal memorandum IM-MJ-87-09."

By now you may have caught on to the analyst's dilemma with verifiable requirements. The more concrete the requirement, the easier it is to verify whether it has been successfully implemented. But if the requirement is totally specific, it may unnecessarily restrict the implementer's design. The level of detail of a requirement will depend on the circumstances and the analyst's professional judgment. But all requirements should be reviewed by both the analyst and user representatives with this question always in mind: "Is there a straightforward way to verify that the completed application satisfies this requirement?"

CONSISTENT REQUIREMENTS

If the functional requirements are inconsistent, it will obviously be impossible to implement the specifications. The developer will be forced to stop some aspects of the development, document the inconsistency and suggested resolution, and meet with users and the sponsor to agree on a workable specification change. Large numbers of inconsistencies will cause delays and extra expense and will create the impression that the development is not going smoothly.

Consistency checking has both mechanical and creative aspects. Mechanical consistency checks include questions like:

- Does the application support input and modification of all data required for system outputs?
- Do high-level user concept diagrams agree with lower levels and the functional requirements?
- Are the data aggregates, record types, and elements referred to in the user concept diagrams and functional requirements consistent with the names used in the data model?

These consistency checks are aided by automated requirements handling tools, which are discussed in Chapter 16.

Creative consistency checking requires senior analysts who can ask penetrating questions. Consider some examples of consistency problems which could arise in the Ace Aerospace example but are unlikely to be caught by an automated consistency checker:

- The Generate Standard Reports functional requirements indicate that standard reports will only contain alpha-numeric output. When compiling material for specific reports, however, the need for time series bar and line charts arises.
- Some project status briefing charts are found to require complex artwork inappropriate for automation in the Contract Tracking System. However, a basic concept in the Generate and Display Project Status Briefing Charts function is that *all* charts will be projectable from a computer menu selection process.
- A general functional requirement is to provide a single menu-driven interface for all user information access. However, user instant ad hoc queries are desired, and these must be specified in a query language rather than selected from a menu.

Checking for such inconsistencies must be done manually and thoughtfully. The guiding principle here is that time should be allotted for a senior analyst who has not been directly involved in the requirements writing to review them (either in writing or orally in a structured walkthrough) from this perspective. Then, when users review draft requirements, they will not have to worry about inconsistencies among the requirements statements. Instead, the users should concentrate on inconsistencies between the requirements and their actual needs.

NONREDUNDANT REQUIREMENTS

Redundancy in requirements causes problems in maintaining consistent requirements over the development cycle. If a requirement is mentioned once, it should not be repeated in another place in the requirements specification. If it is, the redundancy often leads to one of the references being changed (due to later decisions), while the other is overlooked. Then the requirements will become inconsistent.

Ferreting out redundancies is an effort which the systems analysts must constantly pursue. Typical situations in which redundancy creeps in are these:

- *Function redundancy:* A detailed function is discussed in more than one place in the functional decomposition.
- *Horizontal overlap:* A process is split up across several different functions, and the functional requirements concerning the process overlap.
- *Vertical overlap:* Requirements discussed at one level of the functional decomposition are repeated at a more detailed breakout of that function.

All of these problems can occur with a single analyst but tend to be more aggravated when multiple analysts work as a team.

Function redundancy, in which the same requirement is stated in two different places, is the easiest problem to spot. For example, in the Ace Aerospace problem, the system administrator must know about problems in loading the monthly corporate accounting system figures. Hence, there is a requirement for a report describing rejected records. It might easily happen that this report requirement is described under both the Input Corporate Accounting Data function and the Generate Standard Reports function. To resolve this problem, the analyst must decide which functional area should claim this report, and then refine the definitions of higher-level functions accordingly. For this example, it might be appropriate to include the rejected record report with the Input Corporate Accounting Data function. The Generate Standard Reports function definition would then be refined to indicate that standard reports do not include reports needed for data integrity checks.

Horizontal overlap has partial redundancy of requirements for a process which is discussed with several functions. It can be difficult to spot and troublesome to resolve because of the different viewpoints of the various statements which turn out to be redundant. An example often encountered is discussion of privacy controls. These may be discussed in the following places:

- Set Access Controls function, which allows the system administrator to grant access permissions to individuals
- Processing functions which have requirements concerning how these access permissions will be interpreted

- Data requirements which indicate what data will be stored to represent the access controls.

These three kinds of access control requirements may be discussed in a nonredundant manner, but only with substantial intellectual effort. The requirements are so closely related that initial efforts will tend to duplicate the basic concepts of the access control mechanisms. And, in practice, this duplication tends to contain inconsistencies.

In difficult partial-overlap situations like the access control example, there is a systematic procedure for eliminating the redundancy. First, the analyst must decide which requirements area will contain the basic discussion of the functional requirement. In the example, a natural place for the overall view would be with the Maintain Access Permissions function. Other requirements areas can then refer to this basic discussion, while adding special requirements which are unique to their areas. In our example, the Generate Standard Reports function could specify requirements concerning the report generation capabilities which are granted and denied to specific classes of access permissions, while referring to the Maintain Access Permissions function for a definition of the access permission classes.

Vertical overlap refers to requirements which are redundantly stated at different levels of detail. It tends to be easier to spot and control than horizontal overlap, because functional requirements within a hierarchy tend to be discussed in the same general section of the user requirements. Also, the redundancy tends to be stated with similar language. The following example illustrates a typical situation:

The Generate Standard Reports function shall restrict generation of a standard report to individuals who have data read permission for all data aggregates accessed by the report.

The Generate Manpower Planning Report function shall be provided only to individuals who have data read permission for the Cost Element and Contract Structure data aggregates.

These requirements are redundant and will lead to excessive verbiage if repeated for each individual report.

The procedure to eliminate hierarchical redundancy is to pick a unique level to specify the requirement. In the example just given, the access control requirement can probably be stated for all reports at the Generate Standard Reports level. It can and should then be ignored at the more detailed level of the individual report requirements. If, however, each report has unique access requirements that cannot be specified with a general rule at the Generate Standard Reports level, then the requirement will be specified at the lower level. In that case, the detailed access control requirement would be specified by report, and a comment (no requirement) could be made at the higher level mentioning that access controls will be applied.

FUNCTIONAL REQUIREMENTS WRITING STYLES

For lengthy requirements documents it is important to maintain a consistent functional requirements writing style. In addition, it is necessary to distinguish between functional requirements, which describe capabilities the system must provide, and comments, which may give some rationale for why this capability is required or how it is expected to be used. Consider the following example:

> The system shall maintain a Transaction Log file which tracks each person making a data base change, the types of records changed, the number of changed record occurrences, and the day and time of the user's record-changing session. This information will allow the system administrator to monitor whether expected data maintenance activities are in fact taking place. It will also help to track the effect of unauthorized access to the system by individuals who have managed to evade the Contract Tracking System's access controls.

This example contains a functional requirement (to maintain a Transaction Log) and two comments (the Transaction Log will be used to monitor activity and to control damage after break-ins). Since the three ideas run together in a paragraph, it is difficult to extract the requirement.

Requirements should be distinguished from comments. Four different methods are commonly used to achieve this separation:

- Label all requirements with a requirement number, with comments visually separated from this labeled text.
- Use "shall" for functional requirements, "will" for comments concerning how the user expects to employ the capability. This approach is often used for military requirements, as explained in MIL-STD-490A (1). It is illustrated in the previous example.
- Use imperative sentences (imperative verb and object, such as "Maintain a Transaction Log ...") for functional requirements, normal declarative sentences for comments.
- Use a special language and format (such as "Structured English") for requirements, normal text for comments.

Use of imperatives helps condense the requirements and avoids constant use of "the system" as the subject of the sentences describing requirements. It is helpful, though, for some requirements to have an explicit subject. For example, "The terminal shall respond with a beep and an error message" is slightly clearer than "Respond with a beep and an error message." Consistency of style dictates that the requirements not drift between imperative and declarative sentences. The lead requirements analyst must select a style and ensure that all requirements follow this style.

FUNCTIONAL REQUIREMENTS WITH COMPLEX LOGIC

Standard English can bog down with situations in which complex logic must be explained. Typical situations where this problem occurs are integrity checks with input data, processing algorithms, options for reports, and access control logic. Consider the following example:

> The Project Fiscal Year Expenditure Summary report will contain the best estimate of project expenditures for each month of the current Ace Aerospace fiscal year (June to May), obtained as follows: For past months, the figure will be a summation of all expenses which the Corporate Accounting System has reported for that project and month, plus all expenses entered by the program manager which have not appeared in the Corporate Accounting System reports for later months. Future monthly expenses will be estimated by ...

You do not have to read much material like that to realize there must be clearer methods of exposition! One common device is Structured English. Decision trees, decision tables, and other specialized tables and figures may also be used.

Structured English uses special words and indenting format on the page to simplify representation of loops and decisions. Restating the above example in Structured English could look as follows:

> The Project Extended Financial Summary report will estimate project expenditures as follows:
>
> For each month m from June of calendar year x through May of calendar year $x+1$:
>> If m is earlier than the current month, then:
>>> Expenditure(m) = (sum of expenses reported by the Corporate Accounting System for this project and month) + (sum of program manager-reported expenses for that project and month which have not appeared in Corporate Accounting System reports)
>> If m is the current month or later, then:
>>> Expenditure(m) = ...

In other words, the same key words and indenting devices used in structured programming to make software easier to read can be used with English language requirements to make difficult logic easier to read. If a particular Program Design Language, or PDL (2,3,4), will be used later to design the software for the application, then a similar set of conventions should be used for Structured English in the user functional requirements. Consistent PDLs aid the transition to design and minimize the number of new conventions reviewers must learn.

Special tables and diagrams can be helpful to describe requirements which are awkward to express with text alone. Exhibit 7-1, for example, concisely expresses the details behind the following requirement:

EXHIBIT 7-1. Example Use of a Table to Convey Requirements

Access of User Classes to Major Functions

Functions Available	User Type					
	Division Executive	Division Financial Analyst	Project Manager	Contract Administrator	Contract Tracking System Administrator	Data Entry Clerk
Manage Contract Data • Maintain CTS Contract Structure & Mods Data • Input and Delete Project Obligations Data • Input and Reconcile Corporate Accounting Data • Maintain Corporate Rates Data				X	X X	X
Generate Standard Reports • Generate Project Status Report • Generate Labor Utilization Report	X X	X X	X X	X X	X X	
Answer Ad Hoc Query and Report Requests • Answer Ad Hoc Query Requests • Answer Ad Hoc Report Requests	X X	X X	X X			
Generate and Display Project Status Briefing Charts • Generate Status Briefing Charts • Accept User Annotations • Display and Print Charts	X	X	X X X			
Support System Administrator • Set Access Permissions • Generate Data Currency Report • Browse Transaction Log					X X X	

Users shall access the system through menus displayed on their terminal screens. Each type of user shall have a unique menu system which only displays choices of functions which are available to that user type, as shown in Exhibit 7-1.

Note that, like the Structured English example, the special exhibit should be introduced with a normal English requirement statement.

FUNCTION DEFINITIONS

In addition to the functional requirements and associated comments, text is necessary to define the functions on the user concept diagrams. Such a description indicates the scope of the function, such as:

The Generate Standard Reports function includes the generation and output of all preformatted reports which are based on information in the integrated data base. This function does not include reports pertaining to data maintenance or system administration.

Function definitions help the user representatives to understand the function context for associated functional requirements. They also help to maintain the user concept diagrams and specification documents, because they explicitly set the function boundaries.

Sometimes function definitions must be expanded to explain the concept behind a new type of function. For example, before the first commercial electronic spreadsheet product (VisiCalc), it would have been puzzling to readers to see a function titled "Maintain Electronic Spreadsheet." Readers would have required a diagram of the two-dimensional spreadsheet layout with some discussion of cell usage and cell manipulation in order to have sufficient grasp of the basic concept to understand the functional requirements. Now that the electronic spreadsheet is commonplace, such an explanation with new applications is unnecessary.

Function definitions and functional requirements comments should be combined as narrative associated with a function. These narratives should be given for all functions in the functional decomposition hierarchy, not just the most detailed level functions. As previously mentioned, narratives must be clearly distinguished from the functional requirements.

Some analysts object to function definitions for these reasons:

- They may be verbose.
- They may introduce a kind of redundancy similar to vertical overlap.
- Narrative material is hard to write clearly.

However, function definitions are as necessary to analyst and user understanding of requirements specifications as comments in program code are to a programmer's understanding of his software. Nevertheless, the three objections to function definitions are valid concerns and show why the following rules should be used in writing them:

- Keep function definitions brief.
- Emphasize function boundaries. Give guidelines explaining which current and future requirements fit with this function.
- Avoid repeating functional requirements in the function definitions.
- Describe the function philosophy in the case of an unusual function which would otherwise be difficult for the user to understand.
- Do not include any historical discussions of how this function became part of the application.

These rules result in helpful function definitions which avoid redundancy and verbosity problems.

SUMMARY OF KEY IDEAS
FOR FUNCTIONAL REQUIREMENTS

Well-conceived functional requirements should be verifiable, consistent, and nonredundant. There is inevitably a conflict between obtaining high precision to get good verifiability and keeping the requirements sufficiently high level to allow for design flexibility. The functional requirements should be written in a consistent style with clear separation of requirements from comments and function definitions. Structured English, special tables, and diagrams should be used to clarify complex concepts.

Function definitions help define the functional decomposition hierarchy. They should be kept brief, but should explain unusual concepts where the functional requirements would otherwise be difficult to understand.

Functional requirements are a difficult technical writing task, and people generally underestimate how much time the task requires. Fortunately, user concept diagrams provide a system overview which structures the task and helps in making consistency and redundancy checks. The next chapter goes into detail concerning how the user concept diagrams and verifiable functional requirements mesh together in the user requirements and requirements specification documents.

DISCUSSION QUESTIONS

1. What kinds of automated requirements tools would aid generation, maintenance, and consistency checking of verifiable functional requirements?

2. The dividing line between requirements and design is somewhat arbitrary. There is a helpful ground rule: "Requirements cover those aspects that users

feel strongly about having in the implemented system." This ground rule is helpful, but does not change the need for judgment. Who should make the level-of-detail decisions about requirements?

3. It is difficult to write verifiable, consistent, and nonredundant functional requirements. Few software engineers are good writers. Hence, it would be nice to have a method which reduces or eliminates the writing burden.
   a. How could functional requirements be expressed with little or no text?
   b. What problems would arise from this approach?

REFERENCES

1. MIL-STD-490A, *Specification Practices*, Department of Defense.

2. P. Van Leer, "Top-Down Development Using a Program Design Language," *IBM Systems Journal,* vol. 15, no. 2, 1976, pages 155-170.

3. Stephen A. Caine and E. Kent Gordon, "PDL—A Tool for Software Design," *Proceedings of the National Computer Conference, 1975,* American Federation for Information Processing.

4. J. P. Privitera, "Ada Design Language for the Structured Design Methodology," *Proceedings of the AdaTEC Conference,* Association for Computing Machinery, October 1982, pages 76-90.

8

Tying Functional Requirements to the User Concept Diagrams

Poor numbering schemes cause mechanical problems in expressing functional requirements. These problems often result in a necessary restructuring of the requirements specification, with a penalty of one half to two weeks' extra effort. For this reason, what appears to be a simple clerical problem needs to be discussed in this special chapter. The discussion starts with an explanation of the three seemingly contradictory objectives of a numbering system, then presents an approach which has worked best for the author, and finally mentions an alternative worth considering. Examples taken from the Ace Aerospace problem show how the user concept diagrams, function definitions, and verifiable functional requirements can be packaged together in a manner which is easy to review.

NUMBERING COMPONENTS OF THE FUNCTIONAL DESCRIPTION

Three different specification concepts must be numbered in a way which clarifies their individual structures and the relationships among them:

- Application functions
- Functional requirements
- Document sections.

Exhibit 8-1 shows how these could each separately be numbered using straight-forward decimal numbering systems. The function hierarchy (Exhibit 8-1A) can be numbered with digits separated by decimal points indicating the hierarchy level, as discussed with Exhibit 6-4B. Functional requirements (Exhibit 8-1B) pertain to a specific function, so they could possibly be numbered with the function numbering followed by a decimal point and the requirement sequence number within that function. The document sections (Exhibit 8-1C) will be numbered in such a way that the discussion of functions has a section number, and the functional breakouts obtain subsection numbers.

EXHIBIT 8-1. Numbering Objectives

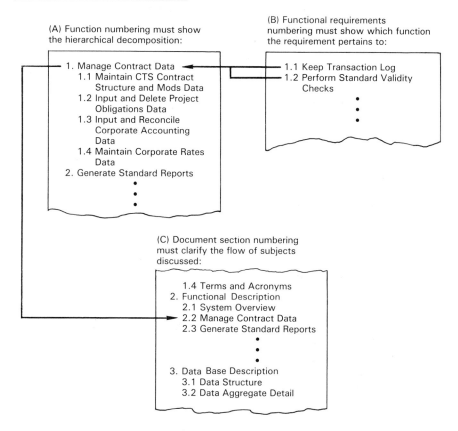

(A) Function numbering must show the hierarchical decomposition:

1. Manage Contract Data
   1.1 Maintain CTS Contract Structure and Mods Data
   1.2 Input and Delete Project Obligations Data
   1.3 Input and Reconcile Corporate Accounting Data
   1.4 Maintain Corporate Rates Data
2. Generate Standard Reports
   •
   •
   •

(B) Functional requirements numbering must show which function the requirement pertains to:

1.1 Keep Transaction Log
1.2 Perform Standard Validity Checks
   •
   •
   •

(C) Document section numbering must clarify the flow of subjects discussed:

1.4 Terms and Acronyms
2. Functional Description
   2.1 System Overview
   2.2 Manage Contract Data
   2.3 Generate Standard Reports
      •
      •
      •
3. Data Base Description
   3.1 Data Structure
   3.2 Data Aggregate Detail

Numbering Difficulties

The direct numbering schemes shown in Exhibit 8-1 lead to several awkward problems. Neither the functional requirements nor the document numbering systems shown are consistent with the function numbering.

It must be possible to state requirements at any level in the function hierarchy, including the entire application. Simply adding a digit to the function numbering leads to ambiguity with subfunction numbers. For example, both the second requirement and the second subfunction of Manage Contract Data would have the same number, 1.2. Moreover, the "add a digit" rule does not work for requirements which cover the whole system, since there is no function number for the whole system.

Exhibit 8-1 shows how the number of a section may be quite different from the number of the function described in that section. For example, section 2.2 discusses the Manage Contract Data function, which is function number 1. This may make cross-referencing difficult. If the user concept diagram refers to function 3.2.1, where should the reader look to find a description of that function?

These difficulties are exacerbated by the desirability of expressing functional requirements as numbered paragraphs in the document. In fact, effective packaging of the functional requirements will present a function's user concept diagram, function definition, and functional requirements all together. Schemes which place the diagrams or requirements in appendices force the reader to flip around through the document, and hence make the requirements tedious to read.

Resolving the Numbering Difficulty

The following rules give a solution to the numbering objectives which is consistent and has sufficient flexibility to support document maintainability:

1. Start with the section number of the major section of the document describing all applications functions (Example: section 2, "Functional Description").

2. Divide this major section into subsections which exactly track the hierarchical decomposition of functions. (Example: section 2.1.2, "Input and Delete Project Obligations Data," will describe the second subfunction of the first major function.)

3. Label requirements by the section number representing the function the requirements are associated with, followed by a dash (-) and the sequence number of the requirement for this function (Examples: requirement 2.1.2-3, "Input Labor Charges" would be the third requirement for function 2.1.2; requirement 2-1, "Provide Menu Access," would be the first application-wide requirement.)

Note that maintainability is supported by this interlocking numbering scheme. A new function can be added without impacting other functions' numbering. It will result in a new document section but will not change sections for previously identified functions. Likewise, new requirements can be added with no more impact than a renumbering of a few requirements attached to the same function.

STRUCTURING THE FUNCTIONAL
REQUIREMENTS DOCUMENTATION

It helps to see how these rules apply when formatting the functional description part of the user requirements document. This section illustrates an effective format, first in outline form and then with an example of pages from the Ace Aerospace user requirements document.

Exhibit 8-2 outlines the general format for the Ace Aerospace example. In this exhibit, section 2 was chosen to discuss functions. An overview description, including the top-level user concept diagram and any system-level comments appear in Section 2. All system-level functional requirements come next, formatted like subsections, but with special requirements dash numbers, like requirement 2-1. The first real subsection, 2.1, covers the first top-level function (Manage Contract Data). Text in this section defines and explains the whole function, using the

EXHIBIT 8-2.   Format for the Functional Requirements Section

Section of Requirements Document	Contents
2. FUNCTIONAL DESCRIPTION	Introduction to the functional model section, top-level functional breakout user concept diagram, and user concept diagram legend
Requirement 2-1 Provide Menu Access • • •	Statement of first globally applicable functional requirement
2.1 Manage Contract Data	Description of first top-level function, user concept diagram for this function
Requirement 2.1-1 Provide Forms-Oriented Data Entry • • •	Statement of first functional requirement applicable to the entire function
2.1.1 Maintain Contract Structure and Modifications Data	Description of first subfunction, User Concept diagram (if any) for that subfunction
Requirement 2.1.1-1 Input Contract and Line Items	Statement of first functional requirement applicable to this subfunction

function's user concept diagram as a helpful aid. Each requirement for Function 2.1 is then given in dash-number labeled subsections starting with requirement 2.1-1. Continuing in this way, each function gets a definition, a user concept diagram (unless it is one of the lowest-level functions), and a set of verifiable functional requirements.

Sample Pages from the Ace Aerospace
User Requirements Document

Exhibit 8-3 shows a few pages of the Ace Aerospace Contract Tracking System user requirements document to illustrate how such a format looks in practice. By allowing parts of the document to have two different kinds of headings (sections and requirements), this format satisfies all the objectives for a consistent numbering scheme.

In order to avoid any confusion with the two kinds of headings, they must differ in appearance. For example, the requirements are distinguished in Exhibit 8-3 by indenting, by using a "requirement" label, and by omitting underlining for the requirement title.

Comments on the Sample Requirements
Document Pages

The sample shown in Exhibit 8-3 raises several interesting points. Since specification readers may be unfamiliar with the exposition approach for functional and data models, they need to have the approach explained. One way is to have introductory material at the start of the functional description and data base description sections, as shown in the first page of the sample. Another way is to have an appendix which can be a lengthier explanation of both the methodology and the exposition approach. The advantage to having the explanation up front is that it catches readers who may not want to interrupt their reading by skipping to an appendix.

The definitions of each function and usage comments are an important part of the functional model. Although not formal requirements themselves, they help to ensure that all readers have a consistent interpretation of the intent of each function. These descriptions help solve the problem that people may agree on the user concept diagrams, but may actually have different processes in mind.

Redundancy in requirements may be avoided by cross-referencing. Instead of repeating data dictionary information, the requirements tell where to find the appropriate material about data elements in the data base description section. Requirement 2-3, which states how access control logic will affect menus, refers to another section for the main access control requirements. Such references avoid redundancy, help keep the document brief, and explicitly show how requirements interrelate.

EXHIBIT 8-3. Sample Pages of the Ace Aerospace Contract Tracking System
User Requirements Document

---

2.   FUNCTIONAL DESCRIPTION

This section describes the functions which the Contract Tracking System
will perform. Functions will be explained in three ways:

- User concept diagrams decompose the functions into
  subfunctions, indicate how data flows among the
  subfunctions and data base components, and show how
  users interact with the subfunctions.
- Descriptions with each function define the scope of
  the function, explain special concepts involved, and
  tell how users expect to employ the function.
- Functional requirements, labeled with dash numbers
  (e.g., Requirement 2.1.2-3 for the third functional
  requirement for function 2.1.2), give formal requirements
  indicating what the processing must perform, and related
  quality factors.

Each subfunction will have its own subsection, and may itself be subdivided as
illustrated by another user concept diagram. Components of the data base are
explained in section 3, Data Base Description. Requirements stated for a function
pertain to all subfunctions of that function. The developer must show that the
Contract Tracking System meets all of the functional requirements.

Exhibit 2-1 is an overview user concept diagram showing the major functions
for the Contract Tracking System. Symbols used in these diagrams are explained
in the legend of Exhibit 2-2. Requirements applicable to the entire system are
listed below.

2-1

EXHIBIT 8-3. (Continued)

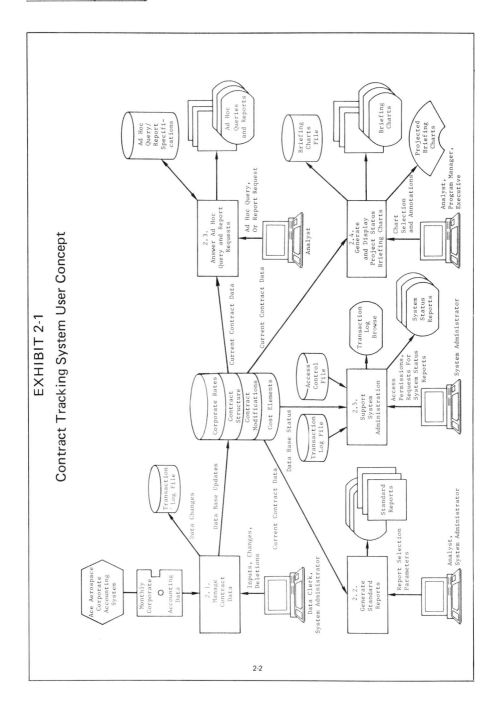

EXHIBIT 2-1

Contract Tracking System User Concept

EXHIBIT 8-3. (Continued)

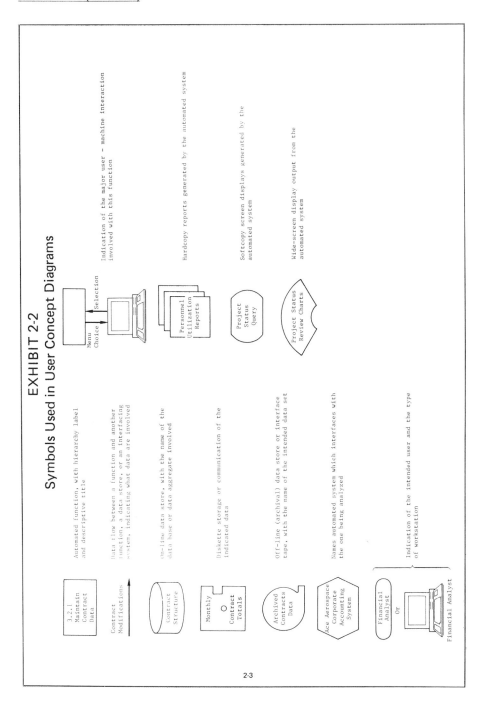

EXHIBIT 2-2

Symbols Used in User Concept Diagrams

Automated function, with hierarchy label and descriptive title

Data flow between a function and another function, a data store, or an interfacing system, indicating what data are involved

On-line data store, with the name of the data base or data aggregate involved

Diskette storage or communication of the indicated data

Off-line (archival) data store or interface tape, with the name of the intended data set

Names automated system which interfaces with the one being analyzed

Indication of the intended user and the type of workstation

Indication of the major user – machine interaction involved with this function

Hardcopy reports generated by the automated system

Softcopy screen displays generated by the automated system

Wide-screen display output from the automated system

2-3

105

EXHIBIT 8-3. (Continued)

Requirement 2-1 Provide Menu Access
> Users shall access all CTS functions through menus displayed
> on their terminal screens.

Requirement 2-2 Support Rapid Function Selection for Expert Users
> The system shall allow experienced users to make a series of
> keystrokes which immediately access the desired function without
> having to wait for display of all intermediate menus.

Requirement 2-3 Hide Denied Functions
> No menu items shall be displayed to a user who is denied access
> to that function (see section 2.5.3, "Set Access Controls")

Requirement 2-4 Mark Outputs Proprietary
> All CTS reports and all screen displays which carry information
> from the CTS Integrated Data Base shall be marked with the
> following message centered at the bottom of each page or screen
> display:
>
> > "* * * ACE AEROSPACE PROPRIETARY DATA * * *"

2.1 Manage Contract Data

The "Manage Contract Data" function includes all automated processes which
add, change, or delete information in the integrated Contract Tracking System data
base. Exhibit 2.1-1 shows the user concept for this function. All functions
modifying the data base must satisfy these requirements:

Requirement 2.1-1 Keep Transaction Log
> Whenever a record occurrence is added, changed, or deleted in the
> CTS data base, the system shall store the transaction log information listed
> in section 3.2.5.

Requirement 2.1.2 Perform Standard Validity Checks
> The Contract Tracking System shall automatically check all occurrences
> of data elements of new and modified record occurrences, to ensure that length,
> type, and allowable values specifications shown in the Data Dictionary tables
> in Section 3 are met. No record occurrences failing these checks shall be
> allowed in the data base.

EXHIBIT 8-3. (Continued)

EXHIBIT 2.1-1
Manage Contract Data Function User Concept

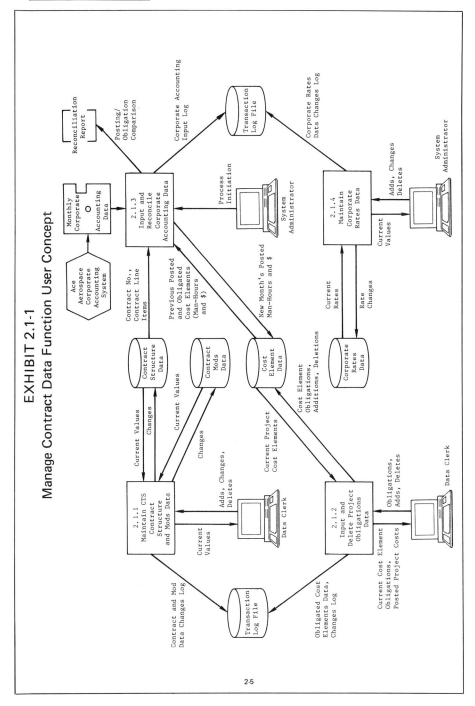

2-5

EXHIBIT 8-3. (Continued)

2.1.1 Maintain CTS Contract Structure and Modifications Data

This function supports interactive entry of information about Ace Aerospace Eastern Division contracts and contract modifications. This function has a relatively small transaction workload, but it is important for the system administrator and Ace Aerospace contract administrators to ensure that this information exactly matches the most recent contract terms (within two working days of contract signing). Checking of data entered by the system administrator occurs primarily by having the system administrator generate tailored Contract Terms Reports (function 2.2.3) and review the hardcopy printout with Eastern Division contract administrators.

Requirement 2.1.1-1 Enter Basic Contract Structure Data
The Contract Tracking System shall support interactive entry of Contract, Contract Line Item, and Deliverable Item data using the following general data entry procedure:

For each new Contract:
Enter Contract record data (record 1 described in section 3.2.1) using a single data entry screen display.
For each new contract line item:
Enter Contract Line Item record data (record 2) using a separate screen display for each line item. For each Deliverable Item under this Contract Line.

Item:
Enter Deliverable Item record data (record 3) using the remaining area of the same screen display used to enter the Contract Line Item. If data for this Deliverable Item sould exceed the number of lines still available on the screen, remove the top-most Deliverable Item from the screen display to make room for this new one.
End deliverable item.
End contract line item.
Permit user review of all data just entered for this contract through screen displays with the same layouts as the data entry screens just used.
End new contract.

2-6

The example helps illustrate the guideline that requirements should be stated to the first verifiable level. For example, requirement 2-2 says that experienced users should have a quick way of getting to desired interactive functions. When the final product is developed, it will be simple to verify whether the user interface allows such a short-cutting of the normal menu sequences. But the stated requirement gives the developer considerable flexibility in the approach used to meet the requirement.

Generally the most detailed requirements will be with the most detailed functional breakouts. For example, the need to use Structured English does not arise in the sample until requirement 2.1.1-1.

Requirements should not be verbose or take a huge amount of time to develop. An analyst should be able to perform all the steps needed to generate the requirements for a problem the size of the Ace Aerospace Contract Tracking System in a month or two. This includes objectives analysis to learn the nature of the problem and a detailed conceptual data base description. Brevity in textual requirements helps to produce the documentation quickly.

Alternative of Display Tables

Purists who argue that document parts should have consistent labeling throughout have an alternative to the requirements dash-number subsections. The alternative is to put all requirements for a function in a table which is referred to in the subsection discussing that function. Exhibit 8-4 shows how a set of requirements in Exhibit 8-3 appears with the requirements display table device. Note that all section, function, and requirements numbering stays the same; the difference is that display tables minimize the possibility of confusing requirements and function subsections in the document.

In practice, display tables are more difficult to produce. Tables are harder to type than straight text. They need to be formatted more carefully and should be boxed to look right. Many of these tables will be on multiple pages, which causes questions concerning table continuation page format and readability. Display tables can work well when the analysts use automated tools which ease these production problems.

COMPARISON WITH OTHER FUNCTIONAL DESCRIPTION APPROACHES

The type of functional requirements exposition described in this book differs in important ways from both common textual requirements and from recommendations of the authors who popularized "Structured Analysis" in the late 1970s. A brief comparison here will put these ideas in perspective.

The most commonly produced requirements specifications have been, and continue to be, nearly all textual material which is divided in an ad hoc fashion into sections. Such specifications can be useful, but generally they suffer from a

EXHIBIT 8-4. Sample Functional Requirements Presentation Using Display Tables

2.1 Manage Contract Data

The "Manage Contract Data" function includes all automated processes which add, change, or delete information in the Integrated Contract Tracking System Data Base. Exhibit 2.1-1 shows the user concept for this function. All functions modifying the data base must satisfy the requirements in Exhibit 2.1-2.

EXHIBIT 2.1-2
Manage Contract Data Requirements

Req't No.	Requirement
2.1-1	Keep Transaction Log Whenever a record occurrence is added, changed, or deleted in the Integrated CTS Data Base, the system shall capture the Transaction Log information listed in section 3.2.5.
2.1-2	Perform Standard Validity Checks The Contract Tracking System shall automatically check all occurrences of data elements of new and modified record occurrences to ensure that length, type, and allowable values specifications shown in the data dictionary tables in section 3 are met. No record occurrences failing these checks shall be allowed in the data base.

set of problems which have caused them to be labeled "Victorian novels." These problems include incomplete, overlapping, inconsistent, and incomprehensible requirements statements. Often they are packaged in a thick document which gives the impression of formidable challenge to the reader—an impression which usually is justified by the negative characteristics just enumerated. These specifications take a long time to develop, are very difficult to review, and lack a clear connection with system design and development.

The DeMarco (1) and Gane and Sarson (2) texts were a revolutionary reaction to the free text specifications. The main points these authors made were:

- Requirements specifications should be structured using data flow diagrams.
- Functional requirements should only discuss the logical algorithmic and processing steps behind the data transformations.

- Normal English requirements should be eliminated in favor of Structured English and decision table logic.

Following this approach to its logical conclusion, DeMarco recommended packaging the Structured English requirements logic in "mini-specs" corresponding to the most detailed functions on the data flow diagrams. Mini-specs would presumably go in their own major section or an appendix.

DeMarco thus got rid of the verbosity and redundancy of "Victorian novel" specifications by eliminating all discussion of functions except for the most detailed breakouts. Even there, the mini-specs leave out overview discussion and comments, restricting the specification to the specific logical processing required.

Such an approach can work well for small in-house applications. It allows a few people to reach agreements and document them with a minimum of paper work overhead. Quality requirements and rationale for functions can be eliminated, because installation standards are well known, and because this small group has talked through the reasons various functions will be performed the way the mini-specs indicate.

For larger applications (say, more than two man-years of implementation effort), such a condensed style is inadequate. In particular, strict reliance on DeMarco's mini-specs fails to give the following information which is necessary for new people joining the project:

- Function definitions (which help a reader to understand the purpose and scope of the functions)
- Comments (which embody key rationale which surfaced during the requirements analysis)
- Requirements at all function levels (so the scope of generality of a broad requirement can be shown clearly, and the requirement need not be repeated for each lower-level function).

Adding such capabilities, as described in *User-Centered Requirements Analysis*, risks the return of Victorian novel problems. The systems analysts must constantly remind themselves of DeMarco's advice to eliminate redundancy and overspecification, while striving for clarity and completeness.

DISCUSSION QUESTIONS

1. Why do the functional requirements need to be numbered?

2. In what ways do the user concept diagrams help users to review the functional description documentation?

3. Well thought-out, brief requirements take time to compose. Once a library of well-developed requirements specifications has been developed, it should be possible to reuse some of this thought.

a. To what extent can the functional description use material from previously generated requirements specifications?

b. What mechanisms should be employed (cut-and-paste, automated libraries, etc.) to assist reuse of previously developed functional requirements?

REFERENCES

1. Tom DeMarco, *Structured Analysis and System Specification*, Englewood Cliffs, N.J.: Prentice-Hall, 1979.

2. Chris Gane and Trish Sarson, *Structured Systems Analysis*, Englewood Cliffs, N.J.: Prentice-Hall, 1979.

9
Output Definitions

How formally should reports and screen displays be defined in requirements specification? This is a subject of endless debate. On the one hand analysts like Ken Orr (1) argue that outputs should drive the whole system development. On the other hand it is often reasonable to argue that concrete definition of reports and screen displays should wait until the design stage. The designers can then take advantage of special characteristics of the selected screen forms manager and report writer tools.

Chapter 9 takes the point of view that a wide variety of output definition techniques can be useful to include in requirements specifications depending on the importance of the outputs to the application being defined. Most of the chapter describes a spectrum of techniques varying from brief identification of an output to a full description of format, content, and logic. The last section summarizes which techniques are most useful in common situations.

OUTPUT IDENTIFICATION

Output identification is the simplest form of report or screen display user requirement. Stated as a verifiable functional requirement, output identification includes at least the report or screen display name and indication of the data it includes. It also may indicate known user options, output medium, and any other operational characteristics important to users. Exhibit 9-1 gives an example of very short output identification.

EXHIBIT 9-1.   Example Simple Output Identification

Requirement 2.2.3-2 Generate Contract Fiscal Year Status
Summary Report

This report will give the budgeted and actual
expenditures for all contracts or contract line items, at
the user's option. Expenditures will be listed for each
completed month of the current Ace Aerospace fiscal year.

Report tailoring options allow users to restrict output to the particular information they want sorted in preferred order. Such options can vastly reduce the bulk of paper printouts needed from a system and reduce the need for extensive manual analysis of results. A tabular form for output identification helps when there are extensive tailoring options and when several reports are listed for a single functional requirement. Exhibit 9-2 shows an example of such a table.

EXHIBIT 9-2.   Example Output Identification with Options Specified

Report Title	Contents	Options
Contract Fiscal Year Status Summary	Budget and actual expenditures for each completed month of the current Ace fiscal year	Level of detail: • By entire contract • By contract line item Scope of report: • All contracts • Contracts with funded value between min and max thresholds • All contract line items with a specified project leader • Line items for a specified contract • Specified line item Sort order: • Ascending contract number/ascending line item number • Descending contract value/descending line item value

If the output requirements are stated with no more detail than the identifications illustrated in Exhibits 9-1 and 9-2, then the implication is that the developers will have complete flexibility in creating formats which are easy to implement with their favorite screen and report implementation tools. These formats should then be reviewed with users during the design stage to obtain agreements on layout wording and dynamic characteristics of screen displays.

MENU STRUCTURE

A particular kind of screen display of great interest to users is the menu. This display gives the user a list of available functions, as in Exhibit 9-3. The user makes a selection by typing the appropriate number or abbreviation letters or by moving the cursor to the desired choice. Control then passes to the selected application area and the terminal displays another screen.

Users sometimes have particular menu structures in mind which they would like for developers to follow. Perhaps experience has shown that certain ways to structure their tasks improve efficiency, and they would like the menus to reflect this task structuring.

EXHIBIT 9-3.   Example Menu Screen Display

```
          ACE AEROSPACE CONTRACT TRACKING SYSTEM
               PROJECT MANAGER'S MAIN MENU



                    1. Standard Reports

                    2. Ad Hoc Query/Report

                    3. Briefing Charts
```

A common way to show menu structure is with a hierarchical tree diagram as shown in Exhibit 9-4. The main menu is shown at the top. Choices on each menu lead either to more detailed menus or to functional screen displays. Such a diagram gives a clear overview of the sequences of choices available to a type of user.

A problem with specifying menus in the requirements specification is that detailed design analysis usually uncovers additional choices which should be included. If menus are included in the formal requirements, the developer and users will have to meet often with the sponsor during the design stage to negotiate changes to these formal requirements. One option is to provide sample menu

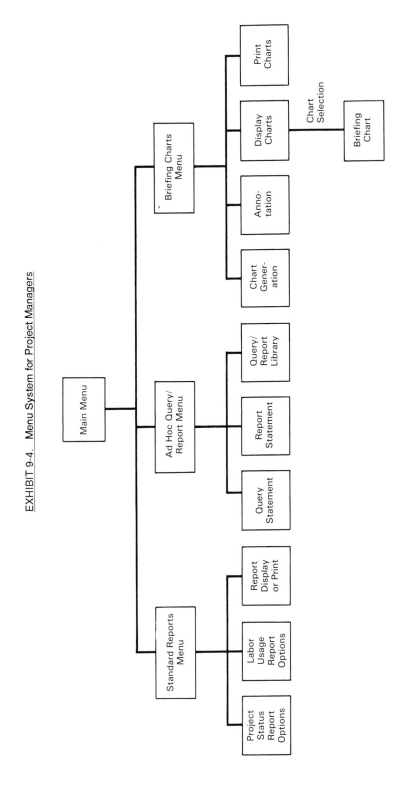

EXHIBIT 9-4. Menu System for Project Managers

structures in an appendix to the requirements specification. These should be clearly labeled as examples for guidance, rather than formal requirements.

OUTPUT EXAMPLES

Examples of actual report and screen displays offer a more concrete view of output requirements. If these results are currently being produced by either automated or manual means, then chances are good that the format of the current products is a useful one.

Exhibit 9-5 shows a typical sample output from the Ace Aerospace application. It shows how Ace Aerospace managers are accustomed to seeing all 12 months in columns and the contracts in rows. A substantial amount of information is conveyed with an example at almost no systems analysis cost. The example was created anyway to support the organization's operations and planning. All the analyst needs to do is determine whether the example is truly representative of the product format, and ensure that it is sufficiently legible to be clear after reproduction.

Although the general layout is clear from an example like Exhibit 9-5 it does not answer detailed questions. For example, what are the rules for labeling the "Actuals" and "Projections" columns when the report is produced near the beginning and end of the fiscal year? How are the expenditure numbers computed from quantities stored in the data base? Because examples, by themselves, do not answer questions of formatting and computation rules, the author recommends including them as an appendix. Like menu structures, they are a useful aid to help users communicate their needs to developers. They do not, however, constitute verifiable functional requirements.

DETAILED FORMATS
AND COMPUTATION RULES

When outputs are particularly critical to users they should be specified in verifiable detail. The goal is to provide clear formatting and computation rules while avoiding long textual explanations and minimizing the time an analyst must spend on these specifications. An approach that works well is *annotated samples*.

Exhibit 9-6 shows the same output sample as Exhibit 9-5 with annotations added. The annotations explain the intended formatting and computational logic, as well as identifying the data items from the data base description (see Chapters 11 and 12) which are needed to produce each field of the report.

EXHIBIT 9-5. Sample Output Report

CONTRACT FISCAL YEAR 1987 EXPENDITURES SUMMARY   FEBRUARY 10, 1987

TOTAL EXPENDITURES BY MONTH ($)

CONTRACT/ LINE ITEM	ACTUALS								PROJECTIONS			
	JUNE	JULY	AUGUST	SEPTEMBER	OCTOBER	NOVEMBER	DECEMBER	JANUARY	FEBRUARY	MARCH	APRIL	MAY
BEAM POINT INT EXP.												
HIGH ENERGY LASER	0	0	0	13975	34278	36734	32760	44607	36029	25780	22887	19731
PLATFORM	0	0	0	0	2619	23937	25138	36925	38105	4126	41096	42398
COMPUTER CONTROLS	0	0	0	21817	39255	40826	36025	50278	47298	49763	50320	51478
MONTHLY TOTALS	0	0	0	35792	76152	101497	93923	131810	121432	116807	114303	113607
FY 1987 TOTAL	905323											
EVASIVE TACTICS SIM.												
MGT & SYSTEM INTEG	30124	31972	29876	29548	31243	29547	26781	28376	12965	0	0	0
AIRCRAFT MODELS	25113	30927	15829	9367	7698	7513	6748	6383	3257	0	0	0
SIMULATION ENVIRON.	118952	140784	139217	78021	25921	12842	10243	8947	4871	0	0	0
TACTICS SIMULATION	0	0	0	12316	32873	33097	31920	35816	23983	0	0	0
MONTHLY TOTALS	174189	203683	184922	129252	97735	82999	75692	79522	45076	0	0	0
FY 1987 TOTAL	1073070											

EXHIBIT 9-6. Annotated Report Sample

CONTRACT FISCAL YEAR 1987 EXPENDITURES SUMMARY ①   FEBRUARY 10, 1987 ②

TOTAL EXPENDITURES BY MONTH ③ ($)

| | | ACTUALS | | | | | | | PROJECTIONS ⑤ | | | |
CONTRACT/ LINE ITEM	JUNE	JULY ④ / AUGUST	SEPTEMBER	OCTOBER	NOVEMBER	DECEMBER	JANUARY	FEBRUARY	MARCH	APRIL	MAY
BEAM POINT INT EXP. ⑥											
HIGH ENERGY LASER	0	0	13975	34278	36734	32760	44607	36029	25780	22887	19731
PLATFORM ⑦	0	0	0	2619 ⑧	23937	25138	36925	38105	41264 ⑨	41096	42398
COMPUTER CONTROLS	0	0	21817	39255	40826	36025	50278	47298	49763	50320	51478
MONTHLY TOTALS ①	0	0	35792 ⑩	76152	101497	93923	131810	121432	116807	114303	113607
FY 1987 TOTAL	905323 ⑪										
EVASIVE TACTICS SIM.											
MGT & SYSTEM INTEG	30124	29876	29548	31243	29547	26781	28376	12965	0	0	0
AIRCRAFT MODELS	25113	15829	9367	7698	7513	6748	6383	3257	0	0	0
SIMULATION ENVIRON.	118952	139217	78021	25921	12842	10243	8947	4871	0	0	0
TACTICS SIMULATION	0	0	12316	32873	33097	31920	35816	23983	0	0	0
MONTHLY TOTALS	174189	184922	129252	97735	82999	75692	79522	45076	0	0	0
FY 1987 TOTAL	1073070										

119

EXHIBIT 9-6.   Annotated Report Sample   (Continued)

Notes

(1) Fiscal year is an option specified by the user when
requesting the report.

(2) This is the date the report was compiled.

(3) "Actuals" and "Projections" headers work as follows:

Condition	Form of "Actuals" Header	Form of "Projections" Header
Last month for which month-end input of corporate accounting system data has been completed is:		
Before June of the specified fiscal year	Not printed	"PROJECTIONS" centered above all 12 months
June of specified fiscal year	"ACTUALS" (no spaces), centered above June	"PROJECTIONS" centered above July-May
July-February of specified fiscal year	"ACTUALS" centered above June through the last month which has corporate accounting inputs	"PROJECTIONS" centered above the remaining months in the fiscal year
March of the specified fiscal year	''	"PROJECTIONS" (no spaces) centered above April and May
April of the specified fiscal year	''	"PROJ'S" centered above May
May of the specified fiscal year (or later)	''	Not printed

(4) Each month has a column of nine spaces. Column headers are
centered in the column.

(5) The column of asterisks separating "Actuals" from "Projections"
(see note 3) is located in the leftmost column of the first
month under "Projections."

EXHIBIT 9-6.   Annotated Report Sample   (Continued)

(6) Contract Name (item 1.2)

(7) Contract Line Item Title (item 2.2)

(8) The "Monthly Actual Expenditures" figure is computed by summing all applicable expenditures:
    Month Burdened Labor (item 12.2)
    + Month Other Direct Cost Items (items 11.3)
    for the month being considered.

(9) The "Monthly Projected Expenditures" figure is computed from the Work Breakdown Element and Milestone records using the following formulas:

Milestone activity start day	=	Work Breakdown Element Start (item 3.4), for the first milestone for that Work Breakdown Element; 1 + Milestone Completion Day (item 6.3) belonging to the preceding milestone, for all other milestones for that Work Breakdown Element
Milestone activity end day	=	Milestone Completion Day (item 6.3)
Milestone fraction in month M	=	(Computed using algorithm A10, Appendix A, from the Milestone activity start day, end day, month M, and the Ace Aerospace business calendar)
Milestone projected cost in month M	=	(Milestone fraction in month M) X (Milestone Cost, item 6.5)
Monthly projected expenditures for Line item L in month M	=	Summation of all milestone projected costs in month M for each Work Breakdown Element in Line Item L and each Milestone for the Work Breakdown Elements

(10) Monthly totals for a contract are summations of the line item expenditures for the contract in that month.

(11) Contract total for the fiscal year is the summation of monthly totals for the contract (see note 10).

Many of the notes identify the data in particular report fields (see notes 1, 2, 6, and 7). Because of the need to have a detailed data model for these references, the author recommends making the detailed output annotations after compiling the data structure diagram and data dictionary. This is why the methodology pyramid (Exhibit 4-7) has output definitions as part of the last step of functional and data base description.

Logic concerning output formatting which is not clear from a single sample needs to be carefully explained. Notes 3, 4, and 5 serve this purpose. Note 3 shows how a decision table can be just as effective in annotations as it is in the verifiable functional requirements.

Computational rules explain how output fields can be computed from fields in the data base. Notes 8, 9, 10, and 11 are of this type. Lengthy algorithms should be carried in an appendix to which the notes can refer. For example, note 9 refers to an appendix which explains calendar computation details for computing the "Milestone fraction in month m."

LAYOUT DESIGN TOOLS

When preparing an annotated output sample the systems analyst often finds it is helpful to invent a sample which shows many of the special cases which can arise. A page of a report already produced by the user organization will generally show only a narrow range of possible situations.

Creating a special example should be assisted by a special text editor designed for that purpose. In particular, a definition of 132-column reports is much easier with a full-screen editor or electronic spreadsheet that allows both up-and-down and side-to-side scrolling. Another dividend is that these tools usually permit the results to be printed out with a "ruler" border, so that row and column coordinates of any field can be quickly identified. Exhibit 9-7 shows a screen display example with such a border. Finally, some tools will even fill out an output shell with random data.

An additional benefit can be gained by using the screen forms package which will be used by the application developer. In that case, the screen definition determined by the systems analysts when defining the application requirements can be given in the most usable digital form for the developers. In practice, this benefit comes most easily when the systems analysts and developers are in the same group.

SUMMARY OF OUTPUT
DEFINITION CONCEPTS

Output specification is one of the areas where the dividing line between requirements and design is unclear. At a minimum, the requirements specification should mention the kinds of information which must be available from particular screen

EXHIBIT 9-7. Screen Display Sample with Ruler Borders

```
         1         2         3         4         5         6         7         8
1234567890123456789012345678901234567890123456789012345678901234567890123456789012345678901234567890
```

CONTRACT DELIVERABLES STATUS

EVASIVE TACTICS SIMULATION CONTRACT   AS OF 11/1/87

OVERDUE DELIVERABLES	DATE DUE	PROJECTED COMPLETION
SIMULATION ACCEPTANCE TEST PLAN	10/1/87	1/15/88
EVASIVE TACTICS SIMULATOR CONTROL PANEL	10/15/87	12/31/87
DELIVERABLES PROJECTED TO BE LATE		
TACTICS MODELS DESCRIPTION	11/30/87	12/31/88
AIRCRAFT MODELS SOFTWARE DEMONSTRATION	11/30/87	12/15/88
DELIVERABLES PROJECTED ON TIME		
SIMULATION USER'S GUIDE	11/15/87	12/15/87
SIM. ENVIRONMENT WS MODULE COMPLETION	12/10/87	12/5/87
PROGRAMMER'S MANUAL DRAFT	1/15/88	1/15/87

```
         1         2         3         4         5         6         7         8
1234567890123456789012345678901234567890123456789012345678901234567890123456789012345678901234567890
```

123

displays and printed reports. At a maximum, detailed formatting, data identification, and algorithmic rules can be given using annotated samples. Likewise, the menu structure for user access can either be identified in the requirements specification or left until later for the application developers to define.

Because of this lack of clear right and wrong in output definition the systems analyst should determine a good approach for each application. Mixed expositions may be necessary when some outputs are substantially more important than others. Important outputs usually require a full annotated sample, like Exhibit 9-6. Detailed output definitions should be given a section of the user requirements or requirements specification document separate from the section containing the verifiable functional requirements. The output definitions section will have a subsection for each critical output. Each detailed output specification will contain:

- Output title
- Purpose
- Options
- Annotated sample.

Separating the output definitions from the functional requirements helps to emphasize the importance of critical screen displays and reports. It also improves readability because the output options and annotated sample are different in appearance from the textual functional requirements.

The analyst should clearly separate output "ideas" from output requirements. Menu structures and sample outputs which are intended to be general guidance to the developers should be included in appendices. This information should be clearly labeled in the documentation to distinguish it from appendices containing formal requirements. A lead-in paragraph explaining the purpose and status of the particular appendix usually suffices.

Chapters 6 to 9 show how to use user concept diagrams, verifiable functional requirements, and output definitions to create functional description for the new system. The functional description cannot stand on its own; it must be closely tied to the application data base description. The data base description is a more technical subject which is described in the next four chapters.

DISCUSSION QUESTIONS

1. What kinds of ambiguities keep an output sample from being useful as a verifiable requirement?

2. You are defining a new application to replace an old system which had a report writer accessible to end users. Many ad hoc reports have been defined and used but you now have several problems which make it difficult for you to capture the essence of these reports as requirements for the new application:

- Definitions of reports are scattered in many places.
- No one knows which old reports are still being used.
- There is no documentation about most of the ad hoc reports other than its 4th generation language code.

    a. How should these ad hoc reports be reflected in your new requirements?

    b. How will you get the requirements detail you need to make sure the new system will support the reports which are still useful?

REFERENCE

1. Ken Orr, *Structured Requirements Definition*, Topeka, KS: Ken Orr and Associates, 1981.

PART FOUR
Data Analysis

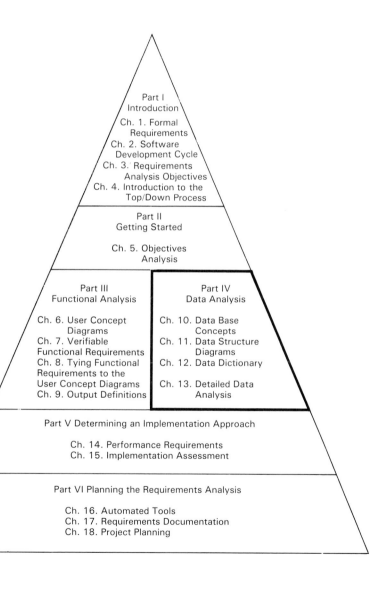

Part I
Introduction

Ch. 1. Formal
Requirements
Ch. 2. Software
Development Cycle
Ch. 3. Requirements
Analysis Objectives
Ch. 4. Introduction to the
Top/Down Process

Part II
Getting Started

Ch. 5. Objectives
Analysis

Part III
Functional Analysis

Ch. 6. User Concept
Diagrams
Ch. 7. Verifiable
Functional Requirements
Ch. 8. Tying Functional
Requirements to the
User Concept Diagrams
Ch. 9. Output Definitions

Part IV
Data Analysis

Ch. 10. Data Base
Concepts
Ch. 11. Data Structure
Diagrams
Ch. 12. Data Dictionary

Ch. 13. Detailed Data
Analysis

Part V Determining an Implementation Approach

Ch. 14. Performance Requirements
Ch. 15. Implementation Assessment

Part VI Planning the Requirements Analysis

Ch. 16. Automated Tools
Ch. 17. Requirements Documentation
Ch. 18. Project Planning

10

Data Base Concepts

Data analysis is the most technical area of systems analysis. This chapter gives a brief overview of data base concepts needed to understand the data analysis techniques described in Chapters 11 to 13.

HISTORICAL IMPACT
OF RANDOM ACCESS TO DATA FILES

Early management information systems were restricted by the need to process magnetic tapes when handling large quantities of data. The programs were carefully constructed to minimize the number of times a tape had to be read, since mechanically moving the tape took long periods of time. As a result, programs were constructed as shown in Exhibit 10-1. Entire tapes would be read in large batch jobs which produced other tapes and/or printed outputs. Tapes were processed sequentially from beginning to end.

There was little flexibility in the management information outputs of such a system. Users got a large computer printout at a fixed frequency. Special requests required moving mountains to get someone in Data Processing to write a new program that would be inserted into the crowded operational job stream. Programs were connected by interface tape files, and there was no real concept of "data base."

EXHIBIT 10-1.   Example of Early Magnetic Tape Processing

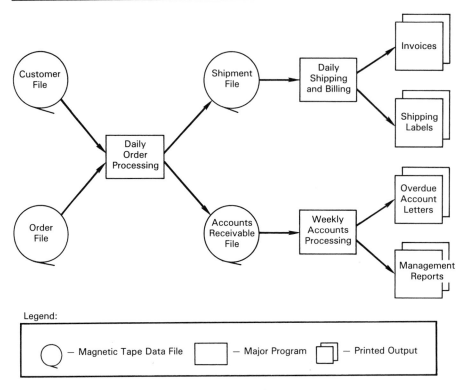

Legend:

⭕ — Magnetic Tape Data File   ▢ — Major Program   ▢ — Printed Output

The late 1960s brought an alternative to sequential access tape files. These were direct access or random access storage devices, primarily disk drives. Small amounts of data could be accessed quickly, regardless of where it was stored physically.

Direct access storage made a new software architecture possible: the integrated data base. Now applications could all run off the same master data base, as illustrated by Exhibit 10-2. Unlike tape files, disk files can be accessed by more than one application almost simultaneously. Freedom from the restriction of sequential processing required for tapes made it easier to design a data base which supported multiple applications. Advantages of the direct access integrated data base approach included:

- Large reduction in redundant data storage
- Corresponding reduction in problems caused by redundant data having inconsistencies
- Ability for applications to process small amounts of data at a time in short jobs
- Possibility for on-line (interactive) processing by a person at a terminal for data input and query.

EXHIBIT 10-2. Integrated Data Base Example

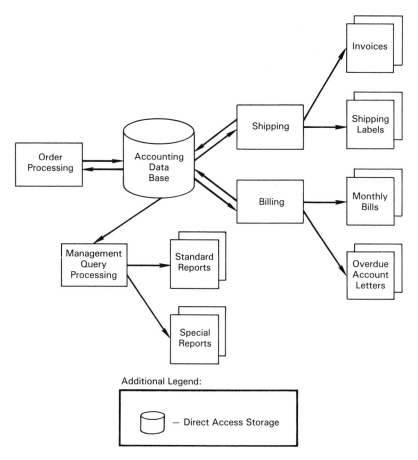

Additional Legend:

⊘ — Direct Access Storage

Corresponding to these changes from sequential to direct access storage, systems analysts found that it was necessary to increase emphasis on data definition when analyzing new applications. In the early 1960s, analysts had emphasized the procedural aspects of programs. Flow charts were a vast majority of the system definition outputs. Most of the rest was input-processing-output material (see Exhibit 6-3). People spent amazingly large amounts of time dreaming up clever algorithms for standard support functions like sorting, so that applications could be made to run in a tolerable amount of time. Defining the data in the interface tapes was generally a dull, straightforward task. By the nature of the processing, these tape formats had to be simple, and needed only to be checked against the needs of two or three programs using the data.

As people began to experiment with the integrated data base concept, however, data definition and management became an important issue. After all, 20 or more programs might have to access this one master source of data! Performance was still a vital concern, since access to disk records was orders of magnitude slower than access to the computer's main memory. Moreover, users were pushing for interactive applications, and would not accept minute-long waits for computer responses. Effective data base architectures were essential for quick access to information.

Two principles for defining and managing data came from the applications developed in the late 1960s and early 1970s using integrated data bases. The first was that powerful data manipulation software utilities were required, because the effort expended with data entry and retrieval programs was swamping all other parts of applications program development. The second need was to handle data with more complex logical relationships than the familiar "flat files" that peo-ple had been using. As illustrated in Exhibit 10-3, these flat files consisted of fixed-length records with fixed-position data fields. Often they were handled originally as punch cards with the data fields entered in prespecified columns.

DATA BASE MANAGEMENT SYSTEMS

A new kind of systems software emerged in the 1970s to provide the necessary data manipulation utilities. Research projects and early commercial products such as IBM's Information Management System (IMS), Honeywell's IDS, MRI's System 2000, and Cincom's TOTAL showed that a data base management system (DBMS) should include the following:

EXHIBIT 10-3. Example Flat File

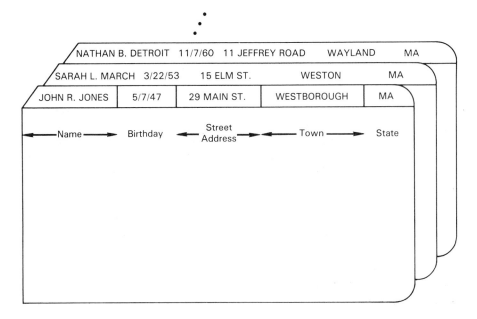

- Data definition language
- Data manipulation language
- Access controls
- Ad hoc query and report languages
- Load and unload utilities.

The following paragraphs briefly describe these features.

The data definition language (DDL) describes the format (often called "schema") of the data base. With the data manipulation language (DML), it acts to isolate the applications programs from the actual data base formats.

For example, suppose an application with a five-digit zip code item must be changed to contain "zip + 4" nine-digit numbers. Classical programming with data definitions in the application code would require changes to all programs accessing zip code. After lengthening the zip code item, the succeeding items in the record will occur in different locations, shifted four character positions. Changes would be required for other programs which access items in the address record, even if they did not need zip code.

Exhibit 10-4 shows how a DBMS isolates the application programs from data (re)definitions. Applications programs call for records and items by name, using DML commands, not by physical location on disk. The DML processor accesses the schema for this application, which tells where these records and items are physically stored, and then uses this information to access the actual data. When the schema needs to be changed (for example, to increase zip code length), the changes must be specified to the DDL processor and the data base may need to

EXHIBIT 10-4. Isolation of Applications From Data Base Format

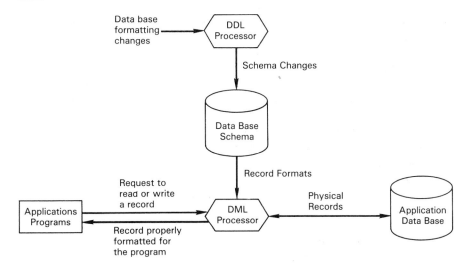

be reloaded. But proven applications programs remain untouched, as long as the record and item names remain the same.

The data manipulation language is a set of utility routines which assist programmers and end-user software in locating, reading, and writing records in the data base. Often an interactive DML capability is available to try out data base access steps. In addition, most DBMS packages allow programmers to access DML routines from one or more high-order languages (e.g., COBOL, FORTRAN, PL1, C, or Ada). The mechanism for implementing the high-order language connection is called the host language interface.

Real data bases have extensive privacy concerns that must be handled properly before people will allow the integrated data base to be assembled. For example, an accounting data base may require employee salaries; yet that sensitive information may be withheld from all but a few people. Access control is the function which allows authorized users to access information, while denying access to individuals who are not authorized to see it. Different individuals and types of users may have varying authorizations for the same integrated data base. The data base management system usually assists access control by allowing the application administrator to specify individual or user group authorizations in a subschema or user view. These authorization tools tell which parts of the overall data base schema are permitted to be seen by a particular user, group of users, or application program.

Users like to be able to fill special information needs themselves, rather than wait for Data Processing to program a new report. A DBMS should provide a general ad hoc query capability for flexible questioning of the data base. This capability is a combination of a query specification language, which lets a user make a request for information, and a query processor, which accesses the data base to satisfy the query. For example, the question, "Which salespeople earned more than $10,000 commission last month in the New York–New England area?" should be simple to obtain from a sales data base. An ad hoc report capability is similar but allows the user to specify how the results of the query will be formatted. For example, the user can specify labels for column headings, spacing of columns, and page breaks.

Since the DBMS usually stores data in special formats with embedded pointers, it is useful to have load and unload utilities. The load utility takes a flat file table such as the one in Exhibit 10-3 and converts it into the DBMS internal format, based on an application schema. The unload utility does the reverse, creating flat files from the DBMS-structured data base. These utilities are used together when restructuring the data base (after a schema change), or separately when interfacing with another system.

In the late 1970s and 1980s, DBMS products have been adding additional features such as:

- Screen forms package
- Business graphics outputs

- Special data integrity checks
- Distributed data base features.

A screen forms package helps the developer set up data entry and formatted query screens easily, with a tool which uses DML utilities. Business graphics provide features like line graphs, bar charts, and pie charts, usually packaged with the ad hoc report writer. Special data integrity checks include a facility to scroll through allowable values for an item on a data entry screen. Distributed data base features allow access of data from multiple physical locations as if they were all part of one logical data base. Through the mid-1980s, the general distributed data base problem has proven to be extremely difficult to solve. Products with good distributed data base capabilities tend to be weak in their other data management capabilities.

TYPES OF DBMS DATA MODELS

As previously mentioned, one of the incentives for inventing data base management systems was the need to handle complex data relationships. Direct use of random access flat files is cumbersome in most real integrated data bases, because they force the programmer to keep track of a variety of codes and pointers. Today's DBMS packages typically use one of the following data modeling viewpoints to handle data structures:

- Hierarchical
- Network (CODASYL)
- Relational.

A particular DBMS works primarily from one of these outlooks, but may have some features of the other two.

Hierarchical Data Model

A hierarchical DBMS (examples: IMS/DL1, System 2000, FOCUS) handles repeating groups found in hierarchical structures. Consider, for example, a typical organization structure, such as the one in Exhibit 10-5. The company has several divisions. Each is composed of several departments which may themselves be divided into multiple sections. When keeping information about various organization units (say, unit name, manager, secretary, and phone number), we would like to be able to track which subunits belong to it. For example, Accounting, Finance, and Personnel departments all fit into the Administration division. Problems in maintaining such a hierarchy with flat files arise from the variable nature of subunit breakouts. A department might have any number of sections between two and ten.

EXHIBIT 10-5. Example Hierarchy

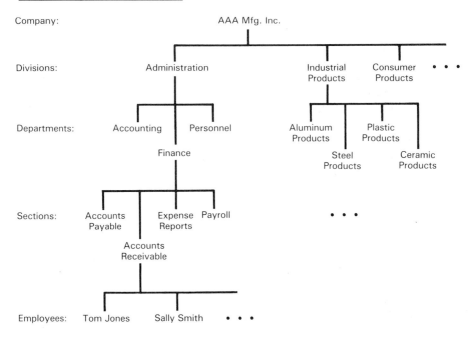

A hierarchical DBMS will allow the data base designer to specify the structural breakdown of the application data hierarchy (e.g., "divisions are composed of departments which have sections which have employees"). The DBMS figures out how the record occurrence will be physically stored.

Exhibit 10-6 shows a common shorthand for diagramming the example hierarchy. The arrows indicate each hierarchical breakout. For example, the arrow pointing from Department to Section indicates that each department may be com-

EXHIBIT 10-6. Hierarchy Diagram

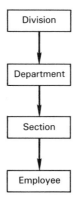

EXHIBIT 10-7. Data Items for the Hierarchy Example

Record	Item	Example
Division	Division Name Division Manager Division Secretary Division Secretary's Phone	Administration Dr. James Broderick Jane Winslow (617) 371-9421
Department	Department Name Dept. Manager Dept. Secretary Dept. Secretary's Phone	Accounting Royce Silver Samuel Hunt (617) 371-9437

posed of any number of sections. The boxes (labeled "Division," "Department," and so on) represent record types. They contain data items (often called fields or data elements) about the entity represented in the record type. Exhibit 10-7 shows what items might be stored for the records in our example. A particular instance of all the data items of a record type, such as shown in the "Example" column of Exhibit 10-7, is called a record occurrence.

Network Data Model

Hierarchical structuring, although significantly more helpful than flat files, was awkward to use in many practical situations. The "College Classes" example illustrates the problem: Consider a data base which keeps track of assignments of teachers to courses and the schedule of course sections. Taking a hierarchical view, there are two hierarchies involved, as shown in Exhibits 10-8 and 10-9. Each teacher may teach several different courses. Likewise, courses may have multiple sections, depending on student demand, with one or more teachers.

EXHIBIT 10-8. Teacher-based College Classes Hierarchy

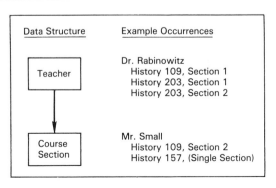

EXHIBIT 10-9. Course-based College Classes Hierarchy

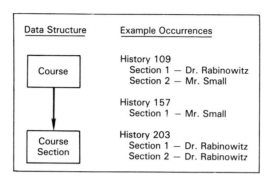

Organizing the data by teacher, the question "Is History 137 being taught?" requires searching the whole data base. Likewise, organizing the data by course, the question "What courses is Dr. Rabinowitz teaching?" requires searching through all the data.

What you would really like to do is store both hierarchies simultaneously as diagrammed in Exhibit 10-10. Course Section acts as a breakdown of *both* Teachers and Students. But when you do this, you break out of the hierarchical tree structure of Exhibit 10-5 into a more general network style of data modeling.

In network data modeling, hierarchical breakdowns are generalized with one-to-many relationships. Record type A has a one-to-many relationship with record type B if some occurrences of A are related to more than one occurrence of B, and all occurrences of B are related to a unique occurrence of A. Any two record types may have a one-to-many relationship (and sometimes more than one) between them. The relationship indicates which record occurrences of the two record types belong together in some sense. For example, in Exhibit 10-10, the Teacher record occurrence for Mr. Small is related to the Course Section records for History 109, Section 2 and History 157, Section 1 by the "Teaches" relationship. We often call Teacher the parent record for the "Teaches" relationship and Course Section the child record.

Typical rules for modeling data with a network DBMS include:

EXHIBIT 10-10. Double Hierarchy for the College Classes Example

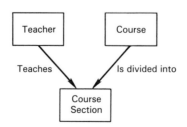

- One-to-many relationships cannot be circular (see Exhibit 10-11). That is, you should not be able to follow a chain of one-to-many relationships and return to the record type you started with.
- Given a one-to-many relationship from record A to record B, the data manipulation language must provide these capabilities:
  - For a particular occurrence of record A, locate all related occurrences of record B.
  - Given a particular occurrence of record B, locate the unique related occurrence of record A and all other occurrences of record B related to it.

These rules are easier to understand and remember if you look at an example showing how they could be physically implemented with DBMS-set pointers. Consider the part of the college classes data base illustrated in Exhibits 10-8 and 10-9. Exhibit 10-12 shows how these data look under the network structure diagrammed in Exhibit 10-10. There are two Teacher, three Course, and five Course Section record occurrences. The one-to-many relationship "Teaches" between the Teacher record and the Course Section record must implement the hierarchical view in Exhibit 10-8. The one-to-many relationship "Is Divided Into" between the Course record and the Course Section record must implement the hierarchical view in Exhibit 10-9.

EXHIBIT 10-11. Examples of Circular One-to-Many Relationships

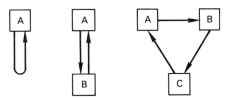

One relationship implementation strategy is to have each record contain a DBMS-set pointer item for each one-to-many relationship it is involved with. Exhibit 10-12 shows how these pointers could be set in the "College Courses" example. The "Teaches" relationship would have a pointer from Mr. Small to the first Course Section (History 109, Section 2) that he teaches. That Course Section occurrence has its "Teaches" pointer indicate the next section taught by Mr. Small (History 157, Section 1). The History 157, Section 1 "Teaches" pointer then points back to Mr. Small's Teacher record occurrence, to signal that he has no other sections and to provide a way to go from Course Sections to the Teacher instructing them. Another set of pointers would implement the "Is Divided Into" relationship between Course and Course Section records. In a network DBMS, the DDL and DML processors take care of all the pointers called for by the data base developer, thus freeing programmers from tedious pointer logic creation and testing.

EXHIBIT 10-12.   College Classes Example Physical Implementation With Pointers

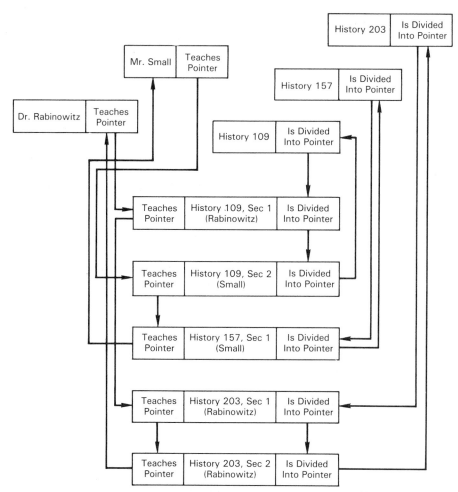

The same organization which created the COBOL language standard, the Conference on DAta SYstems Languages (CODASYL), also produced a standard for network DBMS. The CODASYL Data Base Task Group (DBTG) report in 1971 (1) set the standards followed by most of today's network DBMS. Examples have included Honeywell's IDS and Cullinet's IDMS products.

The DBTG chose the word "set" to mean one-to-many relationship. This has caused great confusion because of the mismatch of this usage with the common mathematical definition for "set," meaning a collection of objects. We will avoid use of this term when discussing data relationships in this text.

You should be aware of how three different types of interrecord relationships are handled in network modeling. A one-to-one relationship between record type A and record type B indicates that every occurrence of A corresponds to a unique occurrence of B. This case is usually handled by combining the items of both record types into a single combined record, AB. A one-to-many relationship between A and B indicates that each occurrence of A may correspond to an arbitrary number of occurrences of B, but each occurrence of B must have a unique corresponding occurrence of A. This case is handled by one or more choices of pointer schemes, as has been discussed. A many-to-many relationship is the most general situation in which an occurrence of A may correspond to an arbitrary number of occurrence of B and vice versa.

Many-to-many relationships can be messy to handle directly. Network data modeling relies on the fact that *every many-to-many relationship can be split into two one-to-many relationships.* Here is how to do it.

If record type A has a many-to-many relationship with record B, create a new link record, A/B, which contains an occurrence for every pair of occurrences of A and B which are related to each other. In essence, you represent the set of ordered pairs in the original relationship by a new record type. Then create a one-to-many relationship from A to A/B which holds whenever the occurrence of A is the first part of the occurrence of A/B. Likewise, create a one-to-many relationship between B and A/B which holds whenever the occurrence of B is the same as the second part of the occurrence of A/B.

In the "College Classes" example, the relationship "Instructs" is a many-to-many relationship between the Teacher and the Course record types. Exhibit 10-13 illustrates the Teacher/Course link record and the two one-to-many relationships.

Note that there may be information content (data items) which should be kept with the link record. Reflection on the meaning of the link and the associated data items may result in a different definition of the link from the "brute force" approach of Exhibit 10-13. For example, the Course Section record in Exhibits 10-11 and 10-12 can also be used to represent the many-to-many relationship between Teachers and Courses. However, Course Section is broken out finer than the Teacher/Course record, since the same teacher can teach more than one section

EXHIBIT 10-13. Splitting the Example Many-to-Many Relationship

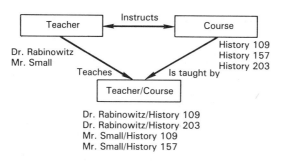

EXHIBIT 10-14. Relational View of the College Classes Example

Teacher   Course

Teacher Name	Date of Birth	Degree	Home Address

Catalog No.	Title

Course Section

CS Teacher Name	CS Catalog No.	Section No.	Time	Room

of the same course. Hence, there can be more than one Course Section occurrence corresponding to a Teacher/Course occurrence.

Relational Data Model

The relational approach is based on pioneering work by E. F. Codd around 1970 (2). Its basic premises are:

- Users find it easier to understand data organized as flat file tables than as a hierarchy or network.
- Relationships should not have to be determined in advance and pointers preset to allow navigation of the data base.

A relational view of the "College Classes" example in Exhibit 10-10 would look almost the same as the network view (see Exhibit 10-14). Relational DBMS practitioners use a somewhat different terminology for the same concepts that appear in CODASYL implementations. Record types are called relations or tables, which are envisioned as a large matrix of rows and columns of data (see Exhibit 10-15).

EXHIBIT 10-15. Teacher Relation Viewed as a Matrix

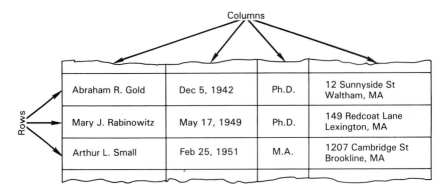

	Columns		
Abraham R. Gold	Dec 5, 1942	Ph.D.	12 Sunnyside St Waltham, MA
Mary J. Rabinowitz	May 17, 1949	Ph.D.	149 Redcoat Lane Lexington, MA
Arthur L. Small	Feb 25, 1951	M.A.	1207 Cambridge St Brookline, MA

Thus, a record occurrence in CODASYL is a table row in relational parlance. CODASYL record items become relational table columns. An item occurrence becomes the data in a specific row and specific column.

EXHIBIT 10-16.   Join of Teacher and Course Section Tables Using Teacher Name

Row *n* :

Mary L. Rabinowitz	May 17, 1948	Ph.D.	149 Redcoat Lane Lexington, MA

History 109	Section 1	TuTh 3-5	Smith 203

Row *n* + 1:

Mary L. Rabinowitz	May 17, 1948	Ph.D.	149 Redcoat Lane Lexington, MA

History 203	Section 1	MWF 9-10	Morse 127

Row *n* + 2:

Mary L. Rabinowitz	May 17, 1948	Ph.D.	149 Redcoat Lane Lexington, MA

History 203	Section 2	MWF 2-3	Morse 121

To navigate a relational data base, there must be some way to use the data in the relations, since there are no preset pointers. This is done by the join operator. Two relations A and B are joined together by matching specified columns *a* of relation A with specified columns *b* of B. The result is a virtual relation AB(*ab*) whose rows contain all the data from rows of A and rows of B which have an exact match in data in the specified columns (*a* and *b*).

For an example of a join, consider the relational "College Classes" model in Exhibit 10-14. Suppose you need to set up a report about the faculty which includes Teacher Name, Home Address, Course Number, Section Number, and Time for each course this teacher leads. First, join the Teacher table to the Course Section table, specifying that the Teacher Name in the Teacher table must match CS Teacher Name in the Course Section table. The result of the join would be a combined virtual table as shown in Exhibit 10-16. This virtual table is highly redundant but does assemble the data you need for your report. A typical relational

DBMS gives you ad hoc query, ad hoc report, and high-order language interface instructions for formatting the items you need from the join table.

Joins can be used to implement one-to-many relationships. For example, the "Teaches" relationship in Exhibit 10-10 can be implemented by joining the Teacher and Course Section relations by matching Teacher Name with CS Teacher Name (see Exhibit 10-14). Likewise, the "Is Divided Into" relationship can be implemented by joining the Course and Course Section records, matching Catalog No. with CS Catalog No.

Relational DBMS concepts were strictly theoretical during the 1970s because of the difficulty in implementing joins efficiently. Searching repeatedly through the two tables to find matches can be extremely time consuming compared to following CODASYL pointers. However, use of algorithmic tools like "B- Trees" and increasing availability of main memory for searches has made relational DBMS implementations feasible. Oracle Corporation's ORACLE product and Relational Technology Inc.'s INGRES product have been trend setters in the relational DBMS community.

Which Type of DBMS Should You Use?

Based on heavy proselytizing by missionaries like Chris Date (3) and James Martin (4), American data processing managers have become increasingly interested in relational data base management systems as the "wave of the future." In fact, they may be. ORACLE and INGRES are rapidly expanding their user base, and every major hardware vendor feels obligated to have a relational DBMS to compete in the 1980s. Hierarchical, CODASYL, and other styles (such as inverted files systems, like ADABAS and Model 204) are joining the relational bandwagon by supporting joins and a relational appearance of their systems. Cincom replaced TOTAL with the relational TIS. Cullinet replaced IDMS with a relational IDMS/R. A particular style of relational query language, SQL (for structured query language) is becoming a true standard for data base management systems. In the late 1980s, most new DBMS purchases will be for relational systems.

The author recommends choosing a DBMS (or deciding to build the application without using a DBMS) based on a thorough study of the needs of the data processing facility or application. Peculiar applications needs, such as the ability to handle textual data well, to implement complex data privacy controls, or to implement a large number of data entry screen displays quickly, may far outweigh advantages of a particular data modeling approach. Difficult performance requirements, particularly in transaction processing, often lead to a custom approach which avoids the run-time overhead of a DBMS. Of course, your DBMS decision may be dictated to you as a standard for the data processing shop which will be building or maintaining the application.

DATA ANALYSIS FOR REQUIREMENTS SPECIFICATION

The material in this chapter is useful background for the discussions in Chapters 11 to 13. These show how an application's integrated data base can be formally described in the system definition phase. Such a description should:

- Support data base design (schema definition) under any data base management system or custom data management approach.
- Be simple for users to understand and discuss.
- Completely specify the application data base contents.

Chapters 11 to 13 use a mixture of relational and network techniques in a systematic data base description approach designed to meet these objectives. Relational theory provides insights on when groups of data items are properly combined into a single record type. Network theory provides a nice way of showing how the record types are related to each other.

DISCUSSION QUESTIONS

1. Most libraries have a manual index file which lists information about each book in the library files, indexed by both author and subject. Usually the title, author(s), short description, publisher, publication date, and location in the library stacks are given for each book.
    a. Sketch out a network model for the book index data base.
    b. Show a relational model for the book index data base.

2. Avoiding circular one-to-many relationships (Exhibit 10-11) sometimes requires a nonobvious trick. One of the relationships needs to be represented as a record type. This is the same trick used to replace many-to-many relationships by a new record and two one-to-many relationships (Exhibit 10-13). For example, consider an Employee record type with a one-to-many relationship "Supervises," to itself. Replace the "Supervises" relation with a new record type.

Supervises

    a. What are the items in this record?
    b. What two one-to-many relationships are required between the Employee record and the new Supervises record?

3. Consider the following relational model for task staffing and schedules for a software implementation project:

Task Leader Table

Task Leader	Task
Chuck Daniels	DBMS Selection
Chuck Daniels	DBMS Checkout
Chuck Daniels	DBMS Support
Jack Jones	Algorithm Design
Jack Jones	Algorithm Prototyping

Task Schedule Table

Task	Start	End
DBMS Selection	10/01/87	1/01/88
DBMS Checkout	3/01/88	5/01/88
DBMS Support	5/01/88	6/15/89
Algorithm Design	10/01/87	2/01/88
Algorithm Prototyping	2/01/88	6/21/88

Task Staffing Table

Task	Worker
DBMS Selection	Chuck Daniels
DBMS Selectiion	Henry Belson
DBMS Checkout	Chuck Daniels
DBMS Checkout	Henry Belson
DBMS Checkout	Lucy Smith
DBMS Support	Chuck Daniels
DBMS Support	Lucy Smith

    a. What join operation will give you a table which shows who supervises whom on tasks? List the part of the join table which you know from the above examples.

    b. Suppose you want to know who supervises whom over particular stretches of time. What additional join is required, and what does the resulting join table look like?

REFERENCES

1. CODASYL Data Base Task Group April 71 Report, New York: Association for Computing Machinery, 1971.

2. E.F. Codd, "A Relational Model of Data for Large Shared Data Banks," *Communications of the ACM*, vol. 13, no. 6, 1970.

3. C. J. Date, *An Introduction to Database Systems*, Vol. 1, 4th ed., Reading, MA: Addison-Wesley, 1986.

4. James Martin, *Principles of Data Base Management*, Englewood Cliffs, N.J.: Prentice-Hall, 1976.

11
Data Structure Diagrams

This chapter describes the powerful technique of data structure diagrams for modeling the logical structure of an application's data. The discussion here relies heavily on the background terminology and concepts presented in Chapter 10. Before going through the steps of data structure diagram generation, it is useful first to examine why analysts should undertake a formal data analysis and what kind of data base definition is needed for the requirements specification.

DATA ANALYSIS OBJECTIVES

The simplest way to model a data base is by following the format of a key input form or report. Although straightforward and quick for implementation, this approach inhibits enhancement flexibility and often slows response of standard applications. For example, if the college classes data base from Chapter 10 was set up according to the course catalog (see Exhibit 10-9), then there would be little flexibility to conveniently add other information about teachers to the data base. Moreover, the simple question of finding out which courses a particular teacher is giving could be very slow. For real-world applications with many relationships among record types, both of these problems become severe. The goal of convenient user interaction with the data base becomes lost in applications backlogs and responses taking many minutes.

Data analysis is the field of study which works to achieve the proper overall data base design for an integrated data base. This design must:

- Accept all inputs into the data base structure.
- Produce all required outputs from the data base.
- Accommodate validation checks of input data in order to maintain data integrity.
- Allow necessary security and privacy controls to be imposed on the data.
- Yield acceptable performance for all applications which will work with the data base.
- Have flexibility to allow data base enhancements while minimizing software reprogramming needs.

The data analysis problem is simplified by splitting it into two parts, performed in different implementation phases. In the application definition phase, development of a conceptual data model documents the user data requirements. In the design phase this is then transformed into a physical data model (using the data definition language of the chosen DBMS), which is optimized for application performance characteristics. The conceptual model is often called the logical data model in data base literature. However, since a good physical model should also be logical, the author prefers to use the adjective "conceptual" to distinguish from the schema-level data base design.

Conceptual data analysis strives to identify all the data items users will need, and to decide how they logically fit together into stable groupings of items called data entities. It also must show how entities are related to each other. In a top-down approach to the analysis, entities and their interrelationships are determined first, and then they are broken down into their component items. This approach is described in this chapter. In bottom-up data analysis, existing lists of data items are analyzed to synthesize data entities and then determine relationships among entities. Chapter 13 describes a bottom-up approach.

The user-centered requirements analysis approach employs two primary documentation tools for the conceptual data model: the data structure diagram and the data dictionary. The data structure diagram should be created by a trained data analyst, using principles discussed in this chapter and in Chapter 13. This diagram has two basic symbols (boxes for record types and arrows for one-to-many relationships) and is easy for users to understand. The data dictionary, described in Chapter 12, uses a familiar tabular form to list the items in each record, including definitions and validity checking information.

CREATION OF THE DATA STRUCTURE DIAGRAM

Creation of a data structure diagram for an application's data base proceeds in four steps:

- Identify data entities
- Identify entity keys
- List entity attributes
- Determine relationships among entities.

The Ace Aerospace sample problem gives examples of decisions made at each step. The discussion leads to a data structure diagram for the Ace Aerospace Contract Tracking System.

The first step is to identify each data entity—a person, object, or concept which is described by data in the data base. When more information is compiled, the data entities will become record types in the data base description. Candidates for data entities arise in most early discussions with users. Many of the special terms discussed during objectives analysis are really data entities. When interviewing a user to determine user concept diagrams, the requirements analyst also asks for data entities with questions like:

- "What things do you need information about in this application?"
- "You used the term 'customer order.' How do you define it? What information about a customer order do you need to retain?"

Candidate entities may also be determined by analyzing materials describing the current system or business process. Each candidate should be approved or declared out of scope for the application in discussions with users.

Example data entities which come from preliminary analysis of the Ace Aerospace contract financial management application include:

- Contract
- Work Breakdown Structure (WBS) Element
- Deliverable Item
- Schedule Milestone
- Monthly Labor Charge
- Monthly Other Direct Costs
- Contract Modification.

Each entity must be defined so that there are rules to help determine what data belong with which entities. Exhibit 11-1 shows two entity definitions. Some of these definitions will have already been made in objectives analysis. For example, Work Breakdown Structure was defined in objectives analysis for the Ace Aerospace example (see Exhibits 5-6 and 5-7).

The process of describing data entities quickly leads to important conceptual decisions for this application. For example, should Other Direct Costs (ODCs) be subdivided into Subcontractor Invoices, Consultant Charges, Computer Time, and Miscellaneous ODCs? Such a split would be useful if different kinds of data are

EXHIBIT 11-1. Data Entity Descriptions

Entity	Description
Contract	Description of an overall contract in which a government or commercial organization pays Ace Aerospace for products and/or services.
WBS Element	A Work Breakdown Structure Element contains the name and description of an element of the hierarchical decomposition of the work in a contract. The Work Breakdown Structure is used by the Ace Aerospace program manager in managing the technical work under this contract.

required for each of these categories. Or perhaps there are reasons to keep track of these ODC components separately for reporting purposes.

The second step is to identify a key for each data entity. This is a special piece of information which uniquely identifies each entity occurence. Exhibit 11-2 shows some candidate keys for data entities.

Schedule Milestone is an example of a data entity requiring a compound key. It would be unreasonable to have an indexing of all milestones across the project. Such an indexing would have an arbitrary sequence and would be difficult to maintain with contract modifications. Indexing the milestones by Work Breakdown Structure Elements makes it possible to associate the milestones with the work leading to the milestone results. In addition, the underlying contract should be part of the Schedule Milestone key to insure that milestones from different contracts do not get confused.

EXHIBIT 11-2. Data Entity Keys

Entity	Key
Contract	Contract Number (assigned by the contracting agency, if a government contract; otherwise, assigned internally by Ace Aerospace management)
WBS Element	Contract Number and Element Index (a digit per breakdown level, separated by periods, as in Exhibit 5-7)
Deliverable Item	Contract Number and Deliverable Item Index (either assigned by the government contracting officer in the contract deliverable requirements list or assigned by Ace Aerospace management)
Schedule Milestone	Contract Number, WBS Element Index, and Milestone Number

The third step is to list attributes of each data entity. These are characteristics of the entity which will become (nonkey) data items after you supply more information about them. For now, they form a list which helps to define the concept of the entity. Exhibit 11-3 gives examples of attributes for Ace Aerospace entities.

EXHIBIT 11-3. Nonkey Data Entity Attributes

Entity	Attributes	
Contract	Contract title Period of performance Total value with options	Type Initial value
WBS Element	WBS Element title Scheduled start/finish	Description Estimated cost
Deliverable Item	Title Data item description Date first delivery required Update frequency or schedule Distribution for delivered product	

The fourth step is to determine relationships among the data entities which have been defined with attributes and keys in steps 1, 2, and 3. This is where the analyst starts sketching the data base road map called the Data Structure Diagram. Analysis of relationships requires a large number of decisions concerning how the real business situation can most effectively be modeled in data structure. The next few pages illustrate this type of decisionmaking, using the Ace Aerospace example.

ANALYZING RELATIONSHIPS
AMONG DATA ENTITIES

The systems analyst should examine the data entities, asking a variety of questions about their interrelationships. These questions can be grouped in four categories:

- One-to-many relationships
- Repeating groups
- Many-to-many relationships
- Anticipated access paths.

The Ace Aerospace sample problem provides examples of each of these sources of relationships.

One-To-Many Relationships

As an example of the kinds of decisions which have to be made when determining one-to-many relationships, consider the question of level of detail for Monthly Labor Charges. Is it sufficient to collect labor costs aggregated for an entire Contract, or should they be collected by a lower level of work breakdown? Keeping data at a lower level means more work in maintaining the data base but may give more insights into the details of project progress.

For the purposes of discussion, let's assume that Ace Aerospace management makes a policy decision that all costs will be collected by the first breakout of the contract. Since this breakout is usually spelled out in the government contracts as "Contract Line Items," a new Contract Line Item entity is broken off from Work Breakdown Structure Element. So far we have a view of the data base as shown in Exhibit 11-4, where boxes represent data entities and arrows represent one-to-many relationships.

For reasons that will be clear when we discuss canonical form data structure diagrams, circular relationships should be avoided (see Exhibit 10-11). Hence, we

EXHIBIT 11-4. Preliminary One-to-Many Relationships

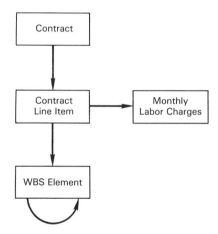

need to fix the relationship between WBS Element and itself. This arrow in Exhibit 11-4 simply indicates that the work breakdown structure can continue to be broken down hierarchically beyond level 3 (level 1 is the whole contract, and level 2 is the contract line items).

One alternative, shown in Exhibit 11-5, is to turn the WBS subdivision one-to-many relationship into another entity called Element Subdivision. Each parent/child pair of WBS Elements in the original relationship becomes an occur-

EXHIBIT 11-5.   Generalized Form of WBS Hierarchy

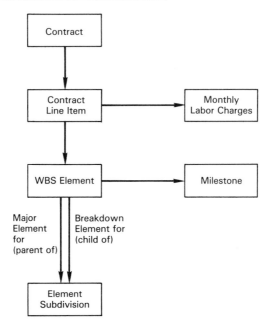

rence of the Element Subdivision entity. Note that this trick is the same as the one used to split a many-to-many relationship into two one-to-many relationships (see Exhibit 10-13 and Discussion Question 2 in Chapter 10). In this case, it allows arbitrarily many levels of hierarchical breakout of WBS Elements. The one-to-many relationships between the WBS Element and Element Subdivision indicate that applications must be able to go from any WBS Element to its component elements and to the next higher level breakout.

Exhibit 11-6 illustrates how this works. From WBS Element 4, we may follow the "Major Element for" relationship down to Element Subdivision occurrences and then come back up using the "Breakdown Element for" relationship to find all information concerning components 4.1, 4.2, and 4.3. Navigating in the other direction from 4.2, following the "Breakdown Element for" relationship first and returning by the "Major Element for" relationship, we find that element 4. is the parent element.

Another option is to fix upon a standard level of detail of the Work Breakdown Structure. For example, Ace Aerospace management may decide that every contract will be managed with a four-level WBS, as shown in Exhibit 11-7. Schedule milestones would be kept only with the most detailed (level 4) WBS elements. Clearly the approach in Exhibit 11-7 is less flexible for individual projects than the approach of Exhibit 11-5. However, it would be the appropriate view if Ace Aerospace management wanted every contract to be controlled with a

EXHIBIT 11-6.   Example Occurrences for the Generalized WBS Hierarchy

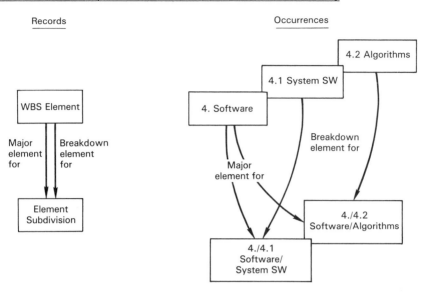

standard four-level WBS. We will assume Ace Aerospace management decides to use the more flexible model of Exhibit 11-5.

Repeating Groups

Repeating groups within an entity need to be examined to decide whether it is best to break them out as separate entities. For example, we found that monthly labor charges should be kept by Contract Line Item and by month, but we did not explore how much detail should be kept. Possibilities could include storing labor costs:

- Per employee working the Contract Line Item
- Per class of employee (salary level or skill type) working the Contract Line Item
- As a single total for all employees working the Contract Line Item.

Suppose that Ace Aerospace managers decide that labor costs should be retained monthly both as a dollar total for the entire line item and as man-hours for each of the ten Ace Aerospace salary levels which had representation on the line item. Then it is appropriate to add an entity for Salary Level Man-Hours, as shown in Exhibit 11-8. An alternative is to add man-hour attributes for every Ace Aerospace salary level to the Monthly Labor Charge entity. This alternative can lead to extensive repetition in the data dictionary. It is usually convenient to create another entity in the conceptual data model when the number of repeats is greater than four.

EXHIBIT 11-7. Fixed Four-Level WBS Structure

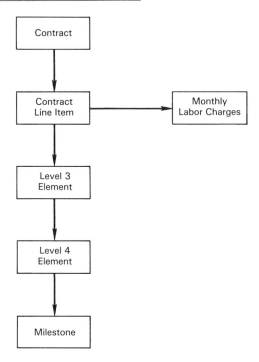

Many-To-Many Relationships

Many-to-many relationships need to broken into two one-to-many relation-ships, as discussed in Chapter 10. For Ace Aerospace, Contract Modifications have many-to-many relationships with Contract Line Items. A single modification may impact several line items, and a single line item may be changed repeatedly by contract modifications. Introducing a new Mod/Line Item entity presents the situation shown in Exhibit 11-9. In cases like this you should thoroughly explore possible data attributes for the Mod/Line Item entity representing the many-to-

EXHIBIT 11-8. Adding an Entity for a Repeating Group

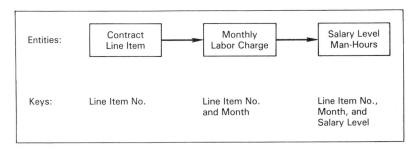

many relationship. For Ace Aerospace, the need is to track changes in overall value of the line item with each modification.

EXHIBIT 11-9.   Splitting the Many-to-Many Relationship Between Modifications and Line Items

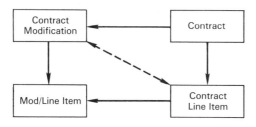

Anticipated Access Paths

A final check needs to be made to examine anticipated access paths. So far, our model makes it easy to access the data by Contract and by Contract Line Item, but what about other access needs? Suppose Ace Aerospace needs to know "billability" of its employees (i.e., fraction of employee time which can be charged to a contract) by salary level to help manpower planning. Then we need to add an entity for Salary Level and connect it to the Salary Level Man-Hours entity, changing Exhibit 11-8 as shown in Exhibit 11-10. This shows explicitly that we will need to access the Salary Level Man-Hours information by salary level across all contracts and months.

EXHIBIT 11-10.   Adding the Salary Level Entity to Show a Data Access Need

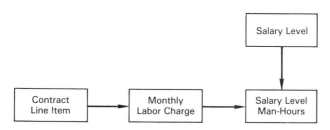

In summary, analysis of one-to-many relationships, repeating groups, many-to-many relationships, and anticipated access paths leads to many decisions which shape the concept and structure of the integrated application data base. These analyses are interrelated and iterative, but when concepts settle down the result is a data structure diagram such as Exhibit 11-11, which forms a basis for the remaining steps of data analysis.

Naming of Relationships

The arrows may be labeled with a name which helps indicate the meaning of the relationship. In real applications it is awkward to name all of the relationships

EXHIBIT 11-11.   Data Structure Diagram for the Ace Aerospace Application

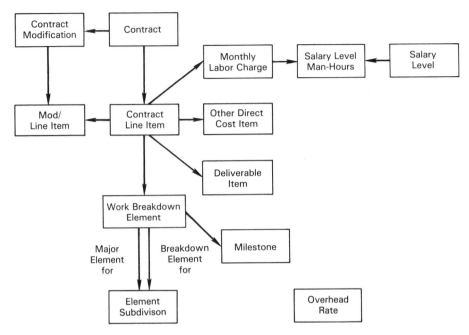

on the diagram, since the names clutter up the diagram and precise descriptions can be difficult to make concise. The following rules of thumb are helpful in deciding which relationships to name:

- Where it is clear from the context what the relationship is, do not name it.
- In particular, if A has a one-to-many relationship with B, A's key is a part of B's compound key, and the relationship holds whenever the B occurrence key includes the A occurrence key, then naming is unnecessary. (Example: Contract → Contract Line Item, where Contract has key "Contract No." and Contract Line Item has compound key "Contract No., Line Item No.")
- When it is not clear what the relationship is, give it a descriptive name.
- In particular, when there are two or more relationships between the same two data entities (such as between Work Breakdown Element and Element Subdivision in Exhibit 11-11), they should be named.

When using a software tool which helps compile requirements (Chapter 16), the relationships will be given some kind of indexing for reference. However, these indices or short names usually do not clarify the relationship meaning.

When relationships are complex, it can be useful to have a separate table which gives a (possibly lengthy) descriptive name to each relationship. This descriptive name is placed between the parent and child record types; for example,

"Contract Line Item has labor charges for one month of the contract specified by Monthly Labor Charge."

CANONICAL FORM DATA STRUCTURE DIAGRAMS

The data structure diagram in Exhibit 11-11 is difficult to understand, because the data entities are scattered randomly across the page. How can they be arranged in a manner which gives order to the data entities? In mathematics, canonical form means the simplest or most natural of many equivalent ways to indicate an expression or equation. Is there a canonical form for data structure diagrams which is natural in some sense?

Yes, there is. The general idea is to arrange the data entities from top to bottom on the page, so that the broadest business entities (used to access the data base) are on top, and increasingly more detailed entities are placed down the page. Canonical form can only be used for data structure diagrams which have split each many-to-many relationship into two one-to-many relationships, and which do not have any circular relationships (Exhibit 10-11 and Discussion Question 2 from Chapter 10).

Here is a simple way to achieve canonical form, based on the one-to-many relationship arrows:

1. Divide the paper into horizontal strips.
2. In the top strip, place all entities which have no parent (that is, no arrow leads *to* any entity in the top strip).
3. In the next strip, place all entities which have a parent but no grandparent (that is, arrows come to these entities from entities in the top strip, but not from any other entities).
4. Continue working down the page with each strip, placing all entities which have a parent from the preceding strip, but not from any entity not yet placed.
5. After all entities have been placed in horizontal strips, arrange entities across strips so that the relationship arrows are easier to draw. In particular, try to arrange a natural hierarchy as a vertical column, as shown in Exhibit 11-5 with the work breakdown structure.

Exhibit 11-12 shows the Ace Aerospace data structure in canonical form. Entities at the top, like Salary Level and Contract, are used to initiate access to the data base. They probably contribute little to the data base storage requirements. By contrast, entities at the bottom, like the Milestone and the Salary Level Man-Hours entities, have detailed data which probably contribute a large percentage of the database physical storage requirements. Entities in the middle provide con

EXHIBIT 11-12.   Ace Aerospace Data Structure Diagram in Canonical Form

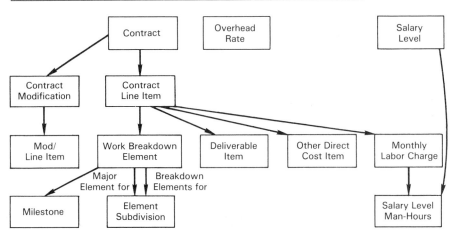

necting structure. Overhead Rate has no relationships, which is true of reference tables which do not need to be tightly integrated with other entities.

Canonical form data structure diagrams also indicate how the data base must be maintained. In order to maintain the relationships, a parent record occurrence must be input before associated child record occurrences. Conversely, the child record occurrences must be deleted before their parent. For example, the one-to-many relationship between Contract Line Item and Deliverable Item indicates that a Line Item occurrence should be input before the associated Deliverable Item occurrences. Likewise, it would be inappropriate to delete a Line Item occurrence while some of its Deliverable Item occurrences are still active in the data base.

IDENTIFYING DATA AGGREGATES
AND ENTITY INDICES

Two final additions should be made to coordinate the data structure diagram with the user concept diagrams (Chapter 6) and the data dictionary (Chapter 12). These are determination of data aggregates and indexing data entities.

Data aggregates are groups of data entities which cover a common subject area. The aggregates are a helpful device for user concept diagrams, because use of individual entities would require too many data store symbols. An easy way to show aggregates on the data structure diagram is to encircle the component data entity blocks by a dashed line and to include a title. For example, in Exhibit 11-13, the Modification Data aggregate includes Contract Modification and Mod/Line Item entities. Likewise, the Contract Structure Data aggregate includes Contract, Contract Line Item, Work Breakdown Element, Element Subdivision, Deliverable Item, and Milestone entities.

EXHIBIT 11-13.   Ace Aerospace Data Structure Diagram with Data Aggregates and Entity Indexing

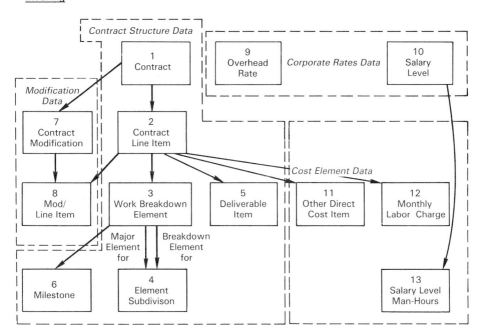

You usually make a first guess at aggregate names and data extent with the user concept diagrams. Then, when you produce a data structure diagram, you check to see if these aggregate names and content make sense. Invariably there are new insights from the data structure diagram which cause changes to data store labels in the user concept diagrams. You must take the trouble to insure consistency of aggregate labels between the two diagram types to avoid user (and analyst!) confusion.

Data entities should be numbered on the data structure diagram when you are ready to generate the data dictionary. This indexing is a handy way to reference entities in the data dictionary. For example, the indexing of entities in Exhibit 11-13 shows that Contract data items will be described first in the data dictionary, followed by Contract Line Item data items, and so on. With more complex data structures it is helpful to index by data aggregate. For example, if Modification Data is the first aggregate, 1.1 would be the index for the Contract Modification reçord and 1.2 would be the index for the Mod/Line Item record.

This indexing should occur when the basic data structure diagram has shaken out to a reasonably stable design. At this point the blocks no longer represent vague notions of data entities. They have become conceptual record types, which will be defined in detail in the data dictionary.

A word of caution: Resist the temptation to make a beautiful 11" X 17" framed print of the data structure which you hang on the office wall as a monument to successful design. New information will come up in later stages of analysis which will require changes to your data structure. Be open to these changes and make sure that you can modify your materials easily, for example by using a word processor or interactive graphics package.

COMMENTS ON THE ARROW NOTATION

Data structure diagrams were described by Charles Bachman in 1969 as a convenient way to model network data bases (1). His arrow notation, used in this book, has been criticized for three reasons: it reverses standard mathematical notation; it does not clearly indicate characteristics of the relationship in both directions; and arrows suggest a flow rather than relationships. These objections and other reasons to add symbols to the diagrams should be understood, while keeping in mind the need for understandable and simple diagrams.

The first criticism, that Bachman arrows reverse standard mathematical function notation, is illustrated in Exhibit 11-14. The "Is Composed of" relation is a one-to-many relationship between the Contract record type and the Contract Line Item record type. In mathematical terms, the "Belongs to" function (the inverse of the "Is Composed of" relation) maps the set of Contract Line Items into the set of Contracts. That is, every Contract Line Item has a unique Contract determined by the "Belongs to" function. Actually, the two notations in Exhibit 11-14 are not completely equivalent. The Bachman arrow makes an additional assertion: "Some Contracts are composed of more than one Contract Line Item." Given the data base emphasis on hierarchical breakdowns, the author believes mathematicians can be comfortable with arrows pointing the Bachman direction when they work in a data base context.

The second criticism is that the simple arrow notation does not allow the analyst to indicate whether participation of the parent or the child record occurrences

EXHIBIT 11-14. Comparison of Arrow Directions Between Bachman Diagrams and Mathematical Function Notation

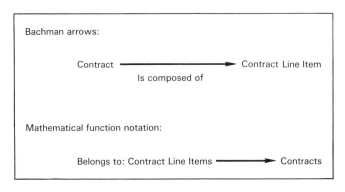

EXHIBIT 11-15. Use of Optional Indicators on Relationship Arrows

Notation	Meaning			
	1. Some Contracts have more than one related Contract Line Item.	2. All Contracts have at least one related Contract Line Item.	3. Every Contract Line Item which is related to some Contract is related to a unique Contract.	4. Every Contract Line Item is related to a unique Contract.
 Contract ⟶ Contract Line Item	Yes	Yes	Yes	Yes
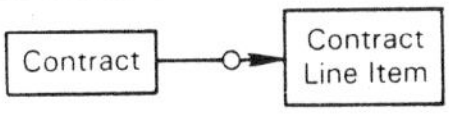 Contract ⟶○ Contract Line Item	Yes	Yes	Yes	No
 Contract ○⟶ Contract Line Item	Yes	No	Yes	Yes
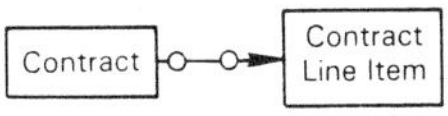 Contract ○⟶○ Contract Line Item	Yes	No	Yes	No

is optional for this relationship. For example, if a Contract may exist without any Contract Line Items, it may be useful to note that fact. Likewise, if some Monthly Labor Charge occurrences may be "orphans" without a parent Contract Line Item, then this fact should be noted in order to ensure that these orphan situations are handled properly. James Martin and Carma McClure suggest using "o" (for "optional") at either end of the relationship arrow to indicate when the corresponding record type may have occurrences not involved in the relationship (2). Exhibit 11-15 shows how this convention can be used.

The third criticism is that arrows suggest flows, rather than relationships. Martin and McClure suggest using the "crow's foot" notation shown in Exhibit 11-16, under the grounds that it is more suggestive of the one-to-many intended meaning (2). Arrows, however, are more commonly used, easier to draw, and give

EXHIBIT 11-16. Example of "Crow's Foot" Notation

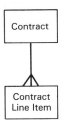

a cleaner appearance in completed data structure diagrams. When the diagrams are in canonical form, the arrows help emphasize the top-down nature of the data structure, with arrows pointing to increasing levels of data detail.

OTHER DIAGRAMMING CONVENTIONS

Data analysts have identified many special situations which can be helped with special diagramming additions to Bachman's notation. Notations described in the following paragraphs portray many-to-many relationships explicitly, show when relationships are mutually exclusive alternatives, and identify subentities. These devices should be used sparingly, because they tend to add complication to the data structure diagrams, making the diagrams difficult to review.

Conventions with Explicit
Many-To-Many Relationships

Peter Chen's work popularized use of diagrams which show data entities and the relationships among them as a tool for conceptual data modeling (3). He calls these entity-relationship diagrams. Unlike the data structure diagrams described in this chapter, Chen recommends showing many-to-many relationships explicitly. He labels each end of relationship lines to distinguish between "one" and "many." As illustrated in Exhibit 11-17A, Chen shows data entities as rectangles. One-to-many and many-to-many relationships are shown with diamonds and lines which connect the entities involved in the relationship. These lines are labeled "1," "M," or "N" to show whether they are one- to-one, one-to-many, or many-to-many relationships, and to show which end of the relationship they are pointing to.

James Martin has a somewhat different notation which also allows one-to-one, one-to-many, and many-to-many relationships (2). Exhibit 11-17B shows an example of his entity-relationship diagrams (also referred to as "James Martin data model diagrams"). Relationships are not necessarily named, use lines instead of the diamond symbol, and can have optional membership.

In both Peter Chen's and James Martin's diagrams, one-to-one relationships are allowed between entities. Normally, user-centered requirements analysis collapses two entities into one when they have a one-to-one relationship. However, there are times when users have strong reasons to think of such entities as being distinct. For example, in Exhibit 11-17 the kinds of attributes thought to be part of the Contract entity (value, period of performance, contract type, etc.) may be different from the kinds of attributes assigned to the Contract Signing entity (managers involved, date of signing, place of signing, etc.), even though there is a simple one-to-one relationship based on a common key, Contract Number.

EXHIBIT 11-17. Data Diagrams Allowing Many-to-Many and Circular Relationships

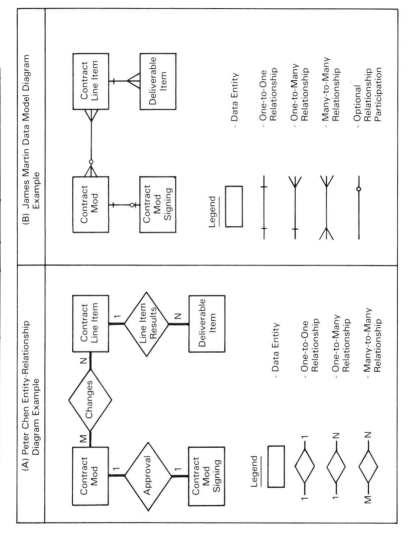

Both types of entity-relationship diagrams shown in Exhibit 11-17 are commonly available in computer-aided software engineering (CASE) environments. You may have to use one of these, because Bachman diagrams are much less commonly supported by CASE products. In that situation, you can get most of the desired effect of canonical form data structure diagrams using James Martin data model diagrams. Just restrict yourself to one-to-many relationships, use the symbol: +─< where you would otherwise use: →, and format the diagram in canonical form.

Mutually Exclusive Relationships

Another complication often added to entity-relationship or data structure diagrams is notation for mutually exclusive relationships. Two (or more) relationships from or to the same record type are mutually exclusive if exactly one of them holds for each occurrence of the common record type. Exhibit 11-18 shows an example in which Deliverable Items can be assigned at either the Contract or the Contract Line Item level, but not both. The diamond (decision) symbol used here is suggestive of the choice which must be made.

EXHIBIT 11-18.   Example of Mutually Exclusive Relationships

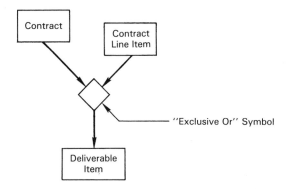

Subentities

The concept of subentity (or record subtype) refers to groups of entity occurrences which require unique attributes. For example, Ace Aerospace Contracts may have two major subentities: Government Contracts and Commercial Contracts. Because Government Contracts are handled somewhat differently from commercial ones, each type will have some distinct attributes. As shown at the bottom of Exhibit 11-19, many attributes are common to both types of Contracts. Government Contracts will have special terms like PCO and COTR based on peculiarities of the government contracting process. Other attributes describing client representatives and contract type pertain to Commercial Contracts.

EXHIBIT 11-19. Examples of Subentity Notations

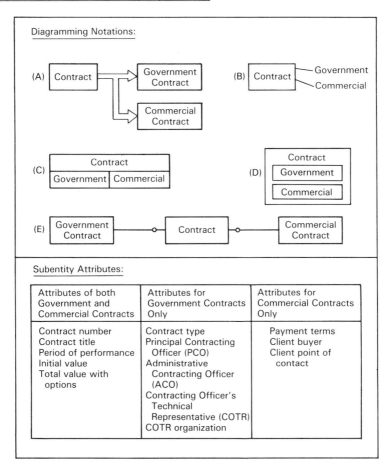

Subentities can be shown on diagrams by devices such as shown on the top of Exhibit 11-19. The first notation (A) is Inmon's (4). The second notation (B) is a simplified form which also lists subentities to the right. Notation (C) comes from Martin and McClure (2). Its horizontal spread of subentity labels takes too much space when there are more than two, so these labels could better be arranged vertically, as shown in (D). The notation of one-to-one relationship with optional participation (Exhibit 11-17B) could be used as shown in (E). The author leans toward notation (B), implemented as annotation on normal data structure diagrams.

RELATIONAL DATA STRUCTURE DIAGRAMS

Because the relational data model supports data base navigation through joins, it is natural to try to diagram a conceptual data model with a notation which explicitly shows join possibilities. Exhibit 11-20 shows how the Contract Structure data aggregate from Exhibit 11-13 would look in such a diagram. Each conceptual record type is shown as a bar with divisions for data items (columns of relational tables) which may be used for joins. Lines connect joinable items from different record types. In cases where joins typically occur for multiple item combinations, they are shown by splitting the ends of the join line to point at each of the items.

EXHIBIT 11-20.   Sample Relational Data Structure Diagram
for the Contract Structure Data Aggregate

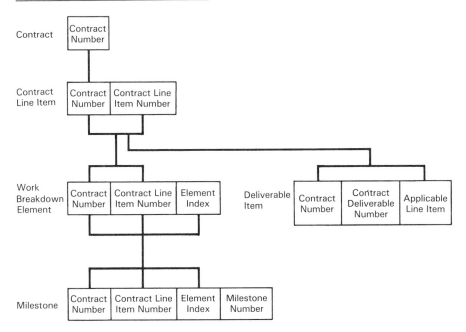

These diagrams tend to be less helpful for conceptual data models than the data structure diagrams based on one-to-many relationships (Exhibit 11-13). Relational diagrams get very cluttered in a hurry, particularly if *all* joinable combinations are shown. They do not lead to a canonical form which shows a progression from indexing record types to most detailed data records. Nor do they support the decisions concerning level of detail of data entities as clearly as one-to-many relationship modeling does.

The relational data structure diagrams (Exhibit 11-20) are most useful in situations where the record types must be existing data files, and the only integration which can be achieved consists of join possibilities among these files. In the development phase, they can also be a useful tool for data base programmers who want to keep handy diagrams of join possibilities.

SUMMARY OF TOP-DOWN DATA ANALYSIS

While developing user concept diagrams for an application, the requirements analysts should develop a data structure diagram. This is done by identifying the data entities involved in system functions, their major attributes, and their one-to-many interrelationships. The conceptual data model for an application can usually be documented in a single data structure diagram consisting of boxes and arrows and arranged in a canonical form which works down from the most basic data base access entities toward the more detailed data content entities. Many different notations can be added to these diagrams, but the more the analyst sticks to the two basic symbols (the box and the arrow), the easier the diagram will be for users to review. Sometimes the analyst must work with existing files which restrict the degree of integration which may be achieved. In this case it can be useful to work with relational data structure diagrams which show join possibilities for pairs of record types.

Following creation of the data structure diagram, data entities will evolve into conceptual record types. These are defined in a data dictionary, as described in Chapter 12.

DISCUSSION QUESTIONS

1. Convert the following Data Structure Diagram to canonical form:

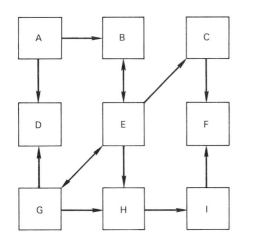

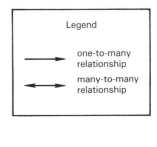

2. One of the subtle conceptual data modeling questions is "When should two data concepts be modeled as separate data entities, and when should they be modeled as subentities of the same entity?"

   a. Which approach is likely to be preferable in the following situations?

- Government Contracts and Commercial Contracts in the Ace Aerospace example (Exhibit 11-19)
- Savings Accounts and Checking Accounts in a data base supporting a bank's operations
- Airports and seaports in a logistics data base used to schedule transportation of people and freight.

b. What problems can arise if the wrong choice is made between subentities and multiple entities?

3. Old Faithful College relies on fund-raising activities for 15 percent of its budget. You have just taken over the job of Fund-Raising Director and are horrified to find that your staff has sloppy records which make it difficult to determine proper mailing lists or understand which fund-raising campaigns were successful. As you settle in at your new desk, you get a phone call from a donor who is upset at lack of acknowledgment of a $20,000 gift to Old Faithful. You determine that an automated data base is your number one priority to get the fund-raising records in order. In reflecting on the needs of the data base, you decide that the following are required:

- Prospective donor lists should distinguish between foundations, alumni, and other individuals.
- Prospective donor lists should include information concerning whether the prospect has given large, moderate, small, or no donations in the past.
- Contributions must all be noted in the data base, as well as the date an acknowledgment was sent.
- The data base must show who failed to respond to initial mailings, so they can be sent follow-up mailings.
- The costs for each fund-raising campaign should be stored, including staff manpower, campaign special help, and other expenses.
- Overhead costs of running the office, including staff salaries and office expenses, should be kept by month.

Using top-down data analysis, interpret these needs as a canonical form data structure diagram. In particular:

a. Identify and define the data entities required.
b. Identify keys and attributes of each data entity.
c. Identify one-to-many relationships among attributes, sketching out a preliminary data structure diagram.
d. Complete the data structure diagram by putting it in canonical form and identifying useful data aggregates.
e. Recheck to see if this data model supports the informal requirements previously mentioned.

REFERENCES

1. Charles W. Bachman, "Data Structure Diagrams," *Data Base*, vol. 1, no. 2, 1969.

2. James Martin and Carma McClure, *Diagramming Techniques for Analysts and Programmers*, Englewood Cliffs, N.J.: Prentice-Hall, 1985.

3. Peter Chen, *The Entity-Relationship Approach to Logical Data Base Design*, Q.E.D. Monograph Series on Data Base Management, no. 6, Wellesley, MA: Q.E.D. Information Sciences, Inc., 1977.

4. William Inmon, *Information Systems Architecture*, Englewood Cliffs, N.J.: Prentice-Hall, 1986.

12

Data Dictionary

This chapter describes how detailed data characteristics may be compiled in concise tabular formats. This work requires careful attention to detail and completeness but does not need much textual writing.

DATA DICTIONARY OBJECTIVES

The data dictionary gives data model details beyond the data structure diagram, just as the verifiable functional requirements give detailed information beyond the user concept diagrams. The data dictionary gives the following kinds of information about conceptual data base records:

- Record description
- List of all record items with:
    - Identification of key items
    - Grouping of items
    - Descriptive item name and example
    - Item indexing for referencing
    - Item input integrity checks
    - Other item characteristics.

Exhibits 12-1 through 12-3 show minimal data dictionary entries for two conceptual record types, Contract and Milestone, in the Ace Aerospace example. These
exhibits illustrate the points made in the rest of this chapter.

EXHIBIT 12-1.   Contract Record Data Dictionary Entry

Record: 1 Contract

Description: Items describing an overall contract in which a
government or commercial organization pays Ace Aerospace
for products and/or services.

Comments: The Contract Number is assigned by the client
contracting officer for government contracts, or by Ace
Aerospace accounting for commercial contracts.

Item	Input Format		Allowable Values/ Units	Example
	Max length	Type		
Key Item 1.1 Contract Number	20	C		F19628-83-C-0166
Other Items				
Items Applicable To All Contracts				
1.2 Contract Name	25	A		QX LASER POINTING
1.3 Client Type	1	A	G = Government C = Commercial	G
1.4 Contract Start	6	N	MMDDYY	120585
1.5 Contract End	6	N	MMDDYY	120486
1.6 Ace Aerospace Project Manager	25	A		STEVE NICKERSON
1.7 Total Funded Value to Date	10	S	NN,NNN,NNN dollars	1,575,000
1.8 Value of Other Contract Options	10	S	NN,NNN,NNN dollars	2,300,850
Items Applicable To Government Contracts				
1.9 Contract Type	6	A	[see Exhibit 12-3]	FFP
1.10 Principal Contracting Officer	25	A		RALPH JOHNSON
1.11 Administrative Contracting Officer	25	A		WALTER MILES
1.12 Contracting Officer's Technical Representative (COTR)	25	A		SUSAN MOORE
1.13 COTR Organization	15	C		SD/XR3
1.14 Fee	10	S	N,NNN,NNN dollars	141,000
Items Applicable To Commercial Contracts				
1.15 Payment Terms	8	A	[see Table B]	NET 30
1.16 Client Buyer	25	A		ETHAN GRIMES
1.17 Client Point of Contact	25	A		ALICE WARREN

EXHIBIT 12-2.   Milestone Record Data Dictionary Entry

Record: 6. Milestone				
Description: Information about the nature and timing of a contract deliverable or decision meeting.				
Comments: Milestones are defined for Work Breakdown Elements.				
Item	Input Format		Allowable Values/ Units	Example
	Max length	Type		
Key Items				
1.1 Contract Number	20	C		F19628-83-C-0166
3.1 Work Breakdown Element Number	15	C	digits separated by decimal points	5.3.2.4
6.1 Milestone Number	2	N	0 < Item 6.1 < 16	4
Other Items				
6.2 Milestone Name	15	C		LASER TEST 3B
6.3 Activity Start Day	6	N	MMDDYY	031586
6.4 Milestone Day	6	N		042186
6.5 Task Leader	25	A	MMDDYY	RAHMID JOSHI

RECORD DESCRIPTION

The record description should be a short explanation of the objects or concepts which are described by items in this conceptual record type. The record description and record key help make decisions about whether an item belongs with the record type or somewhere else in the data base.

It is often helpful to provide comments which assist reader understanding of special aspects of record usage. The comments should also be kept short and to the point.

The record description and comments are an evolutionary result of tentative data entity descriptions created at the start of data analysis (Exhibit 11-1). When creating the data dictionary, the analyst should review the tentative data entity de-

EXHIBIT 12-3.   Allowable Values For Contract Type (Item 1.9)

Contract Type Code	Meaning
CPFF	Cost Plus Fixed Fee
CPIF	Cost Plus Incentive Fee
FFP	Firm Fixed Price
FFPLOE	Firm Fixed Price Level of Effort
FPAF	Fixed Price Award Fee
FPC	Fixed Price Cost Accrual
FPIF	Fixed Price Incentive Fee
TM	Time and Materials

scription against both the data structure diagram and user concept diagrams to see if tentative data entity descriptions are still applicable.

IDENTIFICATION OF KEY ITEMS

A record key is an item or combination of data items used to identify record occurrences. Tentative key attributes were identified early in the data analysis (Exhibit 11-2). Now as more rigor is applied to defining the data items, some changes are likely to be required in key items. As shown in Exhibits 12-1 and 12-2, key items should be listed first in the data dictionary tables. Compound keys are easily handled with multiple rows under the "Key Items" heading, as shown in Exhibit 12-2.

GROUPING OF ITEMS

It is often useful to group items within a record type. One reason is to show record subtypes, discussed previously with Exhibit 11-19. Exhibit 12-1 shows how the items belonging to Government Contracts, Commercial Contracts, and both are distinguished by physical grouping with a caption. Another reason items often need to be grouped is to aid the reader when a record type has a large number of items. For example, a large Personnel record type might have 22 nonkey items. As an unbroken list, it becomes very hard for a reviewer to look over the list, learn it, and decide whether it makes sense. Putting the list in alphabetical order (as in Exhibit 12-4A) makes the problem even worse, because then it is completely random whether any item is related to the preceding one. If, however, the 22 elements are grouped in categories such as "Identifiers," "Business Position," and "Accounting Information," then it is much easier to examine the items in each group. Exhibit 12-4B illustrates such a grouping.

DATA ITEM SPECIFICATIONS

Each data item must be described in the data dictionary so that its meaning and validity conditions are clear to the developer. We now examine how the data dictionary tables as illustrated in Exhibits 12-1 to 12-3 provide the necessary descriptions.

Descriptive Item Name and Example

The example data dictionary tables briefly identify each item with a descriptive name and an example. This is a streamlined approach which is significantly quicker than detailed textual item definitions. The streamlined approach works well for small and medium-sized projects (less than 50 man-years).

EXHIBIT 12-4. Example Groupings of Personnel Record Items

(A) ALPHABETICAL ITEM ORDER	(B) ITEMS GROUPED BY TOPIC

(A) ALPHABETICAL ITEM ORDER

Key Item

Social Security Number

Other Items

Bank
Bank Account Number
Bank Funds Transfer Code
Basic Salary
Business Location
Business Phone
Date Started with Firm
Date Started Current Position
Department
Home Phone
Long-term Disability Insurance
   Coverage
Medical Insurance Coverage
Name
Number of Withholding Exemptions
Position Title
Primary Expertise
Secondary Expertise
State
Street Address
Term Life Insurance Coverage
Town
Zip Code

(B) ITEMS GROUPED BY TOPIC

Key Item

Social Security Number

Other Items

Identifiers

Name
Street Address
Town
State
Zip Code
Home Phone

Business Position

Position Title
Date Started with Firm
Date Started Current Position
Primary Expertise
Secondary Expertise
Department
Business Location
Business Phone

Accounting Information

Basic Salary
Medical Insurance Coverage
Long-term Disability Insurance
   Coverage
Term Life Insurance Coverage
Number of Withholding Exemptions
Bank
Bank Account Number
Bank Funds Transfer Code

Descriptive names should be long enough (say, 40 characters allowed) to convey understanding of the item's meaning. For example, the name of item 1.8, "Value of Other Contract Options," is 31 characters and difficult to shorten without obscuring the meaning. Standard acronyms can be used, like "COTR Organization" for item 1.13, when the acronym is familiar to users. Other abbreviations should be avoided when possible. For example, "Contract Start" is a much clearer name for item 1.4 than "CStart." Spaces should be allowed and encouraged. Adding hyphens or underlines as in "Value_of_Other_Contract_Options" adds a psychological hurdle for users to overcome when reviewing the data dictionary.

The example column gives one or more sample occurrences of the data item. These samples should be chosen to illustrate usage of the item and should be realistic. When an analyst has difficulty coming up with a realistic example, it is an indication that more discussion with users is required to make sure the item and its entire data dictionary entry are appropriate.

For larger applications which must coordinate the requirements of many groups and individuals, more detailed item definitions may be useful. These are phrases like the definitions in a standard English dictionary. For example, "Value of Other Contract Options" could be defined as "Dollar value of all products and services which have been priced for the client in this contract, but have not been funded." Durell's book has some good ideas concerning item definitions and other data administration concepts which are useful at the conceptual data base design level as well as in administering operational data bases (1). Item definitions can help, but they are difficult to write. Their addition to the data dictionary adds a noticeable cost to the system definition effort.

Item Indexing for Referencing

Each item in the data dictionary tables starts with a unique item identifier consisting of the record index and item index within the record. If the item has been listed previously with another record type, it keeps the same name and index, as shown in the first two key items in Exhibit 12-2. This device helps show relational join opportunities, and can act as a substitute for the relational data structure diagrams discussed with Exhibit 11-21.

Items often have a natural decomposition structure. For example, Home Address may be composed of Number, Street, Apartment No., City, State, and Zip. Such a decomposition can be shown in the data dictionary with an indentation approach as shown in Exhibit 12-5.

EXHIBIT 12-5. Example Data Dictionary Representation of an Item Decomposition

Item	Input Format		Allowable Values/ Units	Example
	Max length	Type		
4.5 Home Address				
4.5.1 Number	10	C		121A
4.5.2 Street	15	A		ALGONQUIN ROAD
4.5.3 Apartment No.	10	C		3-32B
4.5.4 City	15	A		BOSTON
4.5.5 State Abbrev.	2	A		MA
4.5.6 Zip Code				
4.5.6.1 Standard Zip	5	N		03135
4.5.6.2 + 4 Digits	4	N		1753

Item Input Integrity Checks

The input and allowable values columns of the data item table give information about how the item will appear on input to the automated application. They do not specify internal storage formats. The information about input appearance provides constraints on input processing and indicates the simple validity checks which must be performed.

The type column tells what kind of input character string will be allowed for each item. Code letters used for the examples are defined as follows:

A = All *alphabetic* upper case letters and blanks
C = Any keyboard *character* string allowed
F = *Floating* point number (number with a decimal point, like 59.735)
N = Nonnegative integer *number*
S = *Special* character string, defined in the allowable values column.

Total Funded Value to Date (item 1.7 in Exhibit 12-1) is an example of a special character string. It is basically an integer dollar amount, but commas are used to separate each set of three digits for easier readability on input.

The max length column of a data dictionary table shows the maximum number of characters which can be input for each item. Users will have to truncate or abbreviate longer names; the developer will have to allow this much space for the items on data input screen displays.

The allowable values column indicates one or more of the following:

- Discrete set of possible values for this item
- Range of possible values for this item
- Input character string format.

Items 1.3, 1.9 and 1.15 in Exhibit 12-1 are examples of items having a discrete set of values. If there are only a few possible values (as with item 1.3), they may be shown in the allowable values column. Otherwise, lengthy sets of discrete values should be given in a separate table. The Contract Type (item 1.9) is an example of an item with a large set of discrete values. The allowable column directs the reader in this case to Exhibit 12-3.

Item 6.1 (Exhibit 12-2) is an example of an item with a range of allowable values. Although the type and max length columns indicate it can be a two-digit positive integer, we see from the allowable values column that it is restricted to integers between 1 and 15.

A number of items show special input formats for dates or dollar figures. In the case of item 1.4, dates are input in a "MMDDYY" format. That is, dates are six-digit integer numbers in which the first two digits give the month, the third and fourth digits give the day of the month, and the last two digits give the last two digits of the year. As already mentioned, the picture for item 1.14 shows that commas are expected for input dollar figures. A notation for monetary figures in dollars and cents up to $999,999.99 could be NNN,NNN.NN.

The application developer must account for these validity conditions when designing and implementing data input processes. The input processes must give positive protection against introducing occurrences of data items which have improper type, greater than the maximum length, or violate the allowable values conditions. Conversely, the developer must ensure that his software will accommodate all inputs which satisfy the integrity conditions in the data dictionary.

Thus, if a name is allowed 25 characters according to the data item table, then a data entry screen display must allow a sufficiently large input field for the user to enter 25 letters. The requirements specification must clearly state that the data dictionary integrity checks are a requirement on the developer. The proper way to do this is with a blanket statement about integrity checking in verifiable functional requirements at the highest level of breakout of the data input processes. This statement refers to the data dictionary for the details of these checks.

Other data input integrity checks will be based on complex conditions, such as dependencies among various input items or between input items and pre-existing data base information. These checks have an algorithmic flavor and should not be forced into the data dictionary. Instead, the specific conditions should be stated explicitly in the verifiable functional requirements. Fortunately, most required integrity checks tend to be the simple conditions which can be listed in the data item tables, thus avoiding cluttering up the textual requirements with excess verbiage.

Other Item Characteristics

The material shown in the data dictionary tables in Exhibits 12-1 and 12-2 should be considered a *minimal* set of characteristics suitable for rapid development of requirements for small-to-medium-sized applications (say, up to ten man-years of effort to develop). Larger systems, particularly those with many users and which replace multiple existing systems, often require more data item characteristics. The draft Information Resource Dictionary Standard recommends that the 15 characteristics of data items shown in Exhibit 12-6 should be maintained in data dictionaries for complex information systems (2). These may be supplemented by additional application-peculiar data item characteristics. Several large Department of Defense systems have maintained data dictionaries with 30 to 50 item characteristics.

Keeping data dictionary tables in a word-processing format becomes unwieldy when there are too many item characteristics to be listed as columns on a printed page. In such cases the data dictionary itself should be kept as an automated data base, allowing printouts or queries of selected characteristics.

DATA DICTIONARY SUMMARY

Chapter 11 demonstrated the intellectual challenge of analyzing the structure of the application data base. This intellectual puzzle solving is replaced in the next step with a methodical enumeration of data items and their main characteristics. Although this is a somewhat tedious exercise, the resulting data dictionary is tremendously useful to the developers. Moreover, the information needed can usually be obtained from the same user representatives being interviewed for the verifiable functional requirements.

The data dictionary effort can be eased by identifying data items with descriptive names and examples (rather than a formal definition), and by minimizing

EXHIBIT 12-6.   Data Item Characteristics Recommended in the Draft Information Resource
Dictionary System Standard

Item Characteristic	Meaning
Identification	
ACCESS-NAME	Abbreviated name of the data item
DESCRIPTIVE-NAME	Longer, descriptive name for the data item
ALTERNATIVE-NAME	Another name (alias) for this item, used by another system or in a different business area. A data item may have several aliases.
DESCRIPTION	Definition of the meaning of this data item
CLASSIFICATION	Item grouping
COMMENTS	Example and/or comments on item usage
Integrity Checking	
REPRESENTED-AS	Type of item (e.g., integer, character string)
ALLOWABLE-VALUE	One of a discrete set of values which may be taken by this item
LOW-OF-RANGE	Lower bound for a range of values which may be taken by this item
HIGH-OF-RANGE	Upper bound for a range of values which may be taken by this item
SECURITY	Security classification or access control information for this data item
Item Requirement Change Tracking	
ADDED-BY	Person or organization adding the requirement for this data item
NUMBER-OF-MODIFICATIONS	Number of times the data dictionary entry for this item has changed
LAST-MODIFIED-BY	Individual who last changed the data dictionary entry for this data item
LAST-MODIFICATION-DATE	Most recent date the data dictionary entry for this item was changed

the number of item characteristics in the dictionary. The analysts must be thorough in filling out examples for each item, and even that can be time consuming for some items. Descriptive item definitions are beneficial for large applications with difficult terminology, but they are expensive to generate. Moreover, large system developments usually need more item characteristics than can fit across a printed table. This situation forces a great deal more data gathering and the overhead of an automated data base for the data dictionary.

An organization may find it useful to keep two data dictionaries. One documents the conceptual data model to support development. The other documents operational data bases and supports application operations and maintenance.

DISCUSSION QUESTIONS

1. Compose formal item definitions for items 1.1-1.8 and 1.15-1.17 in Exhibit 12-1. Then answer the following:
   a. Which item definitions help clarify the meaning of the item?
   b. How should user representatives and analysts interact to determine item definitions?

2. The closing comment in Chapter 12 about data dictionaries mentions that organizations sometimes develop two dictionaries: one for conceptual data models, the other for DBMS schema-level support. The American National Standards Institute Standards and Practices Review Committee (ANSI/X3/SPARC) recommended that *three* separate data models be kept by an organization desiring to achieve full integration of data bases (3). In ANSI/SPARC terminology, these are:

   - Conceptual: logical structure and content of the entire enterprise's data
   - External: structure and content of the data used by particular applications or subsystems
   - Internal: schema-level definition of the data base with physical storage specifications.

   Each kind of data model is isolated from changes in the other two by transformation rules, just as programs are isolated from data models by the schema processing as shown in Exhibit 10-4. Three different organizational functions maintain the three different kinds of data models. Enterprise Administration, Application System Administration, and Data Base Administration maintain the conceptual, external, and internal models, respectively. Cincom Systems has the first available vendor support of ANSI/SPARC with its recently introduced ULTRA DBMS product for large IBM mainframes.
   a. Why would an organization want to add the complexity of a third data model in its data administration?
   b. The ANSI/SPARC proposal has been discussed for over ten years but is only recently getting implementation attention. What is making acceptance so slow?
   c. How does use of the three ANSI/SPARC data models affect the process of compiling data requirements for a new application?

REFERENCES

1. William R. Durell, *Data Administration*, New York: McGraw-Hill, 1985.

2. Daniel R. Dolk and Robert A. Kirsch II, "A Relational Information Resource Dictionary System," *Communications of the ACM*, vol. 30, no. 1, Association for Computing Machinery, January 1987.

3. Dennis Tsichritzis and Anthony Klug, eds., *The ANSI/X3/SPARC DBMS Framework Report of the Study Group on Database Management Systems, AFIPS*, 1977 .

13

Detailed Data Analysis

This chapter describes several techniques for performing detailed checks of the conceptual data model. For many applications the data structure diagram and data dictionary developed as described in Chapters 11 and 12 will be fully sufficient for defining the data model in the requirements specifications. However, for large applications costing millions of dollars, further checking up front is well worthwhile in order to catch mistakes which would be costly to find later.

This chapter discusses four main subjects:

- Record type normalization
- Bottom-up data analysis
- Analysis of data flows
- User views.

Record normalization yields well-formed conceptual record types which are stable and have desirable data maintenance characteristics. Bottom-up analysis determines relationships among data items and then combines related items into normalized record types. Analyses of data flows and user views check the overall data structure against particular uses of the data. These various types of data analyses may not be employed together for the same application but are worth knowing about, so that you can tailor your data analysis strategy to particular applications' needs.

RECORD TYPE NORMALIZATION

The first detailed data analysis subject is record normalization. This is the process of determining whether record types are well formed. Previously the text defined the record key as a set of data items which uniquely identifies record occurrences. Normalization takes a deeper look at the structure of well-formed conceptual record types and the importance of the record key. These concepts originated with theorists examining the relational data model, but normal form applies equally well to applications aimed at hierarchical or network implementation.

Normal form analysis uses the concept of functional dependence between record items. Item B *functionally depends* on the set S of items in record type R if every occurrence of items in S has a unique associated occurrence of item B in record R occurrences. This is quite a mouthful for a straightforward idea. Consider the example where R is a Course Section record consisting of these items pertaining to college courses: Course Number, Course Title, Section Number, and Instructor. Exhibit 13-1 shows some example occurrences.

It would be reasonable to infer that:

- Course Title functionally depends on Course Number. That is, every Course Number has a unique Course Title associated with it.
- Instructor functionally depends on the combination of Course Number and Section Number.

It probably turns out that no two courses have the same title. If so, then it is also true that

- Course Number functionally depends on Course Title.

Note that Instructor does not functionally depend on Course Number alone, since more than one instructor may teach the same course.

Functional dependence cannot be proved from a data table, only disproved. Like the one-to-many relationships among record types, it is a result of people's decisions concerning how their business should be modeled by data.

EXHIBIT 13-1.   Course Section Record Occurrences

Course Number	Course Title	Section Number	Instructor
History 23	Survey of U.S. History	1	Prof. M. Hodges
History 23	Survey of U.S. History	2	Asst. Prof. W. Gold
History 50	Modern European History	1	Inst. R. Lance
History 50	Modern European History	2	Asst. Prof. M. Pace
History 50	Modern European History	3	Asst. Prof. W. Gold
History 69	Origins of Middle East Conflicts	1	Prof. A. Nadine

Third Normal Form

Given the definition of functional dependency, it is possible to define third normal form record types, first described by Codd (1). Informally, a record type R is in third normal form if every nonkey item functionally depends on the record key, the whole key, and nothing but the key. To get a more formal definition, we need to step through definitions for first, second, and third normal forms. Motivation for these definitions will be provided by the Grades Sheet example from Exhibit 13-2.

The first step is to identify data items and place them in candidate record types. Exhibit 13-3A shows the items from the Grades Sheet example, all lumped into a single record type. This initial record type is an awkward mixture of items which will gradually be improved by breaking it up into several record types which have an improved structure.

From Exhibit 13-2, we see that the information for each student forms a repeating group with many occurrences for the single occurrence of items above "Student Grades" on the report. Making a single record type as in Exhibit 13-3A would require considerable duplication of the upper items (see Exhibit 13-4). This duplication results in two problems more important than the obvious problem of inefficient data storage.

The first problem occurs during input or change of a student grade. There has to be a careful check to ensure that the Course Title, Meeting Time, Meeting Place, Instructor, and Instructor Phone Ext item occurrences were all the same as for previously input record occurrences of grades for students in the same course and section. Likewise, if one of those attributes were to change for a course and section, it would need to be changed in many record occurrences.

EXHIBIT 13-2. Grades Sheet Example for Data Normalization

```
┌──────────────────────────────────────────────────────────────┐
│                  Fall Semester 1987 Final Grades List          │
│                                                                │
│   Course: History 103A, Medieval Europe                        │
│           Section 3, TuTh 1-3, Maxwell 207                     │
│                                                                │
│   Instructor: Robert McFarlane   X 3486                        │
│                                                                │
│                          Student Grades                        │
│                                                                │
│       Student              SSN           Level       Grade     │
│                                                                │
│   Adams, Jennifer B.    097-646-3975     Senior       B +      │
│   Brewster, John H.     768-232-6750     Junior       A −      │
│   Bronson, Alan R.      872-192-3478     Junior       B −      │
│   Chu, Won              886-623-4342     Senior       C        │
│                                                                │
└──────────────────────────────────────────────────────────────┘
```

<u>EXHIBIT 13-3.   Normalization for the Grades Sheet Example</u>

(A) Extract items.

Course Number	Course Title	Section Number	Meeting Time	Meeting Place	Instructor	Instructor Phone Ext

Student Name	Social Sec No	Level	Grade

(B) Remove repeating groups to obtain first normal form.

Course Number	Section Number	Course Title	Meeting Time	Meeting Place	Instructor	Instructor Phone Ext

Course Number	Section Number	Student Name	Social Sec No	Level	Grade

(C) For records with compound keys, separate groups of items which depend on only part of the key to obtain second normal form.

Course Number	Course Title

Course Number	Section Number	Meeting Time	Meeting Place	Instructor	Instructor Phone Ext

Course Number	Section Number	Student Name	Grade

Student Name	Social Sec No	Level

(D) Remove items dependent on nonkey items to obtain third normal form.

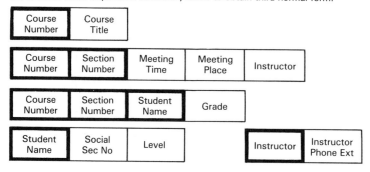

Course Number	Course Title

Course Number	Section Number	Meeting Time	Meeting Place	Instructor

Course Number	Section Number	Student Name	Grade

Student Name	Social Sec No	Level

Instructor	Instructor Phone Ext

EXHIBIT 13-4. Representing the Grades Sheet Example as a Single Record Type

Course No.	Course Title	Sec. No.	Meeting Time	Meeting Place	Instructor	Inst. Phone
Student		SSN	Level	Grade		

History 103A Medieval Europe	3	TuTh 1-3	Maxwell 207	Robert McFarlane	X 3486	
Adams, Jennifer B.	097-646-3975	Senior	B +			
History 103A Medieval Europe	3	TuTh 1-3	Maxwell 207	Robert McFarlane	X 3486	
Brewster, John H.	768-232-6750	Junior	A −			
History 103A Medieval Europe	3	TuTh 1-3	Maxwell 207	Robert McFarlane	X 3486	
Bronson, Alan R.	872-192-3478	Junior	B −			
History 103A Medieval Europe	3	TuTh 1-3	Maxwell 207	Robert McFarlane	X 3486	
Chu, Won	886-623-4342	Senior	C			

The second problem occurs when no grades have yet been received for a course and section, or if the only grade remaining is deleted. In that case, there would be no information concerning title, meeting time and place, and instructor for the course and section.

First normal form record types have no repeating groups of items. They are obtained by removing repeating groups of items to separate record types. In the example, the group of items consisting of Student Name, Social Security Number, Level, and Grade "repeats" with different values for each student while the course section information stays the same. This repeating group must be made into a separate record after adding Course Number and Section to complete the record key. Exhibit 13-3B shows the results of this step. Key items are distinguished with thicker box lines.

Some items in the two records in Exhibit 13-3B functionally depend on only part of the compound keys. Course Title functionally depends only on Course Number in the first record type. Social Security Number and Level functionally depend only on Student Name in the second record type. In essence, the rest of these record types act like repeating groups with respect to these items, and hence this form has all the problems mentioned previously in the motivation of first normal form.

Second normal form record types are in first normal form and have the property that every nonkey item functionally depends on the entire record key. As shown in Exhibit 13-3C, second normal form record types are derived from first normal form records by removing nonkey items which depend on only part of the record key, along with the part of the key they depend on. Thus, Social Security Number and Level form a new record type with their key, Student Name. Also, Course Title forms a new record type with Course Number.

Instructor Phone Ext is an item which has awkward implications in the second record type in Exhibit 13-3C. True, it functionally depends on the compound key of Course Number and Section Number. This is because Instructor Phone Ext functionally depends on Instructor and Instructor depends on Course Number and Section Number. (If item C is functionally dependent on item B and B is dependent on A, then C must be dependent on A. This is often called a transitive dependency.) Awkwardness arises on input because whenever a new occurrence of this record type is added, the Instructor Phone Ext must be checked against all other occurrences for the same Instructor, to ensure consistency. Moreover, if there is no occurrence of the record type which has Prof. Brown (say she is taking a sabbatical to do research, but is still working in her office), there will be no way to record her extension.

Third normal form record types are in second normal form and have the additional property that nonkey items functionally depend *only* on key items. Third normal form records are derived from second normal form records by removing the transitive dependencies. In the example, the Instructor Phone Ext item is extracted with its nonkey dependency, Instructor, to form a separate record type (see Exhibit 13-3D).

Extensions of Third Normal Form

Record normalization has been the subject of extensive academic investigation by data base theorists. Chapter 17 of Date's book gives an excellent discussion of the objectives of normalization and some of the extensions of third normal form (2). Fagin and Vardi give a survey of the various concepts constructed around data dependencies (3).

Extensions of third normal form came from problems observed in special cases. The most common is the case of "candidate keys." Consider the first example of Exhibit 13-5. Course Number and Course Name are functionally equivalent, because they each functionally depend on the other. Hence, both are candidates to be used as the record key. The record is not in third normal form, because Course Description functionally depends on both candidate keys. Hence, there will be a transitive dependency. A nonkey item, Course Description, functionally depends on another nonkey item, thus violating the conditions of third normal form. Yet there appears to be no advantage to split into two record types, (Course Number, Course Name) and (Course Name, Course Description). Both records would describe the same entity, the Course. Likewise, the second example in

EXHIBIT 13-5. Examples of Alternate Keys

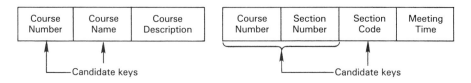

Exhibit 13-5 assumes the school has a Section Code which is functionally equivalent to the compound key of Course Number and Section Number. Again, it would not be useful to split out (Section Code, Meeting Time) as a separate record type, although third normal form demands a breakout.

This discussion motivates a new normal form definition. A record type is in Boyce-Codd normal form if every nonkey item is functionally dependent on candidate keys only. In practice, Boyce-Codd and third normal forms are very similar, with Boyce-Codd leading to a more natural result in the candidate keys situation.

Dependency Diagrams

When normalizing record types, it often helps to diagram the functional dependencies. Typically an arrow is used, so that A→B indicates that B functionally depends on A. Exhibit 13-6 shows examples. Exhibit 13-6A corresponds to the first record type in Exhibit 13-3B. If every nonkey item has one and only one arrow, and that arrow comes to it from the key, then the record is in third normal

EXHIBIT 13-6. Example Item Dependency Diagrams

(A) Unnormalized Data Entity

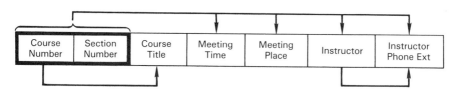

(B) Normalized Data Entity

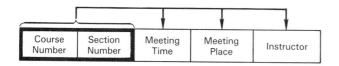

(C) Boyce-Codd Normalized Entity with Two Candidate Keys

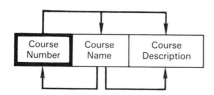

form (see Exhibit 13-6B). The two arrows underneath the record shown in Exhibit 13-6A violate these conditions, and hence that record is not in third normal form. The example shown in Exhibit 13-6C also violates third normal form, since Course Name has two arrows pointing to the other two items. But it does satisfy Boyce-Codd normal form, since these two arrows indicate that Course Name is functionally equivalent to Course Number.

Usage of Normal Forms

Third normal form and extensions have been widely recommended as good standard practices for definition of conceptual record types. Schema-level physical record specifications will often have good reasons to differ from third normal form, in order to tune the performance of key processes. However, most existing information systems have large record types which differ from third normal form for historical reasons and not for performance. Usually the record type corresponds to a lengthy paper form used for input. The arguments for using normalized relations to ease data base maintenance and data base administration are very persuasive. In addition, normalized record types tend to be the easiest for people to grasp, since each record type corresponds to a unique entity. For example, the five third normal form record types in Exhibit 13-3D correspond to these entities: Course, Course Section, Course Section/Student, Student, and Instructor.

BOTTOM-UP DATA ANALYSIS

The second detailed data analysis subject is bottom-up data analysis. This type of analysis makes direct use of the kind of normalization process illustrated with Exhibit 13-3. The analysts first compile a list of all data items needed by the application. Then they determine functional dependencies among these elements. Using a manual or automated record normalization process, such as the third normal form process, the analysts group these items into record types with candidate keys. The analysts or users choose which candidate keys should be considered the primary keys in Boyce-Codd normal form records. The result is a set of normalized record types. Once these are determined, the analysts identify the one-to-many relationships among record types.

Notice that bottom-up analysis differs dramatically from the top-down data analysis described in Chapters 11 and 12. As summarized in Exhibit 13-7, bottom-up analysis starts with detailed listings of data items and their characteristics, while top-down analysis ends with this item-level detail. Both approaches have been used successfully. The two may be used together as a cross-check. For example, bottom-up analysis with functional dependencies among items can be used to determine if the top-down derived record types are in third normal form or Boyce-Codd normal form.

EXHIBIT 13-7.   Comparison of Top-Down and Bottom-Up Data Analysis

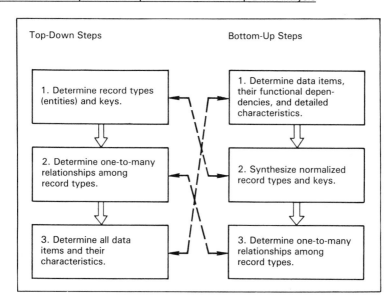

In the author's experience, top-down analysis has usually been more efficient, and bottom-up analysis should generally be reserved for detailed checking. To understand why, consider an application with five data aggregates, 30 record types, and 300 items.

With the top-down approach, the analyst and users are never boggled by staggering numbers of items being analyzed together. If a new item is discovered, the first question is "Which of the 5 data aggregates should include this item?" The next question is "Which of approximately 6 record types represents the appropriate data entity to include this item?" The final question is "Is this item really the same as one of the approximately 10 existing items in the record, or is it a new item which should be added?"

With the bottom-up approach, the analyst or user has to constantly examine lengthy lists. The list of 300 items may cover 5 to 50 pages of the data dictionary, depending on how many characteristics have been stored for each item. Items will have many functional dependencies, which could come from anywhere in the list of 300 items. Sometimes the functional dependencies themselves are unclear, because it is unclear in which context they should be evaluated. For example, within any department it may be true that Course information functionally depends on the Course Title. However, it may not be true over the entire university.

Bottom-up analysis tends to be too tedious and error prone. People who start working bottom-up generally evolve toward a top-down strategy. Henry C. Smith provides an example of such a strategy which is between the top-down and bottom-up approaches discussed here (4).

Many bottom-up data analyses stop after collecting a list of data items and never develop the conceptual data structure. Relationships among items are ignored, so no decisions are made concerning the best ways to model the set of items in record types and interrecord relationships. Users suffer and developers are slowed down. Users must review lengthy data dictionary dumps of item characteristics, but what should they look for? The relationships are the most important part of data modeling for users to agree upon, and the relationships are completely missing from this kind of approach. Developers are forced to synthesize a conceptual data model before they can attack the performance issues involved with a physical data model. This can take a lot of time. It also may result in inadequate review of the data modeling decisions by users, if the developers have less access to users than the requirements analysts had.

Fortunately, there is a quick way to spot when the analysts are merely collecting data items. If the items are kept and distributed in alphabetical lists, it is a sure sign that data structure is lacking. Alphabetical lists tend to randomize the items as far as real data structure meaning is concerned.

ANALYSIS OF DATA FLOWS

The third detailed data analysis subject is analysis of data flows. A comprehensive way for the systems analyst to check the adequacy of the conceptual data model is to verify whether it supports all the data flows on the user concept diagrams. If this check is not performed for the user requirements document, it will have to be performed sooner or later by the application designer. This discussion assumes that, as shown in Exhibit 4-7, both the functional description (user concept diagrams and verifiable functional requirements) and the data base description (data structure diagram and data dictionary) are available in draft form.

Analysis of Data Flows
Using Data Navigation Diagrams

The main tool for top-down analysis of data flows is the data navigation diagram. This is simply a copy of the data structure diagram (Exhibit 11-13) which has been marked up to show how the data base can be accessed to accomplish a particular function. A simple example from the Ace Aerospace application shows the general idea.

In Exhibit 6-17, consider the flow from function 1.3 (Input and Reconcile Corporate Accounting Data) to the Cost Element Data Aggregate. For easier reference, this flow is reproduced as Exhibit 13-8.

The concept of the data navigation diagram is to indicate a path explicitly, following one-to-many relationship arrows, which enables the necessary record occurrences to be located. The path may start at any top-level record type (or other record type intended to be accessed directly from its record key occurrences). The path may then follow any arrow either forward or backward. Lo-

EXHIBIT 13-8. Example Flow for the Data Navigation Diagram Discussion

cated record occurrences can be used for reading or storing data. Exhibit 13-9 shows how the data navigation diagram looks for this example. Numbers within circles indicate the order in which each record type is accessed. The circle is placed either by the one-to-many relationship arrow used to access the record or away from any relationship arrows if the record is likely to be accessed directly by its key.

The actual check of the data base description progresses by comparing the processing requirements against the data dictionary. Exhibit 13-10 illustrates the thinking behind this comparison. The processing steps (shown in Structured English) lead to distinct questions about the data base. These must be answered by examining the data navigation diagram and data dictionary.

For example, the first data model question in Exhibit 13-10 is "How can a Contract and a Contract Line Item be associated with a charge number?" This question may indicate the need to have either a table which shows Contract Line

EXHIBIT 13-9. Example Data Navigation Diagram

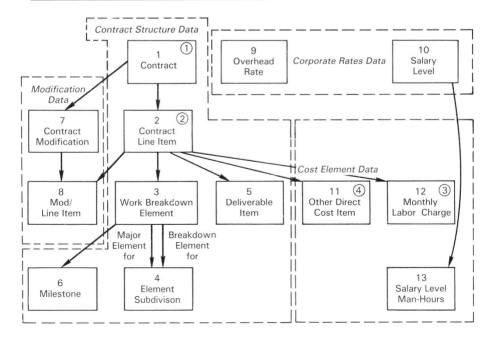

EXHIBIT 13-10.   Data Flow Analysis Using Data Navigation Diagrams

Processing Step	Nav. Step	Data Model Questions
For each charge number reported this month:	① ②	How can the Contract and Contract Line Item associated with this charge number be determined?
Initialize Man-hours = 0 Initialize Labor $ = 0		
For each individual charging this number:		
Increment Man-hours by # hours individual worked this month; Increment Labor $ by individual's fully burdened labor rate X # hours worked Initialize ODC $ = 0		How can the individual's fully burdened labor rate be determined?
For each Other Direct Charge accounted for this month:		
Increment ODC $ by this new charge		
Store Man-hours and ODC $ with the appropriate Contract Line Item for this month	③ ④	Does the data base description support storage of these items?

Items for each valid charge number, or a new charge number item in the Contract Line Item record. After some reflection, the analyst may decide to replace the old Contract Line Item key (Contract Number and Line Item Number) by Charge Number. He may then decide that the Data Navigation Diagram is incorrect; navigation can start with the Contract Line Item record, ignoring the Contract record.

The second question is, "How can the individual's fully burdened rate be determined?" ("Fully burdened" means the individual's basic salary rate is multiplied by a factor which includes overhead and fee.) This question requires some thought, because the data model had not included any information about individuals other than points of contact. However, upon further investigation the analyst finds that there is a simple formula to compute the individual's burdened charge from the information in the monthly corporate accounting report. Thus, burdened labor rates are not required. The result is a change to the formula for computing burdened labor charges in the detailed functional requirements.

The final question is, "Does the data model support storage of the Man-hour and ODC $ items?" This is simple to answer from the data navigation diagram and data dictionary. These items were anticipated, and the data model supported their storage, by month.

Such checks can be made very quickly in the requirements definition phase by making data navigation diagram markups and comparing the data model with the functional requirements. In many situations, these checks themselves need not be documented, but decisions leading from the checks will result in changes to the data model or the functional requirements. When using automated systems analysis tools (see Chapter 16), it is often useful to store results of data navigation analysis in the requirements data base. This gives useful information about which functions use or set which data items. When performing detailed analysis of report and screen display outputs, data navigation diagrams are usually analyzed along with the detailed functional requirements of the outputs. The combined results can be presented as shown in Exhibit 9-6.

James Martin and Carma McClure have some interesting ideas concerning how data navigation diagrams could be structured to obtain formal design specifications for data base access programs (5). Whether the diagrams can be carried this far for real applications is still a research question; however, data navigation diagrams have definite usefulness to application designers at least in giving intuition concerning how the data base will be accessed.

Analysis of Data Flows
Through Chain Decomposition

Both the DeMarco (6) and Gane & Sarson (7) expositions of Yourdon-style systems analysis treated data analysis almost as an afterthought. To them, the primary requirements analysis objective was completion of future physical data flow diagrams (Exhibit 6-10). These diagrams were then supported by process specifications and third normal form data descriptions for stored data. To obtain the detailed data flow diagrams, DeMarco recommended a process of successive elaboration of data flows in "chain decompositions," which appeared to be more fundamental than the third normal form data modeling.

Practitioners following these books tend to conduct data analysis in a five-step process:

1. Construct data flow diagrams as described in Chapter 6.
2. Decompose each data flow on the most detailed data flow diagrams, down to the data item level.
3. Check for data overlaps and repetitions of the same data items. Obtain a hierarchical decomposition of the whole data base.
4. Synthesize normalized record types (as explained earlier in this chapter) from the data items obtained in step 3.
5. Develop a (relational) data structure diagram to show join possibilities.

Exhibit 13-11 helps to visualize steps 2 and 3 in this approach.   In step 2, each data flow is independently decomposed using arbitrary data groupings that

EXHIBIT 13-11. Data Analysis Using Chain Decomposition

(A) Construct Data Flow Diagrams (Step 1)

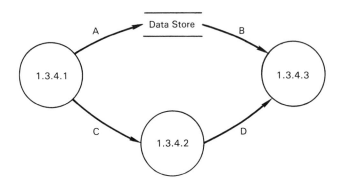

(B) Decompose Flows into Chains (Step 2)

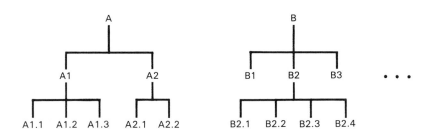

(C) Rationalize Overlaps (Step 3)

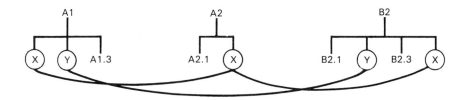

DeMarco called "chains." He represented the hierarchical breakdown of data flows shown in Exhibit 13-11A by algebraic notation as follows:

A   =   A1 + A2   (Data flow A is composed of chains A1 and A2)
A1   =   A1.1 + A1.2 + A1.3 (Chain A1 is composed of subchains A1.1, A1.2, and A1.3)

The process ends when all chains have been decomposed into atomic data items.

In actual application, the chains obtain meaningful names, so that the above schematic might actually appear as:

Class Schedules   =   Course Sections + Instructors
Course Sections   =   Course Catalog + Times + Places.

Step 3, rationalizing the data overlaps, can be extremely difficult, because different terms may be used for the same or similar concepts in different parts of the decomposition. The most methodical approach is to start at the bottom, consolidating data items. Synonyms like "Teacher Name" and "Instructor Name" must be located and a unique label attached to each item in the data base. In many situations this analysis will show that what appeared to be a data item will turn out to be a chain requiring decomposition to rationalize with another chain or item. For example, comparing items Place, Building Name, and Room Number, the analyst may decide that Place should be decomposed as:

Place = Building Name + Room Number.

Following rationalization at the data item level, it is then relatively simple (although it may take many hours) to rationalize chains. Wherever two chains contain common items, the overlapping parts should be specified by one or more common subchains, as illustrated in Exhibit 13-11C.

Often the fourth and fifth steps (obtaining normalized record types and a data structure diagram) are ignored, because all available analysis time has been used up in the rationalization process.

Comparison of the Data Flow Analysis Techniques

Data navigation analysis and chain decomposition analysis investigate data flows in quite different ways. Exhibit 13-12 summarizes major differences. Chain decomposition is a method to provide a list of application data items to be used in bottom-up data analysis which then obtains the entities and relationships needed for a conceptual data model. Data navigation analysis starts with a conceptual data model and uses data flows, data navigation diagrams, and detailed functional requirements to determine if the conceptual data model really satisfies the application's processing needs. Theoretically one could use both techniques, starting with chain decomposition, constructing a data model using bottom-up analysis, and then checking the model using data navigation analysis.

EXHIBIT 13-12.   Comparison of Data Flow Analysis Approaches

Characteristic	Data Flow Analysis Approach	
	Data Navigation Analysis	Chain Decomposition
Intent	Perform detailed check of the conceptual data model	Obtain data items for bottom-up data analysis to create the conceptual data model.
Required Inputs	User concept diagrams and verifiable functional requirements	User concept diagrams only
Difficult Parts	Detailed comparison of data navigation with functional requirements	Rationalization of data items and chains

The author recommends against using comprehensive chain decomposition of data flows. It is a time-consuming approach. The rationalization step is extremely difficult to perform successfully. Since chain decomposition does not require any knowledge of data analysis techniques, it is simple for people untrained in data analysis to attempt. However, all the data structuring aids that would help in the rationalization step are missing. At the end of chain decomposition and rationalization, the analyst is left at the beginning of another tedious process, bottom-up data analysis. This is because the hierarchical chain structure may not correspond to normalized record types, and the chains do not help much in determining one-to-many relationships. Even when groups are successful at chain decomposition followed by bottom-up analysis, they tend to have the feeling, "There must be a better way."

Fortunately, there is a better way—top-down analysis with entity-relationship diagrams—which became widely known several years after the DeMarco and Gane & Sarson books were published. It takes much less time to determine data entities of interest and create a data structure diagram, than to perform a complete bottom-up analysis. The time saved could be used to perform detailed data navigation checks of data flows and have the additional assurance of a robust conceptual data model.

USER VIEWS

The fourth detailed data analysis subject is user views. A user view is that part of a conceptual data model which applies to one user, type of user, or application area. A conceptual data model is generated for each user view, and then these are rationalized to obtain a model of the entire data base. Once a draft data model is available for the entire data base, it can easily be restricted to the records, relationships, and items appropriate to a particular user view. A user representative can then comment on whether this user view represents the data in a manner appropriate to his business area.

The user view is a natural tool when starting top-down conceptual data analysis as described in Chapter 11. Generally the systems analyst interviews functional area experts and gets their advice on the entities, attributes, and relationships which should be stored to serve their functions. These interviews can lead to many user view data structure diagrams. The systems analyst then must consolidate all of these user views into one overall conceptual data model. In most cases, the consolidation is straightforward; Chapter 11 shows how numerous data base decisions combine into one model. In some cases, users may make decisions which are contradictory. For example, for the Ace Aerospace example, contract administrators may want costs retained by Contract Line Item, while project managers would prefer to collect costs by Work Breakdown Element. When such data modeling issues arise, the systems analyst needs to bring up the problem and help the parties involved to come to an agreement.

User views may also be generated for individual application functional areas. In particular, analysis of data input and output processes can verify whether all the data items to be input to the data base have places in the data model ready to accept them. Likewise, analysis of data outputs can identify any problems in generating report or query fields from the data in the data model.

SUMMARY OF DATA ANALYSIS CONCEPTS

The principles of data analysis discussed in Chapters 10 through 13 are vital for defining user requirements of information systems constructed around an integrated data base. Successful application of these principles depends on analysts having a working knowledge of sophisticated data modeling concepts. Hence, data analysis requires more analyst training than does functional analysis. Moreover, user representatives will need more assistance to understand the application data model than they will need to understand the functional model.

The recommended data analysis approach is a top-down style based on the data structure diagram. The analyst starts with data entities and their keys. In the most creative step, one-to-many relationships are identified. These lead to the data structure diagram, which is put in canonical form to portray the structure in the most meaningful fashion. Next, each entity on the diagram becomes a record type, fully described to the data item level in a data dictionary. Detailed checks can be made with data navigation diagrams to ensure that the data base description (data structure diagram and data dictionary) will meet the application's needs. For large applications, it is usually necessary to develop and merge data base descriptions of many user views.

Record types should be in third normal form or Boyce-Codd normal form, in order to support development of a practical, maintainable physical data model for the application. The analysis style described in Chapter 11 tends toward normal form data entities, because the analysis starts with entity descriptions and keys. Nonkey attributes will be selected to be functionally dependent on the key attributes, within the defining concept for the entity. Knowledge of normal form theory helps to keep the normalization goal in mind. Moreover, verifying that record types are in normal form is a useful detailed check.

Bottom-up data analysis and chain decomposition of data flows have been discussed in Chapter 13, as both have been used extensively. However, the greater efficiency obtained with the more recent top-down entity-relationship approach should displace these bottom-up methods in most situations.

Many requirements specifications ignore conceptual data modeling. The only definition of the data base is a list of data items. These specifications are easy to spot, because the items are invariably presented in alphabetical order rather than in meaningful groupings. In these implementation projects, the developer must start working his data base design at the conceptual level. But the developer usually has less access to users than the systems analysts had, for both project organization and cultural background reasons. Hence, implementation is slower, more costly, and less successful than when the users participate up front in developing a clear, complete, agreed-upon conceptual data model.

The functional requirements and data base description are the main user requirements for the new application. There is, however, another area of requirements to consider, namely *performance* requirements. In addition, before the requirements specification can be fully agreed upon, a reasonable implementation approach must be decided which will result in the desired application being deployed at an affordable cost with minimal risk.

DISCUSSION QUESTIONS

1. Consider a data table with the following personnel information:

Employee Name	Social Sec No	Phone No	Spouse Name	Child Name	Supervisor	Department	Department Manager

    a. Diagram the functional dependencies as shown in Exhibit 13-6.

    b. What is the result of normalizing this table to third normal form?

    c. Does Boyce-Codd normal form give a different result?

2. On very large applications which have been split into sizable subsystems, it is common for a data analyst to be assigned to each subsystem. Each individual analyst develops a data model for his subsystem. These subsystem data models can be considered user views of the total application data base.

    a. What procedures need to be employed to meld the subsystem data models into a comprehensive application data model?

    b. What automated tools would assist the user view consolidation?

REFERENCES

1. E. F. Codd, "Further Normalization of the Data Base Relational Model," in *Data Base Systems*, Courant Computer Science Symposia Series, vol. 6, Englewood Cliffs, N.J.: Prentice-Hall, 1972.

2. C.J. Date, *An Introduction to Database Systems*, vol. 1, 4th ed., Reading, MA: Addison-Wesley, 1986.

3. R. Fagin and M. Y. Vardi, *The Theory of Data Dependencies—A Survey*, IBM Research Report RJ4321, 1984.

4. Henry C. Smith, "Database Design: Composing Fully Normalized Tables from a Rigorous Dependency Diagram," *Communications of the ACM*, vol. 28, no. 8, 1985.

5. James Martin and Carma McClure, *Diagramming Techniques for Analysts and Programmers*, Englewood Cliffs, N.J.: Prentice-Hall, 1985. See especially Chapter 21.

6. Tom DeMarco, *Structured Analysis and System Specification*, Englewood Cliffs, N.J.: Prentice-Hall, 1979.

7. Chris Gane and Trish Sarson, *Structured Systems Analysis: Tools and Techniques*, Englewood Cliffs, N.J.: Prentice-Hall, 1979.

PART FIVE
Determining
an Implementation Approach

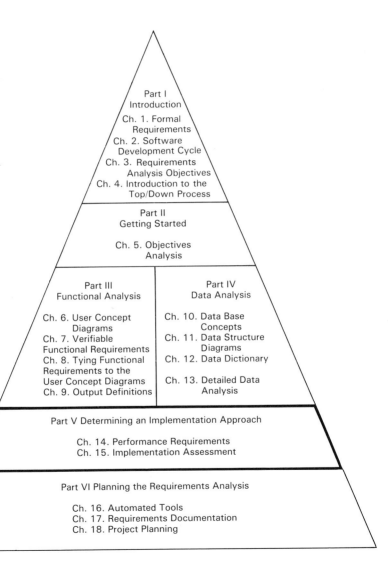

Part I
Introduction
Ch. 1. Formal
   Requirements
Ch. 2. Software
   Development Cycle
Ch. 3. Requirements
   Analysis Objectives
Ch. 4. Introduction to the
   Top/Down Process

Part II
Getting Started

Ch. 5. Objectives
   Analysis

Part III
Functional Analysis

Ch. 6. User Concept
   Diagrams
Ch. 7. Verifiable
Functional Requirements
Ch. 8. Tying Functional
Requirements to the
User Concept Diagrams
Ch. 9. Output Definitions

Part IV
Data Analysis

Ch. 10. Data Base
   Concepts
Ch. 11. Data Structure
   Diagrams
Ch. 12. Data Dictionary

Ch. 13. Detailed Data
   Analysis

Part V Determining an Implementation Approach

Ch. 14. Performance Requirements
Ch. 15. Implementation Assessment

Part VI Planning the Requirements Analysis

Ch. 16. Automated Tools
Ch. 17. Requirements Documentation
Ch. 18. Project Planning

14

Performance Requirements

Most computer applications have important performance requirements. If they are not met, users will be unhappy with the system, and desired productivity gains will not be achieved. However, they must be compiled and published to guide the developer. Otherwise, the developer may not properly understand the users' performance needs.

The subject of performance requirements is often neglected in systems analysis discussions. As a result, analysts often either ignore the subject entirely or waste a lot of time trying to decide what to do about performance. This chapter takes a practical approach which is straightforward but does require users to really think through their performance needs.

In this text performance requirements are statements of how well application functions must perform under expected operational workloads. Emphasis here is on execution speed. Performance depends on the size of the operational scenario, as well as the desired responsiveness. Hence, this chapter discusses the following scenario and response characteristics:

- Number of users
- Data base size
- Function processing rates
- Interactive response times.

Additional comments discuss documentation and interpretation of the performance requirements.

NUMBER OF USERS

The developer should know how many users of each type are expected, in order to plan for terminal support, user interfaces, data base contention controls, and training materials. The number of users is the number of individuals (or groups who share a common terminal) who can access the application. It is *not* the number of people who can all be requesting service at the same time. Simultaneous usage is an excellent parameter to track later when the application is operational. It is not a useful figure to estimate at the requirements specification stage, because it will depend on the design solution. If functions execute quickly, users will have shorter sessions, and hence there will be a smaller number of simultaneous users. Likewise, if batch processes execute quickly, there will be fewer of them queued for execution.

Exhibit 14-1 is a sample table showing numbers of users. This table indicates that Project Managers will be the most numerous users of the Ace Aerospace system. The number of users may grow over time. If so, the anticipated growth rates should be noted in an additional column.

EXHIBIT 14-1.   Number of Users of Each Type for the Ace Aerospace Example

User Type	Number of Individuals
Division Executive	8
Division Financial Analyst	3
Project Manager	60
Contract Administrator	6
Contract Tracking System Administrator	1
Data Entry Clerk	2
Total	80

DATA BASE SIZE

The data base size is important for the designer to know, because processing techniques usually have to be more sophisticated when large volumes of data have to be handled. Three principles summarize what the analyst needs to know in compiling data base size requirements:

Size should be specified by record type (not by whole data base or data aggregate).

- Record data volume should be specified by number of record occurrences (not by physical storage requirements in bytes).
- Growth of the data base should be forecasted for the expected life of the application (rather than giving a single point estimate of data base size).

Data base size should be broken out to the record type level to aid the physical data base design. Record types which have small numbers of occurrences may be stored differently from record types with large numbers of occurrences. The designer will consider both the estimates of record type occurrences and the record access patterns (from the functional requirements and from function processing rates, as will be discussed) to determine how each record type should be physically stored.

Physical storage in bytes is not helpful for requirements specifications, because a wide variety of physical storage options is available to the designer. Knowing the expected number of record occurrences and the number of characters on input for all the items in the record, the analyst could multiply the two numbers together to get an expected number of bytes required for the record type. This may not be reflected in the final physical data base, however, because:

- Items will usually be stored in a compressed form (for example, integers will typically be stored in a binary form, rather than as a byte per decimal digit).
- Data base pointers, hashing space, and so on, will require more physical storage than is required for just the content of the data items.

Hence, number of occurrences is a far better parameter to capture concerning the application data base size requirements.

Growth of the system should also be anticipated. Often a data base will grow over the years as more data are collected. Another possibility is that the data base will be relatively static in size, because old data will be dropped or archived at about the same rate that new data are entered. Growth assumptions should be made explicit.

Exhibit 14-2 shows a simple format which can be used to specify expected data base size, including growth assumptions. Such a table can be filled out through discussions with user representatives, comparison with existing data bases, or a combination of the two.

FUNCTION PROCESSING RATES

The designer needs to know how often the functions in the user concept diagrams will be performed. A data input process performed 1,000 times per day will be designed differently from one occurring an average of once per quarter. To users it is obvious which functions will be frequently invoked and which cover rare situations. To the developer and systems analyst, frequencies of function usage may

EXHIBIT 14-2.   Size of the Ace Aerospace Contract Tracking System Data Base

Data Aggregate	Record Type	No. Data Base Occurrences Expected On Jan. 1, 1989	Expected Yearly Growth in Number of Occurrences
Contract Structure Data	1. Contract	50	10
	2. Contract Line Item	200	40
	3. Work Breakdown Element	1200	400
	4. Element Subdivision	1000	300
	5. Deliverable Item	1000	200
	6. Milestone	3000	1200
Modification Data	7. Contact Modification	500	100
	8. Mod/Line Item	1300	260
Corporate Rates Data	9. Overhead Rate	6	2
	10. Salary Level	10	0
Cost Element Data	11. Other Direct Cost Item	30,000	6000, 1st 3 years 1200, later years
	12. Monthly Labor Charge	6000	1200, 1st 3 years 240, later years
	13. Salary Level Man-Hours	36,000	7200, 1st 3 years 1440, later years

not be at all obvious. Hence, they should be compiled from user interviews. A particularly effective group "Delphi" process for obtaining processing rates is described in a later section of this chapter.

The first two columns of Exhibit 14-3 show a simple scheme for documenting function processing rates. The functions in this table correspond to boxes

EXHIBIT 14-3.   Function Processing Rates for the Ace Aerospace Application

Function	Frequency	Required Completion
1.1 Maintain Contract Structure and Mods Data	12/day	Changes posted by next morning at 7AM
1.2 Input and Delete Project Obligations Data	40/day	Changes posted by next morning at 7AM
1.3 Input and Reconcile Corporate Accounting Data	2/month	Complete process within 3 working days
1.4 Maintain Corporate Rates Data	4/year	(not time critical)

on the user concept diagrams, taken at a level the systems analyst feels is appropriate to obtain useful processing rates.

Besides the function processing frequencies, sessions with users should cover the timeliness requirements of the function processing. Here the systems analysts strive for realistic requirements. Most user representatives start with the feeling that all results should be available interactively in a matter of seconds. Such response for processes which must scan through large data bases is unrealistic. On further questioning, users may admit that a large report requested during the day would be fully serviceable if run overnight and available the next morning. Such a conclusion gives the designer far more flexibility than an overly stringent response requirement. For example, an interactive graphics concept may require review of a draft graphics charts within five minutes to allow the user to modify the results at the same session. This might lead to the purchase of special graphics processors or cause system priority to go to the graphics functions. When the performance requirements are less stringent, the designer can usually come up with a less expensive solution.

The "Required Completion" column of Exhibit 14-3 indicates the time available to process individual functions. These requirements should cover an entire work process (like completion of data entry from a particular form), including both the automated and manual steps. There is an advantage in staying at this higher level, rather than specifying detailed response times such as field-by-field validity check and record commitment response times. Given requirements for completing work processes, the designer has the flexibility to allocate the available time in the way he feels most appropriate for the engineering problems in the application.

A table of function frequency and completion times, such as shown in Exhibit 14-3, gives a simple view of the overall performance requirements. Generally a few functions have the most critical performance requirements. For example, in the exhibit it is clear that maintenance of Project Obligations information occurs much more frequently than the other three functions shown, and hence could be a candidate for performance risk. But the required next morning completion indicates that performance should not be a difficult problem with this function.

INTERACTIVE RESPONSE TIMES

Another kind of execution performance requirement is specification of response times expected when a user interacts at a terminal. These requirements are really a partial definition of acceptable user friendliness rather than an indication of business need. Many users will be familiar with the excellent response obtained with personal computer applications. These users will refuse to work with computer systems which slow down their thought pattern and productivity. The old days of accepting a 15-second delay just to paint a screen at a 120 characters per

EXHIBIT 14-4.   Sample Interactive Response Requirements

User Action	Computer Response	Response Time	
		Usual Response (90%)	Maximum Response
Choice of menu selection	Display of next menu or screen display	5 seconds	10 seconds
Entry of a data field on a data entry screen	Acknowledgement that the field has been accepted by moving cursor to the next field	6 seconds	10 seconds
Selection of a previously generated report for interactive display	Display of the beginning of the report on the user's terminal screen	10 seconds	20 seconds
Completion of an ad hoc query specification	Display of syntax errors or message confirming that the query is syntactically valid	15 seconds	40 seconds

second communication rate are gone for these sophisticated users. The analyst should document response expectations in a table like the one shown in Exhibit 14-4.

These response conditions must be carefully defined to be able to verify whether the implemented system satisfies them. There should be a scenario explaining simultaneous computer usage assumptions, and the response requirements must carefully define the time periods being measured. Response is a statistical quantity which may need to be described by more than one condition. For example, Exhibit 14-4 gives one time that bounds the response 90 percent of the time and another time which is the maximum response under the stated scenario.

The systems analyst needs to act as a broker between the end users and developers to make sure the response time requirements are truly needed, can be met with normal good software implementation practices, and are verifiable. Users may start off feeling that all computer responses must be within two seconds. Reminding them of the ten-second wait that they routinely sit through when loading large spreadsheets, or showing them sample delays for the situations they will encounter in the new application, users may agree to expand the two seconds to more realistic numbers.

Avoid open-ended response conditions. For example, "Provide results of an ad hoc query after user submission of a validated query specification for execution" is an open-ended condition. Most query languages are flexible enough to allow arbitrarily complex queries. These can be made to take arbitrarily long periods of time to execute. Hence, no response requirement can be given unless the type of query is sharply defined.

OBTAINING PERFORMANCE REQUIREMENTS
IN GROUP DELPHI SESSIONS

The preceding sections have indicated what performance information should be compiled. The next question to answer is, "How should it be obtained?" The author has seen systems analysts plead for large amounts of resources to build performance simulators, analyze existing systems, or perform exhaustive interviews with personnel involved in the business area impacted by the new application. Actually, a much more straightforward method can compile a good first draft of performance requirements. It is based on an operations research technique called "Delphi analysis." This is a process for getting a group of experts to agree on numerical estimates. Here is how Delphi analysis has been successfully used by the author to obtain performance requirements.

First, recognize that obtaining performance requirements is more efficient when accomplished in a group setting with user representatives. Reasons for meeting with a group, rather than separately with individuals, include:

- The group can develop a consistent set of assumptions underlying the performance estimates.

- Performance estimates for a functional process should be consistent with estimates for related processes, so coordination of experts from several business areas may be required.

- Differences of opinion on performance numbers are hard for the systems analyst to resolve in isolation; they need to be resolved through discussion among the user representatives who have the differing views.

The need for a group setting for performance requirements contrasts with the desirability of interviewing individuals or very small groups of functional area experts when the systems analyst compiles functional and data requirements. Individual interviews help there, because one or two experts are best able to speak for a particular business area. If experts with other business expertise are present at the same meeting, they will be unable to contribute until their area comes up. Hence, they tend to get bored and feel that they are wasting time. However, with performance requirements, a broad range of expertise is useful to the discussion.

It is best to assemble a performance team of four to eight user representatives who have broad views of their functions in the business areas of the computer application. Such people tend to be mid-level managers with a good deal of responsibility. They expect the meetings to be a productive use of their limited time. The analyst must prepare carefully for the performance meetings in order to meet these expectations.

The performance meetings should start with the analyst describing how they will work. Samples of each of the forms which need to be filled out (like Exhibits

14-1 through 14-4) should be distributed, along with an explanation of their significance. If the lead analyst has properly prepared for the meetings, the user representatives know that they have a few days of hard work ahead of them, but the analyst should confirm expected time requirements for the meetings.

To develop a common frame of reference, the systems analysts should start with the results of objectives analysis (Chapter 5), including purpose, objectives, features, terminology, and user types. At this point, the group should get a form like Exhibit 14-1 with user types already filled in, but not the number of individuals of each type. The analysts then lead the group through the following steps:

1. Each member of the working group should make an estimate of the number of individual users of each type, noting the numbers and rationale on the work sheet.
2. The analyst then compiles the numbers on a master work sheet like Exhibit 14-5 and posts it in view of the whole group.

For each user type:

3. Representatives who had upper and lower estimates (for example, 22 and 6 for division executives) explain their rationale.
4. Other representatives can then explain their rationale, if different.
5. Open discussion continues until the group agrees on a single number to use as the best estimate.

The Delphi approach is very effective at allowing all views to be heard and achieving consensus. It is more effective than taking an average, because it ends up based on a rationale and is backed by the agreement of the performance working group. For example, averaging the estimates in Exhibit 14-5 for number of division executives would result in an estimate of "11," a number that no working

EXHIBIT 14-5. Example Master Work Sheet from Step 2 of Delphi Analysis

User Type	Estimates of Number of Individuals
Division Executive	6, 6, 8, 10, 10, 15, 22
Division Financial Analyst	2, 2, 2, 3, 3, 3, 5
Project Manager	30, 35, 50, 55, 55, 60, 180
Contract Administrator	6, 6, 6, 6, 6, 6, 6
Contract Tracking System Administrator	1, 1, 1, 1, 1, 1, 2
Data Entry Clerk	1, 1, 2, 2, 4, 5, 7

group member likes. But in the group discussions, the user representatives who think "6" is the correct number might have a convincing argument that persuades the others. The number "6" will be more correct at least in that the members of the performance working group believe it is their best estimate.

Numbers of users is a good performance table to start with. It can be attacked early, based on application objectives. It is relatively easy to complete and illustrates well the Delphi decision-making process. Completing the first table quickly gives a feeling of positive momentum to the group's efforts.

The group should next attack data base sizing. A systems analyst should start the discussion by describing the data base, based on the data structure diagram (Exhibit 11-13). A draft data base size table like Exhibit 14-2 with record types but no numbers of occurrences is passed out to each participant. If the data model is large, the analyst may break up the discussions by data aggregate. For example, the analyst may discuss an entire aggregate in some detail, and then the user representatives make number of occurrences for each record type in the aggregate. Record occurrence numbers will then be refined in Delphi steps 3 to 5 as previously discussed.

Experience suggests that the most difficult performance estimates are for the function processing frequencies and response. There tend to be a lot of functions on the user concept diagrams, and these estimates tend to require the most extensive discussion. Twenty minutes to an hour is typical for each function, so this process can be lengthy. Here the systems analyst should avoid the temptation to skip over the hard ones. There will never be a better time, so the group should go ahead and make estimates for each function in the list.

DOCUMENTATION OF PERFORMANCE REQUIREMENTS

Performance requirements can be distributed inside various sections of the user requirements and requirements specification documents, or they can be collected into a separate section. Looking at both approaches, the separate section has definite advantages.

In the distributed approach, the material fits into various sections as follows:

- The number of users of each type fits into the introductory section which describes the application's user types.
- Data base sizes fit into the data dictionary entries with record definitions.
- Function processing times are given with the verifiable functional requirements.
- Interactive response requirements also can be stated with global functional requirements.

Collecting the performance requirements in a separate section makes it simpler to modify them without changing any of the system functions. Such modifications are often necessary to come within budget constraints for the application.

Separation of performance requirements also fits with the general philosophy that the documentation should follow the same top-down structure as the analysis itself. All of the performance requirements can be collected during one set of Delphi sessions with users, after the functional and data requirements are assembled. Hence, it is reasonable to combine performance requirements in their own section of the user requirements and requirements specification documents (Chapter 17).

GETTING THE DEVELOPER
TO SIGN UP FOR PERFORMANCE

An important issue with the performance requirements is deciding how they should be used by the sponsor, users, and developer. There are two general interpretations which can differ significantly:

Users' Interpretation: The performance requirements are just as important as the functional and data requirements. The developer will not be fully paid unless the implemented system satisfies the function completion time and interactive response time performance requirements.

Developer's Interpretation: The performance requirements help describe the intended operational concept, and hence aid the designers in understanding how quickly the system should perform its functions. The developer will provide his best efforts to meet the performance requirements, but myriad circumstances beyond the developer's control may make it impossible to be successful in meeting every performance requirement.

If these two interpretations are not reconciled at the start of development, they can lead later to intense argument and even to legal action.

The developer is well within his rights either to avoid signing up for financial penalties based on inadequate application performance or to demand a high price for a performance warranty. Performance prediction from requirements specifications is not a well-developed part of computer science. However, mathematical models or prototype efforts can clarify what performance expectations are reasonable (as discussed in Chapter 15). Such efforts can reduce the users' and developer's risks, and hence bring their two viewpoints together.

In any event, the legal status of the performance requirements should be clarified before the developer starts out. They can be used as general guidance, as real acceptance conditions, or with a few important performance requirements singled out as acceptance conditions and the rest acting as general guidance. But whatever the final decision, users, developer, and sponsor should have the same interpretation of the nature of the performance requirements when development starts.

DISCUSSION QUESTIONS

1. Designing a system to meet stringent performance requirements is a difficult job. Performance estimation is supported by a large body of literature based on techniques like mathematical queuing theory. Detailed performance modeling is expensive and possibly misleading if some little-understood aspects of the operating system or data base management system drive the achieved response. Hence, it is far more common to "tune" the application for performance after it is developed, than to base the design on performance.

   a. What are the pitfalls of after-the-fact tuning?

   b. How should performance estimation fit into the software development cycle?

2. Despite the general rule that throughput requirements are more meaningful than the number of simultaneous users, the latter figure is often important to the designer. The maximum number of simultaneous users may indicate which computer in a vendor's family of processors is the right one to host the application. It may be easier for a systems analyst to make the estimate with the help of users than for a designer to derive simultaneous usage in an early step of the design process.

   a. If the new application will replace an old system with usage statistics, how should maximum number of simultaneous users be determined for the new application?

   b. If no similar experience is available, how should maximum simultaneous usage be estimated?

3. Many systems have extremely ambitious reliability or availability goals. *Reliability*, measured by Mean Time Between Failures (MTBF), tells how long the system can remain operating without having a problem which takes it out of service. *Maintainability*, measured by Mean Time To Repair (MTTR), tells how fast a problem can be resolved, including restoration of the data base, so that users can get back into the system after a failure. *Availability*, measured by MTBF / (MTBF + MTTR), is the fraction of the time that the system is operable for users. If the application is central to the organization's operations (for example, an airline reservation system), then availability must be kept very high. When the consequences of a failure are drastic, as in an air traffic control system, reliability must be made extraordinarily high. Although availability and reliability requirements are not needed for many applications, they are cost drivers for the systems to which they do apply. They generally lead to much more expensive hardware (redundancy increases reliability) and higher operations costs (to operate redundant equipment and to achieve highly responsive maintenance).

   a. Where do you think reliability, maintainability, and availability requirements should be addressed? Candidates include:

- Purpose/objectives/features statement of application objectives (Chapter 5)
- Verifiable Functional Requirements
- Performance requirements
- Separate analysis with a separate section in the Requirements Specification.

b. How should analysts determine what these reliability, maintainability, and availability requirements are?

15

Implementation Assessment

The previous chapters have explained how to compile a clear, complete, agreed-upon set of user requirements. This wish-list should be tempered by reality factors such as cost, technical risks, and time constraints. Based on rough assessments of these factors, the sponsor may decide to change the application scope, modify major requirements, or develop the application in phases. These decisions should be made before serious software design and development starts. Hence, the author recommends (see Exhibit 4-7) that risk assessment and implementation planning should be the final analysis steps before completion of the Requirements Specification.

Exhibit 15-1 helps to clarify the role of implementation assessment in transforming the user requirements document into an approved requirements specification. After publication of the user requirements, a broad cross section of users should review the document and comment on whether it truly reflects their collective needs. Simultaneously with this review, analysts representing the development organization (or at least taking a development perspective) should perform the implementation assessment. The risk analyses, phasing options, design options, costs, and recommendations in this assessment give the sponsor choices which require his decisions. Based on the sponsor's choices and on user feedback from review of the user requirements document, the user requirements are revised. When additional material is added on implementation environment and require-

EXHIBIT 15-1.   Implementation Assessment Impact on the Requirements

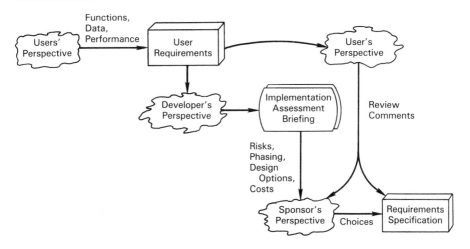

The implementation assessment gives information needed to make the final choices for the requirements specifications.

ments allocation to development phases, the result is a draft requirements specification. This document is then reviewed quickly, modified slightly after final comments, and signed off to drive the application development.

The exact nature of the implementation assessment analyses will depend on the particular circumstances of the application under consideration. The following choices will all make a big difference in implementation of the new application:

- Will it fit into an existing group of MIS applications with a well-established computer hardware and system software environment, or will it be a totally new system needing selection of new hardware and system software?
- Will the application be developed within an internal programming shop or by an external contractor?
- Will the application be implemented using commercially available software, or must the application software be custom developed?

These differing implementation circumstances also make a substantial difference in the nature of issues which must be resolved before generation of a requirements specification.

Because of these differences, it is difficult to give a cookbook approach to risk assessment and implementation planning. However, there are several areas which always should be investigated at this stage:

- Risk assessment
- Implementation phasing analysis
- Cost and schedule estimation.

This chapter discusses general approaches which will be useful in any of the implementation circumstances.

RISK ASSESSMENT

The user requirements document generally has some requirements with high implementation risk. Perhaps the requirements call for a complex processing algorithm which has not yet been developed. Usually there are a few very challenging performance requirements. A combination of functional requirements may stretch the state-of-the-art with commercially available computer and software tools. With military applications, handling of security is often a key risk area; with business applications, adequate privacy controls may be an issue.

The general process for risk assessment follows these steps: First, identify the crucial risk areas for the application. Then, for each risk area, identify implementation approaches for the subject of the risk. Next, analyze or prototype the most promising of these implementation approaches to see if it is likely to overcome the risk. Finally, assess whether the best solution reduces the risk sufficiently to justify beginning development. Two examples described in the following paragraphs indicate how data base performance, algorithm, and software development environment risks may be assessed.

Tri-State Mortgage Company wants to develop a state-of-the- art system to manage its mortgages. A key performance requirement is that 30 people must be able to simultaneously query status of individual accounts, obtaining complete account status within 60 seconds. In benchmark tests on Tri-State's computer with the company's standard DBMS, it appears that queries under this kind of workload will take about five minutes each. Tri-State analysts have three candidate approaches to solve this problem. They could go to a more powerful computer, add a "data base machine," or tune the physical data model to optimize response of the most usual queries. In examining these three candidate solutions further, benchmark tests arranged with the computer vendor show that upgrading to a more powerful computer of the same series which has sufficient power for the queries will cost $300,000. Similar benchmarks with data base machines show that a suitably powerful "back-end" data base processor will cost $120,000, plus an estimated $35,000 additional engineering support. When the analysts try the third possible solution (tuning the data base schema) on a dummy data base, they find that the only physical data model which even comes close to the query performance goals is very inflexible. It would have negative implications on downstream maintenance costs as well as greatly increasing the difficulty of implementing other processes against the same data base. Based on the assessment of these three options, the analysts recommend installing a data base machine. Although it has some technical risk in integrating the data base machine with Tri-State's computer, the risk is more than offset by about $150,000 savings over the first option of upgrading Tri-State's computer to a more powerful model.

Swift Consultants, Inc. wants to develop a graphics-oriented decision support system for personal computers. This application requires a new expert system algorithm for the Swift decision-making process, as well as extensive color graphics capabilities on both input and output. The analysts defining this application are concerned about the risk involved with both the algorithm and the complex graphics. They have tested out two attempts at the algorithm; both came up with undesirable quirks unsuitable for a polished commercial application. On the other hand, they found some personal computer graphics utilities which helped them quickly demonstrate two of the most complex color graphics displays. As a result, the analysts are recommending that Swift engineers rethink their algorithm concept and come up with a workable algorithm before implementing the software using the now-proven graphics utilities.

IMPLEMENTATION PHASING ANALYSIS

It is well known that risks of large MIS developments tend to be lessened by breaking the system into parts that are implemented separately. Lessons learned in development and operation of the first capabilities can be used in "smarter" development of later phases. This can be considered a type of prototyping.

The problem with such a phased approach is that the proper content of each phase is hardly ever obvious in advance just by looking at the user requirements. Each functional and data base component is there for a reason; they fit together into a nicely integrated concept. So how can parts of the system be extracted for separate implementation?

One useful approach to obtain phased implementation options is to determine minimal ways to implement the most valuable capabilities, as follows: First, pick out the single most important (or highest benefit/cost ratio) application capability. Next, decide which functional and data requirements must be available to support generation of this critical capability. Be brutal in dropping every requirement you can, recognizing that cheap partial functions may have to be supplied in some areas for capabilities which will not be implemented until later. This reduced set of functional and data requirements is your candidate for phase 1 implementation. Next, take the most important capability not in phase 1. Again, decide which functional and data requirements must be available to support this second capability and phase 1. Continue in this way (see Exhibit 15-2) until all requirements are exhausted.

With the phases obtained in this way, the analyst can then collapse some phases together if there is a demand for rapid development of the system. On the other hand, if development funds are scarce and a stretch-out is desirable, then the entire phasing structure can be retained.

It is important to start with a capability of high interest to the sponsor, rather than the capability easiest to implement. If the first phase is implemented successfully, then the usage and interest it generates will provide the incentive for the

EXHIBIT 15-2.   Phasing Definition Process

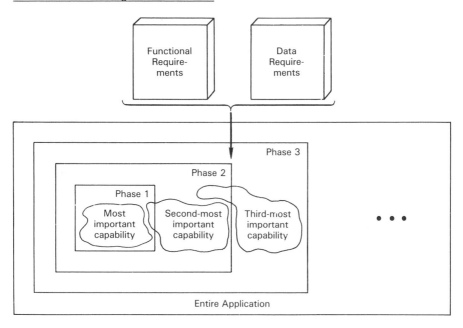

sponsor to continue support for future phases. On the other hand, if the first phase is implemented unsuccessfully or turns out to be of little value to the business, then the whole application is likely to be neglected in favor of more pressing matters.

COST AND SCHEDULE ESTIMATION

Cost realities often lead to a reduction in requirements. Cost estimates at this stage may not be completely accurate and will not necessarily commit the developer to a certain price. But it should be possible to get a good idea of the magnitude of implementation costs and an understanding of the major cost drivers. Then trade-offs can be made of requirements reduction for reduced costs.

Schedule should be examined as well. Smaller development groups will be able to assemble the software with less labor than larger groups who will need extensive intragroup communications. But the small group will take longer. Hence, if the application must be developed quickly, it will be more expensive.

Costs should be estimated using a *reference architecture*. This is a generic hardware suite and set of software modules which appear to be adequate to meet the user requirements. There may be some interesting top-level options in architecture, such as distributed versus centralized computer support. In such situations, more than one reference architecture may be carried through the cost estimates.

The simplest way to estimate costs is to compare the new application with a similar application recently developed by the same developer using the same computer environment. One might, for example, estimate that the new application should take about 75 screen displays, while the old one took 50 screens. Hence, the new application will cost about 50 percent more. Such an estimate would be rather coarse and would apply only to a screen- oriented application.

In the past, such quick estimates have been made first in lines of code, defined as executable instructions (not comments) in a high-order programming language. Then empirical formulas have been used to tell what the total costs, cheapest schedule, and manpower loading should be (1). Unfortunately, with modern application development environments (Chapter 16), lines of code estimates can be misleading. Other parameters like number of screen displays can be more useful in comparing the new application with previous experience.

Such simple comparative software cost estimates are often difficult to interpret. Does the estimate include testing, documentation, and training? What are all the tasks which have to be performed to implement the application? To answer questions like these, the analyst must methodically list the major tasks and estimate their costs.

The work breakdown structure (Exhibit 5-6) is a useful tool to support this more detailed kind of analysis. All the work required to implement the application is split up hierarchically down to the lowest level which the estimator wishes to show. Lowest level tasks should have specific task outputs, whenever possible. Care should be taken to consider *all* required tasks. For example, management and engineering activities are often overlooked. Likewise, care should be taken to eliminate overlap of tasks, which would result in double-counting and an overly high cost estimate.

Exhibit 15-3 shows an example work breakdown structure for the Ace Aerospace example. Note that many other tasks are required besides the software development in task 3.2. This breakdown reflects how the work will be performed. For example, a single project manager will perform all the project management tasks, so there may be no reason to decompose project management. Work tasks in the work breakdown structure should be carefully defined before estimating costs. For example, design of the software may be included in tasks 3.2.n, but documenting and publishing the design belong in task 5.1.

Many of the costs shown in Exhibit 15-3 are significant, but often neglected. Documentation and training can be much more expensive than managers expect. Data conversion can be particularly expensive when the new system is taking over from an old system which must stay on-line until the new system is totally ready to go operational. Operation and maintenance costs are typically 70 percent or more of total life-cycle costs for systems operating over a ten-year period. Data maintenance activities may become a huge burden on the user community. This burden, when surfaced, may cause users to back off on noncritical requirements. People often ignore operation and maintenance costs on purpose. The rationale: If people knew in advance all the problems with children or computer systems, then

EXHIBIT 15-3. Ace Aerospace Sample Work Breakdown Structure

```
1. Project Management

2. Equipment
      2.1 Computer Facility
      2.2 Terminals and Printers
      2.3 Graphics Displays
      2.4 Equipment Integration

3. Software
      3.1 System Software
      3.2 Applications Software
            3.2.1 Manage Contract Data
            3.2.2 Generate Standard Reports
            3.2.3 Support User Queries
            3.2.4 Generate and Display Briefing Charts
            3.2.5 Support System Administration
      3.3 Test and Maintenance Software
            3.3.1 Regression Test Set
            3.3.2 Version Control Library
      3.4 System Tests
            3.4.1 Integration Tests
            3.4.2 Acceptance Tests

4. Data Base Establishment
      4.1 Schema Creation
      4.2 Data Initialization

5. Documentation and Reviews
      5.1 Design Specification
      5.2 Test Plan
      5.3 User Manual
      5.4 Programmer Manual
      5.5 Reviews
            5.5.1 Preliminary Design Review
            5.5.2 Detailed Design Review
            5.5.3 Acceptance Test Review

6. User Training

7. Facility Operation and Maintenance
      7.1 Operation
      7.2 Maintenance
            7.2.1 Hardware
            7.2.2 System Software
            7.2.3 Application Software
      7.3 Data Base Administration
```

they would not give birth to either. A fair cost/benefit analysis should include these very real operation and maintenance costs.

The cost estimator should not assume that all tasks will be performed flawlessly. A management reserve of 10 percent to 20 percent should be added either for the entire job or for each low-level task. Estimates may get overblown when pads are added to each level of the work breakdown, especially when the estimates are assembled by a large group. Such overcaution is also counterproductive, since it leads either to cancellation of the project or a search for another developer.

Given the work breakdown structure and cost estimates, the analyst may go further to the level of detail which shows how particular individuals (or skill types) will be applied to the project. This further analysis can point out problems caused by the need for special skills which are not now available in the developer's organization. Also, adjustments may be made to account for the fact that people come most naturally in integer numbers. It is awkward to split individuals across projects.

Finally, if the analyst adds precedence information to the task definitions (showing which tasks must be completed before other tasks can start), critical path analysis may be applied to determine how long the project should take.

Many commercial project scheduling packages are available which help to portray the work breakdown structure, schedule for the task precedence network, and manpower loading. These packages can help the estimation process for implementation assessment, and then be used in more detail later to support the planning and monitoring of the design, development, qualification, and deployment phases of the development cycle.

PACKAGING THE IMPLEMENTATION ASSESSMENT RESULTS

Typically risk assessments, implementation plans, and cost estimates are reported to the application sponsor in a briefing or short report. It should include options in each area and the analysts' recommendations for the options to choose. The briefing or report could include:

- Risk assessments
  - Statement of the risk
  - Risk reduction strategies
  - Recommended approach
  - Assessment of remaining risk
- Phasing approach
  - Recommended phasing and options
  - Benefits to the business of each phase
- Cost assessment
  - Implementation costs by phase and total
  - Operating and support costs.

This material should be presented with the understanding that the sponsor will probably request changes in the requirements based on this important information about risks, phasing, and costs.

SUMMARY OF THE IMPLEMENTATION
ASSESSMENT STEP

Developing a user requirements document as described in Chapters 5 through 14 gives a clear, complete view of what users want. It lacks, however, information about feasibility. Can the user requirements be implemented with an acceptable amount of financial, personnel, and calendar time resources? Until feasibility is established, the third necessary ingredient of a requirements specification (agreement) will be difficult to obtain. This chapter recommends setting aside some time and effort to address feasibility issues explicitly. The resulting information helps the sponsor to understand business implications of the application development. This understanding is necessary to allow the sponsor to tailor the development to business objectives, and to make the sponsor feel that committing development resources to this project is a good business decision.

There cannot be a cookbook process for implementation assessment, because of the different situations which arise with each application. Hence, it is important for an experienced manager to define the implementation assessment process and responsibilities of each participant. The main subjects which should be addressed are risk assessment, analysis of implementation phasing, and estimation of resource requirements.

The resulting assessments should be discussed in a simple briefing or memorandum form. With advice from systems analysts, users, and developers, the sponsor then makes key scope and phasing decisions which will be formally documented later in the requirements specification.

DISCUSSION QUESTIONS

1. How should implementation costs be estimated for an application which will be implemented with commercially available software?

2. If the developer plans to use the "reusable code" development approach (Exhibit 2-3), how should implementation costs be estimated?

3. How do the cost estimates and implementation phasing results help the sponsor to decide how to use a limited budget?

REFERENCE

1. Barry W. Boehm, *Software Engineering Economics*, Englewood Cliffs, N.J.: Prentice-Hall, 1981.

PART SIX
Planning the Requirements Analysis

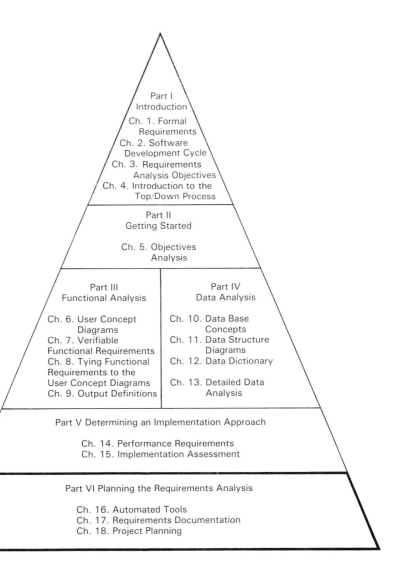

Part I
Introduction
Ch. 1. Formal
Requirements
Ch. 2. Software
Development Cycle
Ch. 3. Requirements
Analysis Objectives
Ch. 4. Introduction to the
Top/Down Process

Part II
Getting Started

Ch. 5. Objectives
Analysis

Part III
Functional Analysis

Ch. 6. User Concept
Diagrams
Ch. 7. Verifiable
Functional Requirements
Ch. 8. Tying Functional
Requirements to the
User Concept Diagrams
Ch. 9. Output Definitions

Part IV
Data Analysis

Ch. 10. Data Base
Concepts
Ch. 11. Data Structure
Diagrams
Ch. 12. Data Dictionary

Ch. 13. Detailed Data
Analysis

Part V Determining an Implementation Approach

Ch. 14. Performance Requirements
Ch. 15. Implementation Assessment

Part VI Planning the Requirements Analysis

Ch. 16. Automated Tools
Ch. 17. Requirements Documentation
Ch. 18. Project Planning

16

Automated Tools

The three chapters in Part VI discuss the concepts which unify the entire requirements analysis effort:

- Automated tools which support requirements analysis
- Organization of the user requirements and requirements specification documents
- Participation of user representatives in interviews, walkthroughs, and reviews.

Planning these three parts of the effort—tools, documentation, and user participation—is the most important contribution of the lead systems analyst. Like all decisions in application definition, however, these three will need to be ratified by the sponsor and users.

Research and development of automated tools supporting systems analysis (discussed in this chapter) is one of the most active areas of computer science in the late 1980s. This work has been stimulated partly by expansion of systems analysis activity, and partly by the availability of low-cost personal computers capable of performing excellent analyst support functions.

Proper application of automated tools requires careful consideration of the analysis methodology and how the tools will assist. The right tools will speed up the analysis and help make it more complete and more presentable. Tools which poorly match the chosen methodology will get in the way, actually increasing the effort required without increasing the quality of the requirements specification.

This chapter shows how an appropriate set of automation tools can be chosen to support an analysis organization or project. The discussion starts with a description of a variety of types of automation requirements. Then it shows how generic types of automated tools satisfy these requirements. No attempt is made to describe particular products, other than listing some commercially available software packages, because products have been changing rapidly with additional developments. A final section describes how the right set of tools can be chosen for a particular analysis situation.

Emphasis is on automation assistance of requirements analysis performed in the definition phase. However, the automated tools often carry through to support design and development. Hence, some of the discussion in this chapter covers a broader view of the software development cycle than simply requirements analysis.

REQUIREMENTS FOR AUTOMATED TOOLS

The two basic requirements analysis uses for automated tools are to assist generation of requirements specifications and to assist transition of the requirements to the design and development phases. Exhibit 16-1 lists 12 types of automated tool requirements in these two areas.

Assistance for Requirements Specifications

The first area of automated tool requirements is assistance for requirements specifications. These capabilities help to compile the application requirements, to generate materials used for reviews and walkthroughs with user representatives, and to generate the user requirements and requirements specification documents.

EXHIBIT 16-1. Automation Can Support Requirements Analysis in Many Ways

Assistance for Requirements Specifications	Assistance for Transition to Design and Development
1. Word processing 2. Interactive drawing graphics 3. Publication system 4. Library of standard textual functional requirements 5. Automated consistency checking 6. Automatic data structuring 7. Configuration management of requirements changes 8. On-line coordination of requirements 9. Analysis methodology enforcement	10. Automated link to the design process 11. Prototyping tools 12. Library of reusable code modules

Word processing is familiar to virtually everyone preparing textual documentation. The ability to edit written material easily and print out clean, revised copy is just as important in requirements specification as with any other kind of document preparation. Some editing tools, often called text processors, give additional print formatting capabilities which aid in production of the requirements documentation by automating heading formats, footnotes, and other page printout concerns. When examining automated tools, you should look carefully to make sure that you will not be hindered by awkward text editing capabilities.

Interactive drawing graphics capabilities help prepare the user concept diagrams, data structure diagrams, and any special-purpose diagrams required to support the requirements analysis. General purpose interactive graphics capabilities like MacDraw™ and Freelance™*, provide capabilities which assist creation and maintenance of line drawings. These include:

- Ability to call up special symbols (such as the terminal symbol in user concept diagrams) from a symbol library
- Use of a mouse to conveniently point to the location where a symbol should be located
- Ability to expand, contract, and move symbols
- Quick drawing of arrows and other straight lines or straight line segments
- User-specified fonts (type styles) of various sizes, with typing placed in mouse-indicated locations
- Capability for the user to move whole sections of a diagram to make room for additions
- Storage of the diagram on hard disk or floppy disk for later modification or printout.

In essence, drawing packages are to line drawings as word processors are to textual documents. They allow analysts to make good-looking, maintainable drawings on their own. Such drawings do, however, take time to assemble, even with the finest drawing packages. Drawing difficulty increases rapidly after about ten symbols are placed on a page; hence a hierarchical approach to user concept diagrams can greatly aid drawing and maintaining these diagrams. It is often helpful to save systems analyst time by using support staff to create the drawings.

A *publication system* aids in composition of documents having both text and pictures. For example, a page might start with a paragraph of text, then have a half-page diagram, and end with another paragraph of text. The publication system allows the user to make these composition decisions, preview the results in softcopy at his workstation, and print out document sections in a high-quality (usually laser printer) output. Examples of such a system are PageMaker™ and

---

*MacDraw is a trademark of Apple Computer. Freelance is a trademark of Lotus Development Corporation.

Ventura Publisher Edition™*. If the requirements are maintained using a more specialized systems analysis tool, the analyst must insure that there is a convenient way to meld text, tables, and diagrams in the necessary hardcopy documentation.

A *library of standard textual functional requirements* can aid productivity by taking advantage of previous thought on the same topic. For example, a crisp description of ad hoc query requirements is difficult to write. However, once an acceptable ad hoc query requirement is worked out for one application, it is likely to be usable for others with minor modification. Ideally, such a library should be maintained in the same environment as the requirements word processor. The analyst could use a menu-driven system to browse for a requirement of interest, take the version which is most appropriate, insert it into his word processing file of verifiable functional requirements, and then edit it as necessary to meet the current need. It may be necessary to build up the library using installation-specific conventions for functional requirements. But the time-saving possibilities of such a library are considerable. Lawyers do not reinvent standard paragraphs for each client; likewise, systems analysts should be able to reuse standard requirements statements.

Automated consistency checking is performed by analyzing a data base of requirements to determine if consistency rules are satisfied. Examples of consistency checking processes include:

- Hierarchical diagram checker which ensures that data flows and external entities on detailed user concept diagrams are consistent with the corresponding flows and entities on the next higher-level diagrams.
- Data base description checker which ensures that each record on a data structure diagram has a data dictionary entry.
- Function-data cross checker which ensures that all data store and data flow terms on user concept diagrams are properly related to terms used in the data base description.

Such consistency checking is a major emphasis of research activity in the 1980s concerning automated support of systems analysis.

Automatic data structuring aids both top-down and bottom-up data modeling. For top-down modeling, the need is for automated assistance in drawing a data structure diagram which is in canonical form and has all lines drawn clearly. The computer should act as an expert graphics artist in determining box and line layout of the diagram, so that the data analyst need only be concerned with identification of the data aggregates, record types, and one-to-many relationships. For bottom-up modeling, the need is to automate normal form processing. Given data items and functional dependencies, the software can automatically generate third normal form or Boyce-Codd normal form record types. The analyst can then

---

*PageMaker is a trademark of Aldus Corporation. Ventura Publisher Edition is a trademark of Xerox Corporation.

modify the results by picking different keys from alternate candidate keys, naming the record types, and making changes which may cause some departure from normal form.

Configuration management of requirements refers to the process of maintaining an agreed-upon requirements baseline. Particularly when the user requirements document has been circulated, users build up an expectation of what functions the system will perform. If these expectations are modified because someone requests a change, there should be agreement by the sponsor, user representatives, and developer on the changes. Confusion can also come from loss of records concerning why a change was made. When that happens, someone may request the original requirement again, only to rediscover later what was wrong with it. To bring order into the change process, requirements can be marked with date, requester, and rationale. Such information is easiest to track if the requirements are in an automated data base to start with.

On-line coordination of requirements aids the process of keeping all analysts on a project informed about the status of the analysis. If Harry can interactively browse Jane's current user concept diagrams, he may be able to avoid horizontal redundancy. Likewise, Jane may want to use data records and items defined by Fred. If the functional and data models are both kept on-line, then the latest versions can be available to everyone. The alternative is to use paper copies which may quickly become obsolete. In on-line coordination, it is important for analysts to be able to browse, but not change, the material generated by other analysts. Setting up and maintaining on-line coordination often requires the services of a project librarian.

Analysis methodology enforcement comes from restrictions imposed by the characteristics of the automated tool or by the way the tool is administered locally. For example, a tool which supports only DeMarco's style of data flow diagrams (Exhibit 6-19) may be limited to four symbols (function bubbles, data flow curved arrows, data store markers, and external entity boxes). In that case, restrictions are enforced by the tool's limitations. A more general diagramming tool which supports the icons of user concept diagrams can be administered locally to restrict to a particular set of external-entity symbols. Analysis methodology enforcement is a two-edged sword. Enforcing methodology conventions by restrictions in the automated support can help standardize the approach taken by an entire group of analysts. However, if the methodology supported is not a close match for the methodology desired, the enforcement capabilities may impose undesirable restrictions in methodology.

Assistance for Transition to Design and Development

Many tools which can be used in systems analysis have important benefits in easing the transition from requirements definition to application design and development. These tools recognize that requirements specifications are not an end in themselves, but serve to support implementation of a software system.

As shown in Exhibit 16-1, the types of tools which assist transition from definition to design and development are:

- Automated links to the design process
- Prototyping tools
- Library of reusable code modules.

These kinds of tools reflect the three kinds of software development cycles discussed in Chapter 2.

Automated links to the design process are most useful when the requirements analysis and design are performed by the same group. They make the two processes flow as one unified process with the same family of tools and application data base. Examples of support requirements of this type include:

- Full decomposition of data flows from high-level data flow diagrams generated in requirements analysis to a level showing the modules in the software design.
- Data navigation diagram preparation using the functional and data models from the requirements compilation.
- Structured English preparation by tools (like ActionDiagrammer™*) creating detailed program logic consistent with the data dictionary and user concept diagrams.
- Screen display and report description with checks for consistency with the application's data dictionary.
- Creation of program structure charts using the requirements functions as a starting point for program modules.
- Initialization of a physical data base design (schema-level definition) from the conceptual data model.

The first four capabilities cover subjects where the dividing line between requirements and design is fuzzy. Linking design to the requirements can be particularly helpful if the requirements functional breakout can be used as a program module breakout. This is not always the case. For example, the developer may choose a DBMS environment that is best used with a different breakout of modules from the ones chosen by users to describe their view of the system.

Prototyping tools can be used for the risk assessment part of requirements analysis, as described in Chapter 13, and also to support design and development. A prototyping tool which can gradually expand in detail until the application is useful operationally will blur the distinctions among definition, design, and development. ADS/Online™** is an example of a product designed to speed application development using a prototyping approach.

---

*ActionDiagrammer is a trademark of KnowledgeWare, Inc.
**ADS/Online is a trademark of Cullinet Software.

Libraries of reusable code modules have shown promise of reducing development costs at large software installations. Efforts to date have been largely installation specific, and do not use commercial products other than general code library tools like PanValet™*. To make the idea work effectively, however, there must be a way to identify which parts of an emerging requirements specification can be handled by existing software modules. An automated tool which assisted location of these matches and then helped modify the requirements specification to be consistent with the existing software modules could maximize the effectiveness of reusable code libraries. Ruben Prieto-Diaz and Peter Freeman describe current research into existing software cataloging and locating methods (1). The Ada™** programming language with public "specification" built into the code modules may provide the right programming environment to allow the code library/requirements matchup to be automated.

TYPES OF AUTOMATED TOOLS

Automated tools supporting systems analysis can be placed in three general classes:

- General purpose software
- Computer-aided software engineering (CASE) packages
- Application development environments.

A gradual blending of the second and third types is occurring over time with extensive product developments. As shown in Exhibit 16-2, the CASE packages start from the need to support the front-end requirements and design engineering. As these packages mature, they are gradually adding executable code and data base schema generation capabilities that assist software development and other downstream activities on the software development cycle. Software development environments, on the other hand, started with the need to develop applications efficiently in a development environment closely tied to the final operational environment. New developments for these tools are pushing them backwards in the software development cycle toward the front-end requirements analysis and design efforts.

General Purpose Software Tools

Four types of general purpose software tools are of interest to systems analysts:

---

*PanValet is a trademark of Pansophic.
**Ada is a trademark of the Department of Defense.

EXHIBIT 16-2.   Automated Tools Perspectives

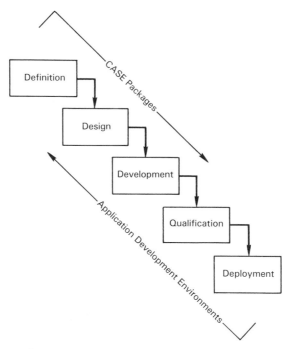

- Word (or text) processor
- Interactive drawing graphics package
- Publication system
- Data base management system.

The first three correspond to the first three requirements in Exhibit 16-1. Their usage was explained in the previous discussion.

A data base management system can be used to produce a custom data base of requirements for a particular application. Such a data base can be used to perform consistency checks, to assist configuration management of requirements changes, and to help coordinate requirements within a group of people (re-quirements 5, 7, and 8 in Exhibit 16-1). Usually it is more cost effective to employ a specialized requirements data base tool like the Problem Statement Analyzer (PSA) developed at the University of Michigan than a general purpose DBMS. Such tools have the benefit of extensive research analyzing and implementing capabilities which serve requirements analysis efforts. But special needs not well served by the existing requirements data base tools can always be met by building a new requirements data base using a general purpose DBMS.

Computer-Aided Software Engineering Tools

Computer-aided software engineering (CASE) packages integrate a large number of analysis-assisting features together. The result is a single system or family of tools which satisfy most of the requirements in Exhibit 16-1. Not only can the individual tools help the analysts, but also the integration of tools around an integrated data base helps perform consistency checks and lets the analysts avoid repeated requirements reformatting.

Exhibit 16-3 is a sketch showing the components of a generic CASE system. The integrated data base consists of textual requirements and design information and graphic application diagrams. For example, a functional hierarchy, related verifiable functional requirements, and data flows are stored in the requirements information. The layout of all the symbols on the corresponding user concept diagrams is stored in the application diagrams part of the data base.

A functional modeling capability (labeled "1" in Exhibit 16-5) supports input and maintenance of user concept diagrams, descriptive text, verifiable functional requirements, and performance requirements. Generally a link with application design is provided, including an ability to maintain program structure charts,* Structured English logic for modules, and cross-references between required functions and program modules. The functional modeling capability may include checking of user inputs to determine if they comply with consistency rules.

A data modeling capability (2) permits analyst input and maintenance of data structure diagram, data dictionary, and data flow analysis information. In addition, a bottom-up data normalization tool is often provided.

An analysis and report capability (3) provides a selection of formatted outputs which aid the systems analysts. In addition, it produces all or most of the requirements specifications and design specifications, according to document formatting instructions given to the system by a system administrator.

A screen/report layouts capability (4) assists design of outputs of the system. This is usually a static view, but some tools allow for dynamic screen characteristics to be displayed using test data.

System administration capabilities (5) provide all the housecleaning support necessary to operate the CASE system for an analysis. This includes setting requirements input and change permissions so that only the appropriate individuals make changes. In addition, the system administrator sets the document formats and keeps proper track of requirements versions.

Exhibit 16-4 shows how the CASE software appears to the systems analyst user. Diagrams can be manipulated on the user's screen display by making menu choices, pointing with a mouse, and using the keyboard to enter text. Diagram components are saved in the underlying application data base. While diagrams and text are being added, the user may browse through other diagrams and text to check for function redundancy, horizontal overlap, and vertical overlap. Some checks which can be automated are performed upon data input; others must wait

---

*Program structure charts graphically identify program modules and show which modules are called by other modules. Often parameters which are passes in these calls are indicated also. David King offers a good description of program structure charts (2).

EXHIBIT 16-3. Generic Model of a Computer-Aided Software Engineering Environment

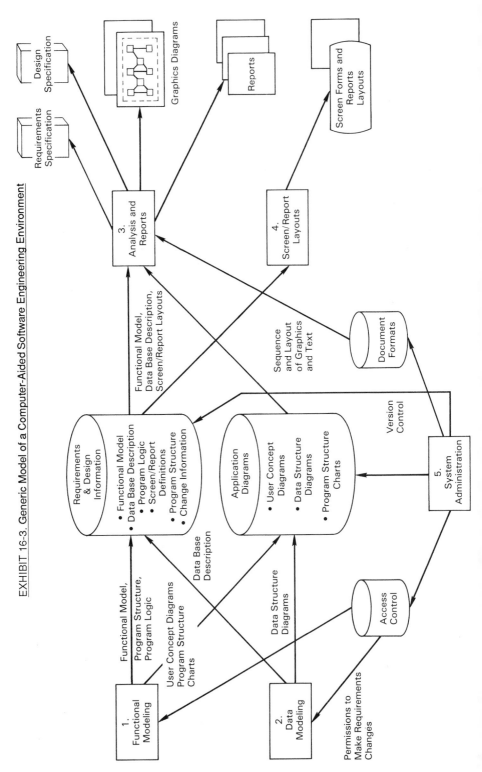

EXHIBIT 16-4.   CASE Packages Feature Interactive Manipulation of Systems Analysis Diagrams

Courtesy Index Technology Corp.

until the user submits the diagram to a comprehensive consistency analysis. Diagrams and text may be printed out and reviewed with users. When complete, entire user requirements and requirements specification documents may be published from the CASE data base.

Appendix A lists CASE systems offered by commercial vendors. These products provide at least some satisfaction for the requirements from Exhibit 16-1, but may not have all the capabilities shown in the generic CASE model (Exhibit 16-3). This is not a complete list, but shows that extensive competition exists in this particular market niche in the late 1980s.

Use of any of these tools requires a considerable initial investment. The software and computer support cost thousands of dollars per workstation, but that may be the cheapest part. Other major costs include:

- Adopting organizational standards for use of the tool
  - View of the software development cycle
  - Structure of documentation products
  - Tailoring of general tool facilities to support organization standards
- Training of analysts in tool usage and organization standards
- Administration of multianalyst CASE data bases
- Extra analyst overhead in working with the CASE environment instead of word processor and interactive graphics.

The benefits of diagramming aids, automated consistency checks, enforced standards, and a data base handoff from requirements to design are real and of considerable value, especially to large projects. However, the costs are also considerable for these CASE environments. Hence, as described at the end of this chapter, a systematic approach should be used for CASE system implementation.

Application Development Environment Tools

Most data base management system vendors provide extensive tools supporting application prototyping and development. These include screen form generators, report writers, conceptual and physical data dictionary assistance, and even test data generators. They argue that these tools enable developers to generate preliminary versions of the application extremely quickly, once user requirements have been compiled.

In essence, the application prototypes, backed by the vendors' 4th generation language (very high-level programming language) tools, become both the detailed design and the code. Because prototypes or early versions can be generated so quickly, users can experiment with executing applications. Based on this experimentation, rapid evolution is possible to obtain design solutions most useful to the people who try out these initial versions. Users tend to get more involved than they would with design documentation, since the early versions are "real."

Users have to be able to review not only the screen displays and reports, but also the overall flow and logic of the application. Such an overview may not be clear from either the user interface or the requirements specification. Hence, the same tools used to develop the prototype should be used to generate design documentation which explains allocation of requirements to modules, menu trees, etc. Such needs are pushing these 4th generation language development environments back toward the design and definition phases (Exhibit 16-2).

Exhibit 16-5 shows a generic model of an application development environment. The application designer, often working in a prototyping manner, gradually builds up all the detail required about the application data (function 1 on

EXHIBIT 16-5.   Generic Model of an Application Development Environment

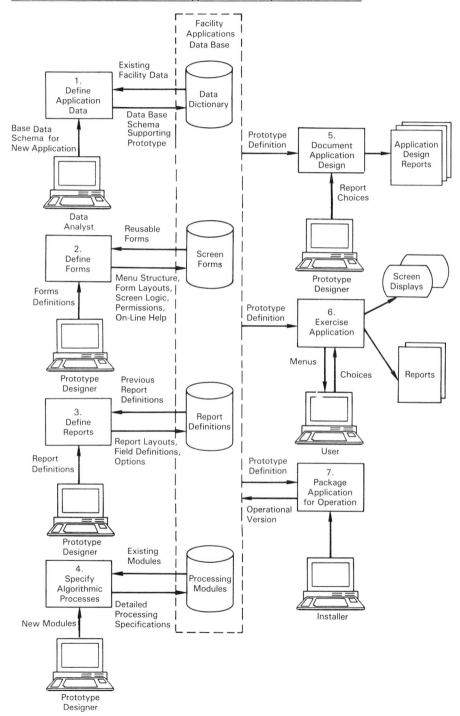

Exhibit 16-5), menus and screen formats (2) reports (3), and algorithmic processes (4) required for the application. For efficiency, for avoidance of duplication, and for consistency with other applications, the designer should be able to retrieve and use existing definitions already used by other applications on the same computer facility.

At any stage of the application development, the designers can call for graphical and tabular reports (5) which document the contents of the application data base, show relationships like set/use matrices, and show prototype response performance characteristics. Some of these reports, like menu structure diagrams and screen format samples, can be used in users' manuals.

A key aspect of the application development environment is the ability to show users various aspects of the application in a prototyping manner (6), in many stages of completion of the application. For example, menu structures and screen formats can be examined first, based on the appearance of static layouts on the target display terminals. After more dynamic aspects of the screens have been defined, test data generated, and some processing modules developed, users can experience how their choices make the application screens react. When the application is complete and satisfactory to users, it can then be installed (7) as an operational application on the facility.

Several aspects of this approach help to collapse design, prototyping, and development into one relatively quick process. These are:

- Construction of a data base which drives the operation of the application
- Ability to demonstrate incomplete versions of the application
- Use of the same application data base for the prototype, evolving application development, and final operational application.

The vendor's data base management system and associated applications development tools remove much of the programming tedium from data input consistency checks, data base accesses, screen display behavior, and report construction. They can even simplify construction of programs which must be written to implement batch and interactive algorithms.

The functions in Exhibit 16-5 work best if a clear, complete, and agreed-upon requirements specification has been generated before prototyping starts. Then the designers can devote themselves to decisions concerning how the application should be implemented. Discussions with prototype screens will usually cause some changes to the user requirements. These should be reflected in the requirements specification as updates.

As the application development environments extend their capabilities toward CASE front-end analysis tools, the hope is that the CASE data base will integrate well with the application development environment data base shown in Exhibit 16-5. Many of the CASE products listed in Appendix A have built bridges between their requirements and design information and various application development environment data base formats.

Some of the more common application development environments are shown in Appendix B. Note that all of these tools are designed for mainframe use. The integration of development and operational capabilities implies an overhead that (in the 1980s) is only reasonable to provide with mainframe support.

Application development environments have been evolving since the late 1970s. Hence, the concept can be considered to be a mature technology in the late 1980s. As suggested by Exhibit 16-2, future advances will be in the direction of support for a greater portion of the software development cycle. In addition, new languages like Ada will need new development environments.

CHOOSING AND IMPLEMENTING
THE RIGHT SET OF AUTOMATED TOOLS

Implementing a helpful automated environment to aid systems analysis has the same difficult problems inherent in any information system application. People have to agree on procedures for using the automation. What aspects of analysis should be automated? Should detailed organization-wide standards be enforced, or should methods and tools be available for project managers to use as they like? Implementation of CASE or application development environments is expensive in software, hardware, customization, management attention, and operational costs. Thus, it is natural to think that a user-centered requirements analysis approach can be helpful in guiding the implementation of these environments.

The alternatives of doing nothing or of falling for a colorful sales demonstration are both likely to be less desirable. Not bringing in any automation may result in forfeiting large productivity gains both from the tools themselves and from the methodologies behind the tools. Likewise, buying a CASE package because the color graphics are beautiful and the system looks state-of-the-art may result in a mismatch between the tools and the organization's real needs.

We can use the reusable code software development cycle (Exhibit 2-3) as an overall model for implementation of analysis tools. The phases are:

- Concept identification
- Definition
- Code reuse assessment
- Development and integration
- Qualification
- Deployment.

The following paragraphs step through the decisions which should be made in each phase.

In concept identification, a sponsor identifies the need for automation and methodology tools to improve systems analysis for a family of applications or for a large specific application. Goals could include:

- Productivity gains: implement in less time with fewer man-hours.
- Quality gains: improve clarity, completeness, and agreement for specifications.
- Management gains: improve predictability concerning cost and schedule of an application development, and establish analysis process uniformity among applications.

The sponsor shows sincere interest by committing analyst resources to investigate the requirements.

In the definition phase, a systems analyst starts by melding the sponsor's concept with views of managers representing users, analysts, and developers. Objectives analysis (Chapter 5) results in a one-sentence purpose, multiple objectives, and features of the anticipated automation assistance. At this level, the decision should be made whether to use general purpose software, CASE, or application development environment tools. In some organizations the answer may be more than one environment, such as word processor and interactive graphics for small applications and a CASE tool for large ones. In making these general decisions Exhibit 16-6 summarizes which approach is best for which situations. Following objectives analysis, the analyst should compile user requirements in discussions with the groups who will be users of the acquired tools. As always, emphasis should be on the functional and data requirements. Since the solution is most likely acquisition of commercial software and hardware, these requirements need not go into great detail. But they should be analyzed before examining any products, so that the vendor demonstrations can point out satisfaction of the users' requirements, not just the product capabilities.

EXHIBIT 16-6.   Ideal Circumstances for Each Type of Automated Tool

Analysis Automation Approach	Most Useful Situations
General Purpose Software	Small- to medium-sized unrelated applications; document handoff required between requirements analysts and developers; implementation through slightly customized commercial software.
CASE Environment	Requirements and design performed by the same set of analysts who work on projects for a variety of target computer environments; definition of very large applications.
Application Development Environment	Large number of individual applications performed for the same mainframe (possibly distributed) facility.

The code reuse assessment phase in this case consists of investigation of commercial products which might be appropriate and deciding upon the required customization. Decisions will have to be made about where to sacrifice requirements to enable convenient use of a good existing tool. For example, the icons in user concept diagrams may have to be sacrificed to use a tool which supports DeMarco's data flow diagrams only (Exhibit 6-19).

When choosing the commercially available automated tools, the following quality factors should be considered:

- Consistency of tool capabilities with the organization's systems analysis methodology.
- Degree of tool satisfaction of the requirements areas in Exhibit 16-1.
- Tool reliability, documentation, and vendor support.
- Ease of use.
- Cost of the software and associated hardware.
- Vendor viability (Is the vendor financially sound and continuing to upgrade the product, so that the tools will be supported for years to come?).

Since these factors take time to assess, they are usually evaluated only for a few of the most promising tools, determined by a filter of gross tool requirements.

A result of code reuse assessment is the decision whether to base all tools on a highly integrated CASE or application development environment product, or whether to adopt a mixture of special purpose tools which will have to be integrated by the analysts.

Development consists of acquisition of the commercial products and customizing them. This is usually the easiest part, but still not trivial. CASE and application development environments are powerful, but complex. They can take days to learn and weeks to understand how the systems analysis group can best use the tools.

In the qualification phase, a test project of moderate size is used to try the acquired tools and associated methodology standards. Care should be taken to obtain productivity and quality data during the test. These results will either show that the automated tool objectives were met or else indicate the reasons they were not met.

If the qualification test shows that the new tools work for the organization, then the deployment phase should make the automated tools generally available. Deployment should include a strong internal selling and training campaign. Training courses tailored to the organization and descriptive user manual materials are required. Also, experts need to be on call to answer questions. Such a fully planned and managed implementation approach is most likely to achieve desired productivity gains for the organization.

DISCUSSION QUESTIONS

1. Integrated CASE tools may be most beneficial on large projects, where the tools help integrate the efforts of many analysts.

   a. Estimate the costs and benefits of a robust CASE tool on two projects:

      - A single-analyst three-month application definition and design project
      - A large application definition and design taking ten analysts eight calendar months.

   b. Do these estimates support the initial hypothesis that CASE benefits are higher with large projects?

2. Some analysts argue that fully integrated CASE systems are inherently weaker in satisfying the tool requirements of Exhibit 16-1 than special packages which each optimize one of these functional needs. For example, an integrated package's text editing capability is likely to be weaker than a dedicated word processor's. Likewise, the CASE package's data flow diagrammer is likely to have weaker interactive diagramming features than is obtained in a general-purpose drawing package. The integrated CASE package may also be more difficult to mesh with the systems analysis group's chosen methodology. Yet the integrated CASE concept clearly has advantages in having an integrated data base of nonredundant requirements and design information.

   a. Which approach do you think is better, a highly integrated CASE tool or many specialized systems analysis tools?

   b. How could you set up a test case to prove or disprove the hypothesis that an integrated CASE package works better for your analysis team than separate specialized tools?

REFERENCES

1. Ruben Prieto-Diaz and Peter Freeman, "Classifying Software for Reusability," *IEEE Software*, IEEE Computer Society, January 1987.

2. David King, *Current Practices in Software Development*, New York: Yourdon Press, 1984.

17

Requirements Documentation

Clarity is one of the three major goals of the requirements specification. Previous chapters showed how the analysts and the users can clearly view the individual requirements areas: objectives, functions, data, and performance. This chapter shows how the material can be assembled into an entire document which is easy to read and to use as a reference document. The approach is similar to the *IEEE Guide to Software Requirements Specifications* standard (1).

The outline of the requirements documentation depends on whether the sponsoring organization has a standard format that must be followed. If the analysts have the freedom to choose format, then they should consider a "natural" user-centered outline, as discussed in the first section of this chapter. If they must follow a prescribed format, then a top-down user-centered approach should still be used to compile the necessary material, which is then formatted as required. The second section uses a military standard format as an example to show how this can be done. A third section summarizes general principles for assembling the user requirements and requirements specification documents.

NATURAL USER-CENTERED
REQUIREMENTS DOCUMENTATION

Exhibit 17-1 shows a logical table of contents outline for a requirements specification. It has the same top-down flow of thought as the user-centered analysis process behind the requirements. Exhibit 17-2 shows how the outline appears for the specific example of the Ace Aerospace financial system. Sections 1 to 5 appear first in draft form as the user requirements document. The final requirements specification contains these sections as changed by user review, and two additional sections. Sections 6 and 7 give the design and development constraints which result from risk assessment and implementation planning (Chapter 15). The following paragraphs quickly trace the contents of each section.

The Foreword gives a short description of the purpose of the document, including how it fits into the application's development cycle. Exhibit 17-3 shows how the Foreword would change between the User Requirements draft and final Requirements Specification for the Ace Aerospace Contract Tracking System.

Although not shown in Exhibits 17-1 and 17-2, an Executive Summary section or cover letter is often included. This gives a two-page description of the importance of the system, what it will do for the organization, how the implementation project is scheduled to proceed, and status of major project issues.

Section 1, General Description, gives an overview of the application requirements without going into details. A reader who wants to know the nature of the application should be able to get a quick understanding by reading the five to ten pages in this section.

Application Characteristics, section 1.1, lists the purpose, objectives, and features of the application. These were compiled in the Objectives Analysis at the start of the analysis, and should have been kept current through changes introduced by the functional and data analyses. Exhibit 5-4 shows this short-form software description.

Special terms identified at the start of analysis should be defined in section 1.2, Definitions and Acronyms. All acronyms used in the document should be spelled out here. This section should define any term used in the document which has a special meaning different from ordinary English usage. As mentioned in Chapter 5, particular attention should be given to terms, like "contract line item" in the Ace Aerospace example, which are vital to understand the application. The reasons for the definitions to be up front rather than in an appendix are to make sure that the reader:

- Knows that the list of special terms exists and where to find it.
- Glances through the definitions to have them in mind when starting to read through the functional requirements.

This is a professional touch that readers appreciate.

Intended Users, section 1.3, describes the direct users of the system. Characteristics of these users will be taken into account by the screen display designers when they design the appearance and logic of the interactive sessions.

References, section 1.4, should contain both the documents explicitly referenced in the requirements specification and related documents which may help the reader. For example, if the application charter emerged from a strategic

EXHIBIT 17-1. Natural User-Centered Requirements Specification Outline

Foreword

Table of Contents

List of Exhibits

1. General Description

    1.1 Application Characterization
        1.1.1 Purpose
        1.1.2 Objectives
        1.1.3 Features
    1.2 Definitions and Acronyms
    1.3 Intended Users
    1.4 References
    1.5 Overview

2. Functional Description

    2.1 (First functional area)
        •
        •
        •
    2.n (Nth functional area)

3. Data Base Description

    3.1 Data Structure Diagram
    3.2 Data Dictionary
        3.2.1 (First data aggregate)
          •
          •
          •
        3.2.n (Nth data aggregate)

4. Performance

    4.1 Number of Users
    4.2 Data Base Size
    4.3 Workload and Throughput
    4.4 Interactive Response Times

5. Application Outputs

    5.1 (First output type)
        •
        •
        •
    5.n (Nth output type)

6. Design Constraints
    6.1 Hardware Environment
    6.2 Software Environment
    6.3 Implementation Standards
    6.4 Maintenance Policy

7. Implementation Phasing

Appendices

EXHIBIT 17-2. Requirements Specification Outline for the Ace Aerospace Example

Foreword

Table of Contents

List of Exhibits

1. General Description

    1.1 Contract Management System Characterization
        1.1.1 Purpose
        1.1.2 Objectives
        1.1.3 Features
    1.2 Definitions and Acronyms
    1.3 Intended Users
    1.4 References
    1.5 Overview

2. Functional Description

    2.1 Manage Contract Data
    2.2 Generate Standard Reports
    2.3 Support Ad Hoc Query
    2.4 Provide Management Analyses
    2.5 Generate Briefing Charts
    2.6 Display Briefing Charts

3. Data Base Description

    3.1 Data Structure Diagram
    3.2 Data Dictionary
        3.2.1 Contract Structure Data
        3.2.2 Modification Data
        3.2.3 Corporate Rates Data
        3.2.4 Cost Element Data
        3.2.5 Transaction Log
        3.2.6 Access Control File

4. Performance

    4.1 Number of Users
    4.2 Data Base Size
    4.3 Workload and Throughput
    4.4 Interactive Response Times

5. Application Outputs

    5.1 Department Business Summary Report
    5.2 Department Profitability Projection Chart
    5.3 Contract Summary Report
    5.4 Contract Status Chart

6. Design Constraints

    6.1 Hardware Environment
    6.2 Software Environment
    6.3 Implementation Standards
    6.4 Maintenance Policy

7. Implementation Phasing

    7.1 Phase 1: Project Financial Status
    7.2 Phase 2: Briefing Support

Appendix A. Corporate Contract Accounting Standards

Appendix B. Sample Briefing Chart Menu Structure

EXHIBIT 17-3.   Foreword for the Ace Aerospace Example

(A) User Requirements Document Foreword

> This document specifies user requirements for a new Ace
> Aerospace Contract Tracking System (CTS), designed to help
> the Capital Region Division manager and his program managers
> to keep closer track of the financial progress of each
> contract. This draft is being circulated to determine if
> the view of CTS automation needs presented herein supports
> the Capital Region's business objectives. Comments received
> by February 15, 1988 will be factored into an expanded
> version of this document which will be the requirements
> specification used to develop the CTS software.

(B) Requirements Specification Foreword

> This document specifies the requirements for a new Ace
> Aerospace Capital Region Divison Contract Tracking System
> (CTS), designed to help the Capital Region Division's
> manager and his program managers to keep closer track of the
> financial progress of each contract. It includes both user
> requirements and design constraints, plus a description of
> the two-phased development approach chosen for CTS. This
> document will be used by the competitively selected software
> developer as the contractually binding specifications for
> his efforts.

planning exercise, then the documentation of that plan should be referenced. The list should be numbered in a way that allows simple referencing in the text to the document number.

The Overview, section 1.5, is a short introduction to the application functions and data aggregates. The application context diagram, a list of top-level functions, and a list of data aggregates should be given here to show the reader the major conceptual divisions of the application.

Section 2, Functional Description, is the heart of the user requirements. It is here that you present the user concept diagrams, plus the verifiable functional requirements. As discussed in Chapter 8, the narrative descriptions and numbered requirements must be explicitly tied in with the functions in the user concept diagrams through a common numbering system. It is amazing how many requirements specifications miss this simple and useful idea; often the system diagrams are relegated to the back of the book in an appendix. Even when you find the diagrams, you cannot tell how they shed any light on the functional requirements.

The functional description section should start with a legend of user concept diagram symbols and an explanation of how the user concept diagrams, descriptions of individual functions, and functional requirements are organized. Experience has shown that this explanation must be given with examples from this application or business area, in order for the user representatives to grasp it quickly.

The Data Base Description, section 3, gets a separate major section directly after the functional description. This is the closest the documentation can get to reflecting the parallel nature of the functional and data base descriptions.

For relatively simple data bases which can be represented by a single data structure diagram, section 3 should be divided into two subsections. Section 3.1 discusses the Data Structure Diagram, and section 3.2 presents the Data Dictionary. A textual description accompanies the data structure diagram. It explains data base terms like "records," "items," "occurrences," and "relationships," as well as the symbols used in the diagram. Then it explains the overall philosophy behind the data model for this application. The Data Dictionary section starts with a brief explanation of the tabular format. It should have a page for each conceptual record type, as in Exhibits 12-1 and 12-2. Separate pages for each record type enhance maintainability of the requirements specifications. Ordinarily, tables of allowable values, like Exhibit 12-3, are included as part of section 3. Long allowable values tables (more than five pages) can be made an appendix or can be included by reference to another document.

For more complex data bases, it is better to divide up section 3 by data aggregate. The start of section 3 discusses the data base description methodology. Then section 3.1 discusses the first data aggregate, including the aggregate's data structure diagram, data dictionary, and allowable values. Sections 3.n discuss each of the other aggregates.

Performance, section 4, concentrates on data sizing and throughput needs. Section 4.1 tells the Number of Users expected of each user type. Section 4.2 indicates the Data Base Size, including estimated growth rate of the data base. Section 4.3 explains the Workload and Throughput requirements for each of the functions from section 2 (see Chapter 14). Interactive Response Time figures may be placed in section 4.4. At the time of the user requirements document, many performance requirements may be marked TBD (To Be Determined) or otherwise indicated to be preliminary performance goals. Following risk assessment and implementation planning, the TBDs will be replaced by firm numbers based on benchmarking which shows what response is reasonably achievable and worthwhile.

Application Outputs, section 5, contains detailed definitions of critical application reports, plots, and displays, as described in Chapter 9. This section describes only the outputs whose detailed definitions are real user requirements. When the general content of the report is all the users care about, and details can be left until the design process, the general content is described in the verifiable functional requirements and the report is omitted from section 5.

The proper location of detailed output definitions in the requirements specification is an arguable point. They could be given with the verifiable functional requirements in section 2 or they could be considered details best left to an appendix. The author has found the best solution is to place definitions of reports (and other outputs) as the last section of the user requirements document for these reasons:

- Detailed descriptions of reports are usually tied to samples of the reports, not to the user concept diagrams.

- Key system outputs are more than just details for bookkeeping; they are critical application requirements which may drive the software design.
- Report descriptions tend to be the most detailed material in the user requirements document.

These principles suggest that you separate output definitions from the rest of the functional requirements, keep these definitions in the main body of the document, but present them at the end of the user requirements.

Sections 6 and 7 (Design Constraints and Implementation Phasing) are added to the user requirements document to form the requirements specification. They result from the risk assessment and implementation planning analyses. Both discuss general aspects of how the implementation will be designed, not just what the software must accomplish.

Sections 6.1 and 6.2, Hardware Environment and Software Environment, pin down parts of the hardware and system software environments which must be used in the application. For example, it might be advantageous to host the new application on the company's IBM 3033 computer which has related interfacing applications using IBM's Information Management System (IMS). If risk assessment showed that the 3033 has sufficient excess capacity, then the IBM 3033/IMS solution may be the only environment which makes sense. Similarly, a corporate standard for COMPAQ personal computers may make it sensible to specify COMPAQ intelligent workstations in section 6.1. Detailed specification of the environment should be resisted when it is worthwhile giving the designers freedom to examine various hardware and software environment options. On the other hand, if the software is to be developed in a fixed price contract, then the developer will usually insist on having all the environmental constraints spelled out. Even with in-house development, it is best to be explicit on the environment by the time software development starts, in order to avoid misunderstandings.

Implementation Standards concerning documentation, reviews, structured programming, user screen display formats, configuration control, testing, user training, and so on are examined in section 6.3. The development team needs to know the development policies they must adhere to, before giving cost estimates or starting on the work.

The Maintenance Policy (section 6.4) is critical to life-cycle cost. Time after time we see applications implemented without regard to software maintenance, followed by hand-wringing over maintenance costs and over the growing application backlog. The addition of comparatively small initial costs (in version control libraries, menu maintenance tools, capturing regression test sets, and so on) can reduce future maintenance costs considerably. Having a section for the maintenance concept in the requirements specification forces people to think about these critical issues before development of the system.

Section 7 describes Implementation Phasing of the application. If the software is developed in more than one block (version), then this section needs to describe which requirements will be met in which block. In straightforward cases, you can give a table showing which verifiable functional requirements are met in which block. For more complex situations where an initial block may implement transient requirements to be replaced in another block, you may need to use one or more appendices. These give the specific verifiable functional requirements to be satisfied by early blocks. Or you may treat the entire requirements specification as a Block 1 definition and mention in section 7 what kinds of future enhancements are likely. Implementation Phasing may also indicate how the application will be tested, how data bases will be initialized, how users will be trained and start operating the application, and what old system/new system parallel operations are expected in an initial shakedown period.

Appendices should give detailed supporting material which would be too detailed or too specialized to fit conveniently in the main document. Appendices are often bound in one or more physically separate volumes. Examples of material for appendices are the following:

- Derivation of a mathematical algorithm to be used by the application.
- Cross-reference matrix showing how the requirements in this document relate to requirements from an earlier analysis or preceding application.
- Non-binding samples of menus or screen displays, showing the kind of interface expected by the users.
- Verifiable functional requirements for multiple implementation phases.
- Lengthy tables of allowable values.

Each appendix should clearly indicate whether it is included to supply non-binding background information or whether it contains verifiable requirements for the application.

Appendices should not be short and should not contain material the reader must know to be able to follow the requirements specification. A short appendix tends to get lost in the reader's scanning of the document. A few pages which are important enough to include in the requirements specification can always be added in the most relevant section in the body of the document. Likewise, if the appendix contains material that is vital for understanding of the application, either the entire appendix or a short summary of it should be included in the relevant section (e.g., Definitions or Functional Description) of the main document.

Now look again at the "natural" table of contents outline in Exhibit 17-1. All the information assembled in the steps described in Chapters 5 through 15 fit into this format. Since the material is presented in the same order that it was developed, a reader approaching this application for the first time will go through the same natural top-down thought process that the analyst and users went through.

WORKING WITH A PRESCRIBED FORMAT:
DOD-STD-7935 EXAMPLE

When the sponsor prescribes a particular requirements specification format, it is no longer permissible to use the "natural" outline previously described. In this case, the material should still be assembled in the top-down manner illustrated by Exhibit 4-2, rather than in the order the sections appear in the final document.

As an example of how to document application requirements using the sponsor's standards, this section has selected a common Department of Defense standard. DoD-STD-7935, *Automated Data Processing Systems Documentation*, describes a set of documentation for software applications supporting management activities (2). The functional description (FD) document is the requirements document in this standard. This is a useful example, because the United States armed services are the largest sponsors of management information systems in the world, and because the standard is public.

According to DoD-STD-7935, the functional description table of contents should appear as in Exhibit 17-4. Sections 1 through 3 contain user requirements, and are intended to be compiled by or with the users involved. Sections 4 and 5 contain design material generated by the in-house ADP shop or by a software development contractor after analysis of the implications of the user requirements. Cost estimates and implementation planning material come last in sections 6 and 7. For simple applications, code is implemented directly from the functional description design material. For more complex applications, one or two levels of design documentation are generated beyond the functional description.

The DoD-STD-7935 functional description is difficult to produce and difficult to use in managing the application implementation, because it is really three documents in one:

- User requirements document
- Computer program implementation plan (including cost-benefit analysis)
- Preliminary design document.

Keeping this material up to date as a single document is a challenge. Are the user requirements in sections 1 through 3 still valid after extensive design changes make the FD design material in sections 4 and 5 obsolete? How are programmatic changes introduced into the document's sections 6 and 7? Melding the requirements and design material works best on small projects (see Discussion Question 3 from Chapter 2).

The top-down analysis approach of Exhibit 4-2 can be used to generate a DoD-STD-7935 functional description document by following these steps:

1. Generate most of the user requirements document (FD sections 1 through 3) using the correspondence with the natural requirements specification as shown in Exhibit 17-4.

2. Complete FD sections 1 through 3 by adding the required material on background, existing methods, benefits, and assumptions. This material is usually brief, but may be expanded if you had to make a thorough analysis of the existing procedures during objectives analysis (Chapter 5).

3. Circulate FD sections 1 through 3 for review as a user requirements document, but title it "Preliminary Draft Functional Description."

EXHIBIT 17-4. DoD-STD-7935 Functional Description Table of Contents

FD Section	Corresponding Section in the "Natural" Outline (Exhibit 17-1)
1. General	
1.1 Purpose of the Functional Description	Foreword
1.2 Project References	1.3 References
1.3 Terms and Abbreviations	1.2 Definitions and Acronyms
2. System Summary	
2.1 Background	1.1 Application Characterization
2.2 Objectives	
2.3 Existing Methods and Procedures	
2.4 Proposed Methods and Procedures	1.4 Overview
2.4.1 Summary of Improvements	1.1.3 Features
2.4.2 Summary of Impacts	[Shown partially in user concept diagrams]
2.4.2.1 User Organization Impacts	
2.4.2.2 User Operational Impacts	
2.4.2.3 User Development Impact	
2.5 Assumptions and Constraints	
3. Detailed Characteristics	
3.1 Specific Performance Requirements	(Embedded in verifiable functional requirements)
3.1.1 Accuracy and Validity	
3.1.2 Timing	4.3 Workload and Throughput 4.4 Interactive Response Times
3.2 Functional Area System Functions	2. Functional Description
3.3 Inputs-Outputs	2. Functional Description 5. Application Outputs
3.4 Data Base Characteristics	3.2 Data Dictionary, 4.1 Data Base Size

FD Section	Corresponding Section in the "Natural" Outline (Exhibit 17-1)
4. Design Details	
4.1 System Description	
4.2 System Functions	
4.2.1 Accuracy and Validity	
4.2.2 Timing	
4.3 Flexibility	
4.4 System Data	
4.4.1 Inputs	
4.4.2 Outputs	
4.4.3 Data Base	
5. Environment	
5.1 Equipment Environment	6.1 Hardware Environment
5.2 Support Software	6.2 Software Environment
5.3 Interfaces	
5.4 Summary of Impacts	
5.4.1 ADP Organization Impacts	
5.4.2 ADP Operational Impacts	
5.4.3 ADP Development Impacts	
5.5 Failure Contingencies	(Discussed in section 2, Functional Description)
5.6 Security	
5.7 Assumptions and Constraints	
6. Cost Factors	
7. System Development Plan	6.3 Implementation Standards 7. Implementation Phasing (partial discussions)

4. Perform risk assessments, design trades, and implementation planning as discussed in Chapter 15.

If the application is simple:

5a. The developer should carry a chosen design to a level suitable for implementation.

6a. The developer should fill out sections 4-7 of the FD as instructed in DoD-STD-7935. This material takes the place of design documentation.

If the application is complex:

5b. Try to convince the DoD program manager that it is in his interest to treat FD section 4 as "not applicable." Likewise, section 6, Cost Factors, should be skipped unless it is being used as a device to obtain an informal implementation work estimate from the in-house ADP shop. Material in these sections will be better covered in a separate proposal from the developer and in the developer's design documentation.

6b. Complete sections 5.1 and 5.2 (Equipment Environment and Support Software) and section 7 (System Development Plan) using the information gathered in implementation assessment. Fill out remaining subsections of FD section 5 as applicable.

SUMMARY OF PRINCIPLES
FOR REQUIREMENTS DOCUMENTATION

Whether the analysts can select a documentation format or have to deal with a prescribed standard, the following constant principles apply to the requirements documentation:

- Be open to special needs of particular applications.
- Get early agreements with the sponsor.
  - Point out standard sections which are not applicable to this application.
  - Understand implications of prescribed sections.
  - Make sure sponsor and analyst have the same understanding of the contents of each section (requires an annotated outline explaining each section).
- Conduct the systems analysis using the top-down user-centered requirements analysis approach.
- Fit results into the chosen format, with as much readability as possible.
- Split off the user requirements document as a separate draft from the requirements specification. (Distinguish the "what" from the "how" in the review process.)
- Include a sign-off page in the front of the requirements specification to ensure formal agreement.

Use of these principles can help to avoid messy battles with the sponsor and awkward floundering when trying to design documents while analysts are writing up their results. The resulting clear, complete, agreed-upon requirements specification serves as a reference for sponsors, users, and developers.

DISCUSSION QUESTIONS

1. In the DoD-STD-7935 functional description format (Exhibit 17-4), the only place that the user concept diagrams and verifiable functional requirements can be included is FD Section 3.2, Functional Area System Functions.
   a. How can the numbering principles described in Chapter 8 of this text be used to tie the verifiable functional requirements and FD sections to the functions in the user concept diagrams?
   b. Sketch out how FD section 3.2.1 would look in the Ace Aerospace Contract Tracking System example (Refer to Exhibit 8-2.)

2. One of the weaknesses of many existing standards for requirements specifications is that there is no place for the conceptual data base description. For example, in the DoD-STD-7935 FD format, section 3.4 (Data Base Characteristics) calls only for a list of data items. Section 4.4.3 (Data Base) also is inappropriate, because all of section 4 should be written by the *developer* in response to the user requirements of sections 1 through 3. The record type interrelationships and data item functional dependencies are user decisions which should be defined in the user requirements. Where should the data structure diagram and related discussion be placed in the DoD-STD-7935 functional description document?

REFERENCES

1. "IEEE Guide to Software Requirements Specifications," ANSI/IEEE Std 830-1984, Institute of Electrical and Electronics Engineers, Inc., 1984.
2. "Department of Defense Standard 7935: Automated Data Processing System Documentation," Department of Defense, 1983.

18

Project Planning

The requirements specification provides the detailed application definition which permits the developer to estimate calendar time and resources needed to implement the computer application. But how can the effort required to develop the requirements specification itself be estimated? This is a question several people asked the author after reading initial drafts of this book. Even experienced analysts have a difficult time with this question.

APPROACH TO PROJECT PLANNING

So many major surprises can impact the definition phase efforts that the process hardly ever is executed precisely as planned. The application may turn out to be much more (or less) complex than anticipated from the application charter. Key user representatives may not be available for major review steps. Risk assessment may point out the need for a special study before completing the requirements specification. Even the business need may change, so that the application's objectives need to be modified.

The lead requirements analyst should establish a project plan with expected time and resource requirements for each small step of the definition phase. Everyone involved should recognize that this plan is subject to the realities of the evolving situation for this project. But the detailed baseline schedule, when reviewed carefully with the sponsor and user representatives, gives the individuals involved a good understanding of the requirements generation process and where it stands at the moment.

Because it is critical for success of the analysis that user participation be carefully managed, the best way to construct a project plan is to use mini milestones of particular analyst-user interactions. The technical work to be performed by the analysts can be estimated by considering the work required to prepare and execute each user interview, walkthrough, or formal review.

USER PARTICIPATION MILESTONES

Objectives for the analysts' meetings with the sponsor, user representatives, and developer include:

- Obtain necessary detail on user requirements.
- Have sponsor and users understand and critique the evolving requirements.
- Make intellectual progress with each meeting.
- Obtain formal approval for the requirements specification.
- Minimize the time these busy people have to spend working the application definition.

There should be an aura of excitement, accomplishment, and fun about the project, and not the feeling of long hours of drudgery on small details.

Exhibit 18-1 shows a generic model of 13 main review step mini milestones which should accompany the analysis steps shown in Exhibit 4-7. These meetings are usually less formal discussions than the formal design reviews required in development.

Different reviewers look for different things. The sponsor is concerned with the overall concept, costs, schedules, and degree of user cooperation and satisfaction with the evolving requirements. The users fight for a set of application capabilities which will make their jobs easier, less tedious, and more productive. If the application will be developed by the in-house programming staff or by an already chosen software development organization, then a representative of that staff should be involved in reviews concerning implementation feasibility. Otherwise, someone knowledgeable about software development and distinct from the systems analysis team should give an independent assessment of development issues.

The first review step occurs after analysts examine the sponsor's application charter and perform objectives analysis. In this review analysts describe their understanding of the scope and objectives of the application. The sponsor must hear this understanding to ensure that it is consistent with his intentions. He also should give rough constraints on costs and schedule.

EXHIBIT 18-1.   Key Reviews with Sponsor and Users

Analysis Step		Review Step			
		Reviewers			Material Reviewed and Discussed
Chapter	Step	Sponsor	Users	Developer	
5 Application Concept		X			1. Results of objectives analysis
		X	X		2. Objectives, requirements approach
6 User Concept Diagrams			X		3. Initial diagrams
11 Data Structure Diagrams			X		4. Second cut at diagrams
7,8 Verifiable Functional Requirements 12 Data Dictionary			X		5. Draft functional and data requirements
9 Report Definitions 13 Detailed Data Analysis			X		6. Reports and results of detailed data analysis
14 Performance Requirements			X		7. Initial throughput and response goals
17 User Requirements Document		X	X	X	8. All user requirements
15 Risk Assessments and Implementation Planning		X		X	9. In-progress review of risk assessments
		X	X	X	10. Recommended approaches, costs, and schedule
17 Requirements Specification			X		11. Changes to user requirements and implementation approach
		X	X	X	12. Draft requirements specification
		X		X	13. Signoff of requirements specification

The second review step is a "kickoff meeting" with users which informs them about the general objectives of the application and systems analysis approach. If possible, the sponsor should start the meeting with a discussion of the application and its importance to the organization. Then analysts discuss the application terminology, objectives, and intended users. The systems analysis discussion should outline the project plan and the major techniques which will be used. The analysts should carefully explain why their approach will work well for this application. The audience knows its business, but probably does not know systems analysis. The analysts should clarify how they will interact with users. Some users will need to spend a substantial number of man-hours on the project. Analysts should discuss when and why these hours are needed, and should tailor the plan to reflect concerns and opportunities brought up by the users. The sponsor and other cognizant managers should verify that the necessary user representative time will be available to the project.

The third review step is the first working session with users. It should occur immediately after the general kickoff meeting.

Working meetings discussing requirements options should be held with small groups to make effective progress. The sponsor and user representatives will help determine the proper way to manage small groups. Options are:

- Sponsor appoints a small number of user representatives to work closely with the systems analysts.
- Analysts work with a large number of users in small groups or in one-on-one situations.

Meetings with 30 people in which someone decides to pick apart the syntax of detailed verifiable functional requirements can be an extremely inefficient use of people's time. And busy people will resent any waste of their time.

The subject of the third review step is a first cut at the user concept diagrams and data structure diagram. The analysts' first set of diagrams, possibly including options, is intended solely to focus users on the problem at hand and diagramming style. This step will be successful if user reactions to the first set of diagrams results in extensive markups of these samples.

Based on user interactions in the third review, analysts need to revise the diagrams and add fragments of detail concerning verifiable functional requirements and attributes of data entities. In the fourth review step, analysts review these redrawn diagrams with a small group of users. Again, there will be some substantial changes, but the diagrams tend to stay reasonably stable after making the third cut. More meetings are necessary when the application is large and requires additional levels of user concept diagrams or additional data views.

Following the fourth review, analysts redraw the diagrams to obtain the third set and perform detailed analysis to get a cut at the verifiable functional requirements and data dictionary. This work goes on with informal visits or phone calls to individual users to answer specific questions. It takes some time, particularly in deciding upon wording for the textual requirements and obtaining data item examples.

The fifth review is a lengthy one, since it covers all of the draft verifiable functional requirements and data dictionary. The third set of user concept diagrams and data structure diagram is used to remind participants what part of the application is being discussed. But emphasis is on the detailed material. Users often agree at the diagram level, but then violently disagree on the meaning of a functional activity when discussing the verifiable functional requirements. The fifth review serves to uncover and resolve these detailed issues. Given the amount of discussion which should take place, it may be necessary to break up the fifth review step into two or more sessions. If a review employs four-hour or eight-hour meetings, it should have hourly breaks to help people concentrate.

The sixth review step examines key application outputs and the results of data navigation analysis. Analysts should also report all changes from the fifth review.

The seventh review step is the Delphi sessions with a working group of users to determine initial performance requirements. As discussed in Chapter 14, the user concept diagrams should be used to illustrate functional activities to help user representatives determine throughput requirements. The data structure diagram serves a similar reference function for data base sizing estimates. After this step the requirements analysts have all the material they need to get from users to assemble the user requirements document.

The eighth review step is review of the user requirements document by sponsor, users, and developer. Since the document has significant content and each reviewer should have many comments, analysts should work to collect and resolve comments as follows:

- Give a separate copy of the user requirements document to each reviewer.
- Collect comments in writing from each reviewer.
- Analyze the comments. Prepare lists of recommended changes and issues with divergent views.
- Hold a meeting to discuss these changes and conflicting comments.
- Change the user requirements document based on the results of the meeting.

This meeting on the user requirements document changes ends the period of most concentrated user involvement in the systems analysis.

As described in Chapter 15, implementation assessment tends to be somewhat less structured, since the analyses, benchmarking, and experimentation done here depend heavily on the implementation issues with the particular application. Depending on the particular circumstances, this phase can be accomplished by the intended developer or the requirements analysts. A mid-term review (review step 9) during this phase is helpful to keep the sponsor aware of the evolving implementation concepts. It also gives a chance for the sponsor to make some initial cost/capability tradeoffs.

In review step 10, analysts give the sponsor and a few senior user representatives one or more carefully worked out implementation options. Each option should have benefits, cost, and schedule estimates, plus an assessment of remaining risk. At this meeting the sponsor gets advice from the users and chooses or affirms an implementation approach.

The final steps complete the requirements specification, based on the sponsor's choice. Review step 11 is a meeting with users to discuss the selected approach and associated changes in user requirements. Review step 12 is circulation and discussion of a complete draft of the requirements specification. Like the user requirements document, analysts circulate the draft for written comments, assemble the comments, and resolve issues at a meeting of the participants. The resulting new draft requirements specification is given to the sponsor and developer for final negotiations before it is signed off.

ESTIMATING EFFORT FOR MILESTONES

The lead requirements analyst must make experienced judgments about the proper amount of time necessary to prepare for each review step. The work estimate depends partly on the size of the problem. For example, preparing the data dictionary for a large system which consolidates 1000 data items from five pre-existing systems will probably take considerably longer than preparing a data dictionary for a new application with only 100 data items. Another consideration for the estimate is the depth of analysis required. In several areas (procedural logic, output definition, user interface details, and data navigation analysis) the division between requirements definition and design is fuzzy. The amount of effort needed for application definition will depend on where the dividing line is drawn.

In general, it is better to shorten the definition phase to allow design and development to proceed as soon as possible, given complete functional and data base descriptions and a demonstration of feasibility. However, the more detailed the requirements analysis, the more likely a firm fixed price contract can be reached with the developer. The user-centered requirements analysis approach, proceeding in the thirteen-step process outlined in Exhibit 18-1, compiles the desired detail over a short period of time.

COMMON QUESTIONS CONCERNING
USER-CENTERED REQUIREMENTS ANALYSIS

People often ask the author the following questions concerning requirements analysis project planning. These questions give additional insights concerning the resources needed for a requirements analysis.

Question: Can junior staff be used as systems analysts after reading this book?

Answer: Bright junior staff with experience in computer science can be productive after a seminar or studying this book. However, they should have the guidance of an experienced analyst who can look over each step and help sharpen the approach. Case-study courses using this book will provide much of the training that otherwise comes only from working projects and having either an apprentice relationship to a master craftsman or years of trial-and-error practice.

Question: Can users perform the analysis themselves?

Answer: Users can perform the analysis themselves, just as an individual can design his own house, but in both cases it is probably unwise in most circumstances. Better results will be obtained by bringing in trained systems analysts, because:

- Much less time is required of the users, who are often buried by the needs of the business.

- Uniform quality of results is easier to achieve with experienced systems analysts.

- Sophisticated data analysis techniques, which are not easily learned in a short amount of time, can be used.

- Analysts are more likely to understand the technology possibilities and types of generic automation functions which should be performed.

- Outside consultants can help focus attention on the engineering issues and cut through political issues among groups of people who work with each other all the time.

On the other hand, there are sometimes problems using trained systems analysts. They must be taught the characteristics of the users' business, and there are sometimes sensitive issues or security concerns which make users leery of bringing in outsiders. Given this background, if there is still a desire to have users define the application themselves, here are some helpful ideas: The users can prepare themselves through extensive reading and training preparation, so that they understand what is required of the analysis. The objectives of the requirements definition should be simplified to ignore complexities of data modeling and implementation strategies. (See for example Carolyn Shamlin's book (1) for an example of a simplified style.) And a methodology expert needs to be available to answer questions about how to express requirements.

Question: In my experience, situations often occur which are so indefinite that I have to generate data flow diagrams of the existing organization in order to understand the business which will be helped by the new application. How does this organizational data flow analysis fit into the conceptual framework of user-centered requirements analysis?

Answer: Data flow diagrams of the current business (Exhibit 5-2) tend to be needed when the application charter is unclear, when the organizational structure is awkward for the functions being performed, or when both problems occur. In these situations, the organizational data flow diagrams should be treated as part of the concept identification (Step 1 in Exhibit 2-2), the phase which leads to an application charter. Often the diagrams show why and how the organization needs to be restructured. Such organizational change should be separated from the engineering of an MIS. Remember Ed Yourdon's claim that overemphasis on analysis of the existing system was one of the biggest problems in applying Yourdon-style systems analysis in the early 1980s (2).

Question: How should I define the structure and content of a data flow directly between two functions? A data store and corresponding data dictionary table should be used only when data must be held over time.

Answer: The need for detailed descriptions of interprocess data flows happens less frequently than one might expect, because once an integrated data base philosophy is adopted, most flows do go through a data store. However, interprocess flows are sometimes needed, and they may be complex. Your choices are to describe the flow with the verifiable functional requirements of the function generating (or receiving) the data flow or to treat the data flow like a data aggregate in the data base description. The latter approach is usually reserved for very complex interprocess data flows.

Question: What should I do if someone has achieved a partial definition of the application, but the definition did not follow the concepts of user-centered requirements analysis? For example, I was assigned to fix up an application which went through an unsuccessful software development. Its documentation was just a programmer's notebook.

Answer: You should always attempt to use any intellectual progress already achieved. In the situation described, available resources include the user interface in the implemented programs, the programmer's notes, and source code. Analyzing these can yield a first draft of user concept diagrams, verifiable functional requirements, and a conceptual data model. Having this start, you could then rapidly work through the steps of user-centered requirements analysis. User review of your materials will point out the requirements that the previous implementer did not understand. And the first cut from the previous effort will remind everyone of issues discussed the last time around.

Question: What should I do if there doesn't seem to be any top management support for the application?

Answer: This is a difficult situation for you, and a fairly common one. Typically it happens when a manager has an application idea and some extra resources to use to define the idea, but not extensive organization support. The sponsor must at least make it possible for you to talk to some intended users. When working through the analyses, you should be looking for other managers who could benefit from the application and thus might support the implementation. In this situation it is more important to "sell the idea" than to have a detailed engineering specification. Given the large risk that the idea will be discarded, it is good to stop with a quickly assembled user requirements document and a rough cost-benefit analysis. If more support emerges, based on this material, then a full requirements specification can be generated later.

Question: What if there is an unreasonable deadline imposed? For example, we signed up a large new customer and had to complete a complex new automated ordering system in 45 days as a condition for the contract.

Answer: In that situation, do whatever you have to do to get a minimum capability in place quickly, but make sure everyone in your company knows it is a temporary solution. Call it a rapid prototype. If this contract is temporary and you only need a short-term solution, that may suffice. However, if automated ordering is part of a new corporate marketing strategy, you'd better figure out what capabilities are really needed with a requirements specification, and rebuild the initial system in a more relaxed schedule. When the real capability comes online, tell the customer using the prototype that you have made the ordering system even better.

Question: What effect does scale have on the analysis?

Answer: As the size of the application increases, the following changes allow more analyst manpower to be applied to limit the required calendar time:

- Make one analyst responsible for the functional model, another responsible for the data model.

- Divide up the top-level functional breakouts among functional analysts, and the data aggregates among data analysts.

- Divide the entire system into subsystems, each with its own team of requirements analysts.

In the last case, splitting the application into subsystems, there must be a clear definition of each subsystem's place in the total system and how the subsystems interface with each other. To do that, the requirements documentation should include system-level, subsystem-level, and interface requirements, as shown in Exhibit 18-2. Often the interface requirements can be inserted into the subsystem specifications rather than standing alone as separate, possibly redundant documentation. The important thing is to make sure somebody has the responsibility to ensure that subsystem interfaces are sensible.

Question: Can there be more meetings than the thirteen reviews shown in Exhibit 18-1?

Answer: Certainly. Larger projects in particular will require more interaction. Smaller projects will be able to combine review steps. The thirteen steps shown in Exhibit 18-1 act as conceptual milestones which help track the overall intellectual progress toward a clear, complete, agreed-upon requirements specification.

EXHIBIT 18-2. Requirements Documentation for Large Systems

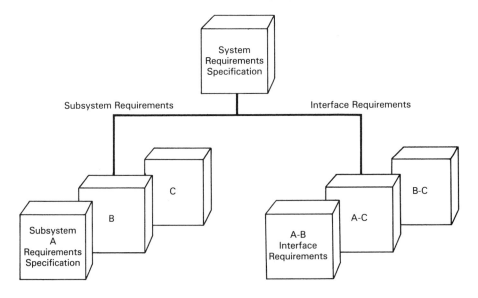

EXHIBIT 18-3.   How Requirements Specification Parts Are Used for Design

Part of Requirements Specification	Is Used as Follows, Depending on the Software Development Cycle		
	Classical	Prototyping	Reusable Code
Functional Description	Decompose functions into modules. Build structure charts. Design menus, screen displays, and reports.	Use as guide for screen applications and process logic.	Use to find candidate modules. Integrate modules with a standard user interface.
Data Base Description	Initialize physical data model.	Initialize physical data model.	Use to identify best fit of candidate modules.
Performance Requirements	Determine hardware requirements. Allocate performance requirements to modules. Obtain special benchmarks and perform queueing theory analysis.	Identify performance problem areas using prototype benchmarks.	Benchmark candidate modules for acceptable performance.

Question: How should requirements transition to design?

Answer: This is an important question for the analysts responsible for the definition and the design phases. The answer depends on the type of software development cycle used (Chapter 2) and whether the same group of systems analysts are involved with both definition and design. Exhibit 18-3 summarizes the main transition processes for the classical, prototyping, and reusable code software development cycles. In all three cases, design should stress the user interface (menu, screen display, and report design) as a key preliminary design activity. In the classical software development cycle, design should take a structured approach to decomposing requirements functions into software modules which are documented with structure charts and Structured English (3). The conceptual data model expands and changes to add the storage concerns necessary in a physical data model which recognizes performance needs. Performance requirements are analyzed and benchmarked to document how the design will meet performance goals. In the prototyping software development cycle, emphasis is changed from creation of paper design documentation to creation of the application development environment's application data base for prototyping. Prototypes are then iterated with users to ensure that the user interface and design concept are appropriate. In the reusable code software development cycle, the requirements specification is used to determine the most appropriate set of reusable modules and a design approach for integrating them. If the same group of systems analysts works both definition and design, and if a set of CASE tools is used for the requirements analysis, then the requirements CASE data base should extend naturally to a requirements-and-design CASE data base in the classical software development cycle or automatically initialize the application development environment data base in the prototyping software development cycle.

SUMMARY OF THE USER-CENTERED
REQUIREMENTS ANALYSIS APPROACH

Requirements analysis is a difficult but important problem which can only be solved in a reasonable amount of time by a well-thought-out analysis approach.

Difficulties come from both political and technical sources. In order to reach agreement on the requirements, a number of different people—sponsor, user representatives, analysts, and developers—must come to mutual understandings. Cultural and educational backgrounds of these people are often widely divergent, so that it takes adroit politicians to bring the group to consensus requirements. Difficult technical issues come up both in understanding the business function to be served by the new application and in specifying capabilities within the current state-of-the-art of software applications.

Because of the inherent difficulty of the requirements analysis process, many projects dispense with requirements after developing a high-level application concept. They go directly to design, and hope that after-the-fact "tuning" will resolve any problems with the implemented code. Such short-circuiting of requirements can lead to disastrous results when it turns out that the application must be rebuilt. At best, it puts a heavy burden on the designers and developers, because they must play the role of requirements analysts (in an unstructured way) while trying to proceed with the application implementation. Development is then slower, more difficult to manage, and likely to miss the target of real user needs.

User-Centered Requirements Analysis takes the view that it is possible to develop good front-end requirements in a reasonably short amount of time. Intellectual progress and agreement are both easiest to achieve with an approach of successive refinement. This starts with a statement of objectives for the new system (Part II) and then continues with overview diagrams and verifiable detail.

For computer applications with extensive user interaction and an integrated data base, the focus of the requirements analysis should be on construction of functional and data base descriptions (Parts III and IV). Performance requirements (Part V) and any other descriptions needed to indicate algorithms, real-time requirements, or other special requirements for the particular application are then added. User concept diagrams give an overview of the functional model, including a view of how the computer functions will interact with users. Verifiable functional requirements, tied to the user concept diagrams, give definite instructions to the implementers about what the application must accomplish. Canonical form data structure diagrams provide a similar overview of the conceptual data model, with details filled in by the data dictionary. The diagrams and detailed requirements must be developed with users and reviewed by them both in rough form and in the formal requirements documentation.

It is helpful to produce the requirements specification first as a draft document, called the user requirements document, and then as a final version that guides development (Part VI). In between, the user requirements are reviewed both to make sure that they match the users' desires and to determine whether they can be implemented at a reasonable cost. In addition, the implementation assessment (Part V) often comes up with desired phasing of capabilities, since it is usually best to implement large applications in stages.

Requirements analysis projects must be individually planned (Part VI) to account for their special circumstances. A small vendor list application implemented on a personal computer using simple data base software might be defined by an analyst in two days. A large cost accounting system covering 10,000 employees at 25 locations might take a year for ten analysts to define. For large projects, modern automated tools can greatly simplify the documentation and analysis burdens of the job.

An advanced methodology greatly improves chances of success, but does not by itself guarantee success. Creativity and technical knowledge are just as essential in requirements analysis as they are in any other kind of architectural work. And the result of requirements analysis is merely the input to the design and development phases which have difficult management and technical hurdles of their own. Still, a clear, complete, agreed-upon requirements specification is a sponsor's most effective tool for achieving a successful computer application on time and within budget.

REFERENCES

1. Carolyn Shamlin, *A User's Guide for Defining Software Requirements*, Wellesley, MA: QED Information Sciences, 1985.

2. Edward Yourdon, "What Ever Happened to Structured Analysis?", *Datamation*, June 1, 1986, pp. 133-138.

3. David King, *Current Practices in Software Development*, New York: Yourdon Press, 1984.

Appendix A

Commercial Computer-Aided Software Engineering Environments

Vendor	Product Line	Environments				Comments
		IBM PC	DEC VAX	Large IBM	Other	
Adpac Corp. 120 Howard St. P.O. Box 3337 San Francisco, CA 94119	Adpac Productivity Tools			X		Constructs diagrams from input specifications or existing COBOL source code.
Advanced Computer Concepts P.O. Box 15710 Sarasota, FL 33579	Advanced Program Design Language		X			
AGS Management Systems 880 First Ave. King of Prussia, PA 19406	Structured Analysis/Design			X		
Arthur Anderson & Company 33 West Monroe St. Chicago, IL 60603	DESIGN/1	X				Automates proprietary METHOD/1 methodology, plus Yourdon and Warnier/Orr approaches.
ASYST Technologies 50 Staniford St. Suite 800 Boston, MA 02114	The Developer	X				Supports Yourdon, James Martin, and other methodologies, and can be tailored.

Vendor	Product Line	Environments				Comments
		IBM PC	DEC VAX	Large IBM	Other	
Bachman Information Systems 11 Percy Road Lexington, MA 01773	IBIS family			X		Models business functions.
M. Bryce & Associates 777 Alderman Road Palm Harbor, FL 33563	PRIDE Information Systems Engineering Methodology		X	X		Provides life-cycle support for the PRIDE, methodology, including generation of COBOL file descriptions and PL1 structures.
Cadre Technologies 222 Richmond St. Providence, RI 02903	Teamwork PCSA	X			Apollo, Sun, IBM RT, Vaxstation II	Teamwork focuses on embedded (real time) software applications and uses powerful workstations to speed analysis functions. PCSA is an inexpensive PC-based data flow diagramming tool.
The CADWARE Group, Ltd. 869 Whalley Ave. New Haven, CT 06515	The Design Graphics System	X				Provides general capabilities designed to support construction of a CASE environment for a custom methodology.
Caine, Farber & Gordon 750 East Green St. Pasadena, CA 91101	Program Design Language		X	X		This is a Structured English tool.

Vendor	Product Line	Environments				Comments
		IBM PC	DEC VAX	Large IBM	Other	
Cap Gemini Software Products 2350 Valley View Lane, Suite 420 Dallas, TX 75234	MultiPro	X		X		Supplies documentation aids for traditional software projects, including graphics for data flow diagrams and flowcharts.
CGI Systems 1 Blue Hill Plaza Pearl River, NY 10965	PACBASE	X		X		PC-based front end provides structured analysis functions which feed COBOL generator for IBM mainframes.
Chen & Assoc. P.O. Box 25130 Baton Rouge, LA 70894	ER-Package	X				Provides systems analysis tools based on entity-relationship diagrams.
Cortex Corp. 138 Technology Dr. Waltham, MA 02154	CorVision, Cortex Application Factory	X	X			Cortex systems analysis techniques automated on PCs provide inputs used by VAX application generator.
Cullinet Software 400 Blue Hills Dr. Westwood, MA 02090	IDMS/Architect, ADS/Online	X		X		Family of CASE tools on PCs will collect specifications for IDMS application development environment on IBM mainframes.

Vendor	Product Line	Environments				Comments
		IBM PC	DEC VAX	Large IBM	Other	
D. Appleton Company 1334 Park View Ave. Suite 220 Manhattan Beach, CA 90266	JANUS		X	X		Supports Appleton's data analysis approach and provides links with other vendors' tools.
Econix Software Engineering 1037 3rd St. Santa Monica, CA 90403	PRISM	X	X		MacIntosh, Sun, Apollo	
Future Tech 724 West Hi-Crest Dr. Auburn, WA 98001	Future Tech CASE System	X				
Index Technology 101 Main Street Cambridge, MA 02142	Excelerator	X	X			Provides PC-based support of systems analysis and interfaces with many other vendors' products.
InfoModel, Inc. 137 West 25th St. Room 508 New York, NY 10001	InfoModel	X				Supports data analysis based on data model diagrams similar to James Martin's.

Vendor	Product Line	Environments				Comments
		IBM PC	DEC VAX	Large IBM	Other	
Interactive Development Environments 150 Fourth St. Suite 210 San Francisco, CA 94103	IDE family		X		Sun	Family of tools provide CASE and application development environment support.
KnowledgeWare, Inc. 3340 Peachtree Road, N.E. Suite 2900 Atlanta, GA 30326	Information Engineering Workbench	X		X		Automated tools supporting James Martin's techniques of information engineering and Structured English diagrams will be combined with a COBOL generator for IBM mainframes.
Leading Software Technologies Corp. 26250 Euclid Ave. Suite 307 Cleveland, Ohio 44132	The Intelligent Assistant			X		Generates IBM mainframe COBOL and JCL based on data flow analysis.
Manager Software Products, Inc. 131 Hartwell Ave. Lexington, MA 02173	Manager Family of Software Engineering Tools			X		PC-based CASE tools link with the DataManager IBM mainframe data dictionary product.

Vendor	Product Line	Environments IBM PC	DEC VAX	Large IBM	Other	Comments
McDonnell-Douglas P.O. Box 516 St. Louis, MO 63166	ProKit Analyst	X				Automates the Gane & Sarson methodology.
Meta Software Corp. 55 Wheeler St. Cambridge, MA 02138	design				MacIntosh	General network "design" diagramming tool can be customized to serve particular systems analysis diagramming approaches.
Meta Systems 325 East Eisenhower Parkway Suite 103 P.O. Box 4179 Ann Arbor, MI 48106	Structured Architect, PSL/PSA	X	X		Apollo, Sun, IBM RT PC	A DeMarco-style structured analysis tool on IBM PCs links with PSA analysis data base on more powerful computers.
Nastec Corp. 24681 Northwestern Highway Southfield, MI 48075	Case 2000	X	X			Supports Yourdon-DeMarco style systems analysis and links with several other vendors' CASE and ADE tools.
Ken Orr & Ass. 1725 Gage Blvd. Topeka, KS 66604	Design Machine	X				Automates Warnier/Orr methodology based on hierarchical decompositions.

Vendor	Product Line	Environments				Comments
		IBM PC	DEC VAX	Large IBM	Other	
ProMod, Inc. 22981 Alcalde Dr. Laguna Hills, CA 92653	ProMod	X	X			Supports Yourdon-DeMarco style systems analysis with emphasis on real-time systems. Includes code frame generators for Ada, C, and Pascal shells.
Rand Information Systems 1201 Harbor Bay Parkway Alameda, CA 94501	Rand Development Center (RDC/IDMS)			X		
Sage Software, Inc. 3200 Monroe St. Rockville, MD 20852	Application Productivity Systems (APS)	X		X		Systems analysis capabilities feed application generators for several IBM mainframe data management environments.
Softlab, Inc. 188 The Embarcadero 7th Floor San Francisco, CA 94105	MAESTRO	X	X		Motorola 4500/UNIX computers	Provides general capabilities allowing user-tailoring for specific methodologies. Includes partial support of code generation.
SYSCORP International 12710 Research Blvd. Suite 301 Austin, TX 78759-4324	MicroSTEP	X				Supports data flow diagrams with user-definable symbols. Will expand in the future to code generation.

Vendor	Product Line	Environments				Comments
		IBM PC	DEC VAX	Large IBM	Other	
Technology Information Products Corp. 12 New England Executive Park Burlington, MA 01803	TIP Product Line			X		Automated tools supporting TIP methodology from planning and analysis through IBM mainframe code generation.
Tektronix Inc. Computer-Aided Software Engineering Division P.O. Box 14752 Portland, OR 97214	CASE Software Factory	X	X		Apollo, Sun, IBM RT PC	Tools automate DeMarco-style structured analysis, Paige-Jones structured design, and generate C and Pascal code for various microprocessors.
Teledyne-Brown 300 Sparkman Dr. Huntsville, AL 35807	Technology for Automated Generation of Systems (TAGS)				Apollo	
Texas Instruments Incorporated P.O. Box 869305 P.O. Drawer 8466 Plano, TX 75086	Information Engineering Facility (IEF)	X				Automates James Martin's Information Engineering methodology.

Vendor	Product Line	Environments				Comments
		IBM PC	DEC VAX	Large IBM	Other	
TSI International 295 Westport Ave. Norwalk, CT 06856	Facets			X		
Visible Systems Corporation 336 Baker Ave. Concord, MA 01742	Visible Analyst Workbench	X				Supports DeMarco and Gane & Sarson data flow diagrams.
Yourdon, Inc. 1501 Broadway New York, NY 10036	Analyst Toolkit, Designer Toolkit	X			Wang	Inexpensive tools support Yourdon analysis and design methodology.

Appendix B

Some Common Application Development Environments

Vendor	Data Base Management System	Application Development Environment	Computer Family
Applied Data Research Rt. 206 & Orchard Rd. Princeton, NJ 08540	Datacom/DB	IDEAL	IBM
Cincom Systems 2300 Montana Ave. Cincinatti, OH 45211	SUPRA ULTRA	MANTIS	IBM DEC
Computer Corporation of America 4 Cambridge Center Cambridge, MA 02142	MODEL 204	Workshop/204	IBM
Cullinet Software 400 Blue Hill Dr. Westwood, MA 02090	IDMS/R	ADS/OnLine	IBM
International Business Machines Old Orchard Road Armonk, NY 10504	DL/I, IMS	DMS, CSP, ADF	IBM

Vendor	Data Base Management System	Application Development Environment	Computer Family
Oracle Corporation 2710 Sand Hill Rd. Menlo Park, CA 94025	ORACLE	IAF	IBM DEC
Relational Technology 2710 Sand Hill Rd. Menlo Park, CA 94025	INGRES	Application-By-Forms	DEC
Software AG of North America 11800 Sunrise Valley Dr. Reston, VA 22091	ADABAS	NATURAL	IBM DEC
Unify Corporation 4000 Kruse Way Lake Oswego, OR 97034	UNIFY	ACCEL	Variety of computers with UNIX
Wang Laboratories 1 Industrial Ave. Lowell, MA 01851	PACE RDBMS	PACE	Wang

Appendix C
Glossary

ad hoc query Capability provided with a data base management system for users to obtain answers to any questions which can be answered from the content of the data base. It consists of a query language which allows the user to express the question and a query processor which finds the answer. Results are usually displayed on the user's terminal screen.

ad hoc report Same as ad hoc query, except that additional capabilities are provided for user-specified formatting of the query answer. Results are usually printed out on a hardcopy device.

alpha testing System tests that determine whether an application satisfies its user requirements.

application An automated system designed to help users to work a business process.

application charter Broad statement of need for a new application. It results from the initial (concept identification) phase of the software development cycle, and gives application bounds and rough objectives to the analysts in the definition phase.

application concept Identification of objectives, users, and key terminology for an application. It is developed by systems analysts at the start of the definition phase of the software development cycle.

application development environment Software tools which assist developers in defining the data base schema and in preparing menus, screen displays, and reports. Usually provided by the DBMS vendor, these tools make rapid prototyping possible.

attributes Characteristics of a data entity which should be maintained by the software application. Attributes become data items when data dictionary information is compiled.

beta testing System tests that determine whether an application meets its objectives in actual use.

bottom-up data analysis Development of a data base description starting with a complete set of data items and then combining these into normalized record types and data aggregates.

candidate key Set of items in a record type which has the characteristic that all other items in the record type functionally depend on this set. There may be more than one candidate key, but all will be functionally equivalent.

canonical form data structure diagram Data structure diagram in which record types are arrayed in generation levels, so that data base entry points are at the top and the most detailed data records are at the bottom.

CASE Computer-aided software engineering.

child record Record type related to a parent record type under a one-to-many relationship. Each parent record occurrence may be related to many child record occurrences, and every child record occurrence has a unique related parent record occurrence.

circular one-to-many relationships Chain of one-to-many relationships in a data structure which returns to the record type at the start of the chain.

CODASYL DBTG COmmittee on DAta SYstems Languages Data Base Task Group, the organization which generated standards for network data base management systems.

computer-aided software engineering environment Interactive system which provides assistance to systems analysts in creating and maintaining diagrams and specifications concerning definition and design for new computer applications. The scope of this term is rapidly expanding to include any collection of software tools which aid software development.

concept identification First phase of a software development cycle. It results in an application charter, which describes the broad purpose and scope of the intended application.

configuration management Control of changes to the application requirements, design, and implementation.

context diagram Top-level data flow diagram which has a single functional activity representing the entire computer application.

critical success factor An area of business activity which must be successful for a manager to achieve his goals.

CSF Critical success factor.

data aggregate A combination of record types representing a general information subject.

data base description Combination of a data structure diagram and data dictionary, used to describe the information content in an application data base.

data definition language Computer language provided by a DBMS that allows the application developer to specify the precise data structure and format for the application data.

data dictionary Collection of definitions and attributes of record types and data items.

data element Data item.

data entity A person, object, or concept which will be described by data in the application data base. Data entities become record types after compilation of the data dictionary.

data field Smallest meaningful unit of data in an interface data file or an application output (corresponds to a data item in the data base).

data flow diagram A diagram which shows functional activities, data stores, and the data flowing among them.

data item Smallest breakout of information in the data base. Attributes of data entities become data items when the data dictionary is prepared.

data manipulation language Utilities provided by a DBMS which allow an application to add, change, delete, and access data.

data model (1) Data structuring philosophy (e.g., hierarchical, network, or relational); (2) Diagram showing the entire structure of a data base.

data navigation diagram Data structure diagram marked to show the data access paths needed for a process.

data structure diagram Type of entity-relationship diagram which represents entities (or record types) as boxes and one-to-many relationships as arrows. Many-to-many relationships and circular relationships are not allowed.

DBMS Data base management system.

DDL Data definition language.

definition phase Phase in the software development cycle which generates the requirements specification.

Delphi estimates Group estimates obtained by an iterative process in which the nth set of estimates is available to each member of the group to help decide upon (n+1)st estimates. This process is particularly helpful to obtain performance requirements.

DeMarco progression Systems analysis approach which develops four types of data flow diagrams in the following order: current physical, current logical, future logical, and future physical.

dependency diagram Diagram showing functional dependencies among items in a record type.

deployment phase Software development cycle phase that makes the new application accessible to users.

design phase Software development cycle phase that generates design specifications.

design specification Document describing the physical design of the application, including breakout of software modules, use of system software and application utilities, format and content of application outputs, and the schema-level (DDL) definition of the physical data structure.

developer Organization that programs the application.

development phase Classical software development cycle phase that generates tested programs and companion documentation, such as a user's manual and a programmer's manual.

direct users Individuals who will interact with the computer application using a terminal or output device.

DML Data manipulation language.

entity-relationship diagram Diagram which shows normalized data entities and the relationships among entities.

feasibility study Rapid assessment of the application concept to determine whether the desired automation can be implemented in a practical manner.

flat file Data organization using a rectangular matrix of data fields in fixed locations.

fourth generation language Language allowing end-users to specify information which must be extracted from the data base. (See ad hoc query and ad hoc report.)

function A component in the hierarchical decomposition of the automated processing needed from the application.

function definition Brief summary of the scope of a function, sometimes augmented by an explanation of unusual processing concepts.

function redundancy Type of redundancy in functional requirements in which the same processing function is discussed in two different places.

functional dependency Relationship between an item and a set of items in a record type. Item B functionally depends on a set of items S if every occurrence of items in S has a unique related occurrence of item B.

functional description Combination of user concept diagrams, verifiable functional requirements, and output descriptions, which describe the functions an application must perform.

functional equivalence Relationship between two sets of items in a record type in which each set functionally depends on the other.

hierarchical data model Data structuring philosophy which explicitly represents a tree-like breakout of one-to-many relationships. That is, each record type may have only one one-to-many relationship leading to it.

hierarchical decomposition Process of successively splitting objects (such as functions, data groupings, and data flows) into smaller component objects.

HIPO Hierarchical input-process-output diagrams.

horizontal overlap Partial redundancy of requirements for a process which is discussed with two or more different functions.

implementation assessment Process of assessing risks, analyzing phasing options, and estimating resource requirements for a new application.

indirect users Individuals who will compile data used by the system or use outputs from the system, but will not interact directly with the application.

key Set of items (attributes) which uniquely identifies a record (entity) occurrence.

key attribute An attribute in an entity key.

key item An item in a record key.

link record Record type representing a many-to-many relationship.

load utility Software which inserts data from flat files into a structured data base.

many-to-many relationship Kind of relationship between two record types in which occurrences of each record type can be related to more than one occurrence of the other record type.

network data model Data structuring philosophy which indicates one-to-many relationships among record types. More general than the hierarchical data model, the network model allows any number of one-to-many relationships to lead to a record type.

normal form record type Group of data items that fit together according to a set of rules chosen to maximize data base integrity, flexibility, and maintainability.

objectives analysis Process of developing the application concept and a feasibility study at the beginning of the definition phase for a new application.

occurrence Individual instance of an item or record type. For example, an Automobile record with a Fuel Economy item might have a record occurrence "Ford LTD" and item occurrence "22 miles per gallon."

one-to-many relationship Kind of relationship between two record types. Record type A has a one-to-many relationship with record type B if some occurrences of A are related to more than one occurrence of B and all occurrences of B are related to a unique occurrence of A.

organizational data flow diagram Data flow diagram which shows how information flows (or will flow at some future time) among functions carried out by the organization.

parent record See child record.

PDL Program design language.

phased implementation Construction of a software application in two or more separate developments. For example, in a two-phase implementation, phase 1 will implement part of the application for users. Later, phase 2 will add the additional functions needed to complete the application.

programmer-centered requirements Requirements expressed in a form designed to minimize the effort required to program an acceptable solution.

prototyping software development cycle Implementation approach in which quickly generated versions of the application are critiqued by users and repeatedly changed until the application satisfies the users.

qualification phase Software development cycle phase that determines whether the programmed application meets its requirements and helps users.

record subtype Grouping of record occurrences which has special data items. For example, the Contract record type could have record subtypes for Commercial Contracts and for Government Contracts.

record type Group of data items, usually assembled in a normal form, which is fully described in a data dictionary (See data entity.)

reference architecture Generic hardware suite and set of software modules which appear to meet the user requirements (used for implementation assessment).

relational data model Data structuring philosophy which represents both data and relationships as tables.

relational data structure diagram Diagram which shows relations and join possibilities between relations (used with the relational data model).

requirements analysis Process of developing clear, complete, agreed-upon and feasible requirements for a computer application.

requirements specification Formal definition of a software application, including user functional, data, and performance requirements, plus implementation constraints. It is used to give the application developer a clear, complete, and agreed-upon understanding of the application.

reusable code software development cycle Implementation approach which maximizes use of pre-existing software modules.

risk assessment Analysis of major implementation concerns to find ways of minimizing error in schedule or cost estimates and maximize the chance of achieving functional and performance requirements.

SADT Structured analysis and design technique.

skeleton diagram Top-level data flow diagram which shows only the major application functions and data base.

software development cycle Breakdown of the process used to develop a computer application into phases. Each phase ends when a specific major goal is achieved.

sponsor Individual or group of people who must commit the resources required to implement the application.

structured analysis and design technique One of the earliest formal data flow diagramming techniques, developed by Douglas Ross of SofTech. Its most noticeable characteristics are a diagonal waterfall arrangement of function boxes and special meaning given to each of the four function box sides when used to connect data flows.

Structured English Natural language exposition of algorithms which uses special words and an indenting format to represent loops and decisions.

subentity Group of data entity occurrences which require special attributes not needed for other occurrences of the same data entity.

successive elaboration Analysis or presentation of system concepts starting with systemwide considerations and gradually decomposing the problem into progressively smaller and more detailed pieces.

systems analysis Combination of requirements analysis and application design.

TBD To be determined.

top-down See successive elaboration.

top-down data analysis Development of a data base description starting with a data structure diagram and then adding data dictionary detail.

top-level functional breakout user concept diagram Skeleton diagram with major external entities, data aggregates, and data flow labels added.

unload utility Software which creates flat files of data from a structured data base.

user Person or type of individual who will work with the application.

user-centered requirements Requirements expressed in terms which are easy for users to understand.

user-centered requirements analysis Approach to requirements analysis which obtains the detail developers need in a form that users readily understand. Developing the functional description and data base description in parallel, it uses user concept diagrams, verifiable functional requirements, data structure diagrams, and data dictionary tables to document the users' view of the system.

user concept diagram Type of future physical data flow diagram which represents user interactions and distinguishes among external entities using physically suggestive icons. These diagrams are a key tool for developing and describing user functional requirements.

user requirements Characteristics of a computer application which users need or desire.

user requirements document Compilation of functional, data base, and performance requirements for an application. This document is circulated for review and then combined with implementation constraints to obtain the requirements specification.

user view Part of a conceptual data model which applies to one user, type of user, or application area.

verifiable functional requirements Instructions concerning the actions the implemented application must perform, stated in sufficiently precise terms that the final application can be checked to see if it satisfies the requirements.

vertical overlap Type of redundancy in functional requirements in which the same requirement is stated at more than one level of detail.

work breakdown structure Hierarchical breakdown of an entire project or contract into successively more detailed work elements.

Yourdon data flow diagrams Style of data flow diagrams popularized by Ed Yourdon and his associates, most notably Tom DeMarco, Chris Gane, and Trish Sarson. These diagrams are restricted to four types of symbols: processes, data flows, data stores, and external entities.

Index

A

ADABAS, 144
Ad hoc query, definition of, 284
Ad hoc report, definition of, 284
Agreement, requirement
   specifications, 23-24
Alpha testing, 13
  definition of, 284
Analysis methodology enforcement,
  233
Annotated samples, 117
Application, definition of, 284
Application charter
  definition of, 284
  refining of, 26-27
   steps in, 27
Application concept
  application objectives, 47-48

system users, identification of,
  48-49
definition of, 284
parts of, 47
special terms, definition of, 49-50
Application definition phase, classical
  software development cycle, 13
Application development
  environment, definition of, 284
Application development
  environment tools, 240-44
CASE system, 243-44
purpose of, 240
uses of, 243
Attributes, definition of, 284
Automated consistency checking,
  232-33
Automated links to design process,
  234

U

Unload utility, definition of, 290
Unreasonable deadlines, 265
User, definition of, 290
User-centered approach, philosophical
  principles behind, 7
  user-centered requirements, definition of, 17, 290
User-Centered Requirements Analysis, 13
User centered requirements analysis, definition of, 291
User concept diagrams
  agreement on, 56
  automation support for, 79-80
  compared to other data flow diagramming styles, 80-83
  completion of, 75-76
  data store/data flow labels, 76-78
  definition of, 291
  DeMarco progression, 62-65
  evolution from HIPO to data flow diagrams, 57-62
  generation of, 69-78
    detailed user concept diagrams, 72-75
    software packages, 79-80
    top-level user concept diagrams, 69-72
  handdrawn diagrams, 79
  hierarchial diagramming, 62
  interaction between analyst and users, 78-79
  symbols for, 65-66
    requirements for, 65
  tied to functional requirements, 98-112
  versus other data flow diagramming styles, 80-83
  working with users, 78-79

User requirements
  classifications of, 28
  compilation order, 28
  concept diagrams, 29-30
  data base description, 29-31
  data structure diagrams, 30
  definition of, 291
  functional description, 29
  user requirements document, 32-33, 36, 291
User requirements document, 32-33, 36
  definition of, 291
Users, number of, 206
User views
  detailed data flow analysis, 198-99
  definition of, 291

V

Vague generalities specifications, 19-20
Verifiable functional requirements, definition of, 291
Vertical overlap, definition of, 291

W

Word processing, 231
Work breakdown structure, definition of, 291
Writing styles, functional requirements, 92

Y

Yourdon data flow diagrams, definition of, 291

Announcing. . . .

The Annual Prentice Hall Professional/Technical/Reference Catalog: Books For Computer Scientists, Computer/Electrical Engineers and Electronic Technicians

- Prentice Hall, the leading publisher of Professional/Technical/Reference books in the world, is pleased to make its vast selection of titles in computer science, computer/electrical engineering and electronic technology more accessible to all professionals in these fields through the publication of this new catalog!

- If your business or research depends on timely, state-of-the-art information, The Annual Prentice Hall Professional/Technical/Reference Catalog: Books For Computer Scientists, Computer/Electrical Engineers and Electronic Technicians was designed especially for you! Titles appearing in this catalog will be grouped according to interest areas. Each entry will include: title, author, author affiliations, title description, table of contents, title code, page count and copyright year.

- In addition, this catalog will also include advertisements of new products and services from other companies in key high tech areas.

SPECIAL OFFER!

- Order your copy of The Annual Prentice Hall Professional/Technical/Reference Catalog: Books For Computer Scientists, Computer/Electrical Engineers and Electronic Technicians for only $2.00 and receive $5.00 off the purchase of your first book from this catalog. In addition, this catalog entitles you to special discounts on Prentice Hall titles in computer science, computer/electrical engineering and electronic technology.

Please send me _____ copies of The Annual Prentice Hall Professional/Technical/Reference Catalog (title code: 62280–3)

SAVE!

If payment accompanies order, plus your state's sales tax where applicable, Prentice Hall pays postage and handling charges. Same return privilege refund guaranteed. Please do not mail cash.

- ☐ PAYMENT ENCLOSED—shipping and handling to be paid by publisher (please include your state's tax where applicable).
- ☐ BILL ME for The Annual Prentice Hall Professional/Technical/Reference Catalog (with small charge for shipping and handling).

Mail your order to: Prentice Hall, Book Distribution Center,
Route 59 at Brook Hill Drive,
West Nyack, N.Y. 10994

Name _____

Address _____

City _____ State _____ Zip _____

I prefer to charge my   ☐ Visa   ☐ MasterCard

Card Number _____ Expiration Date _____

Signature _____

Offer not valid outside the United States.

Dept. 1   D-PPTR-CS(9)